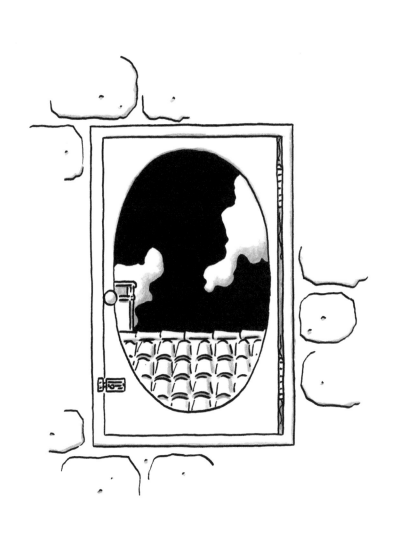

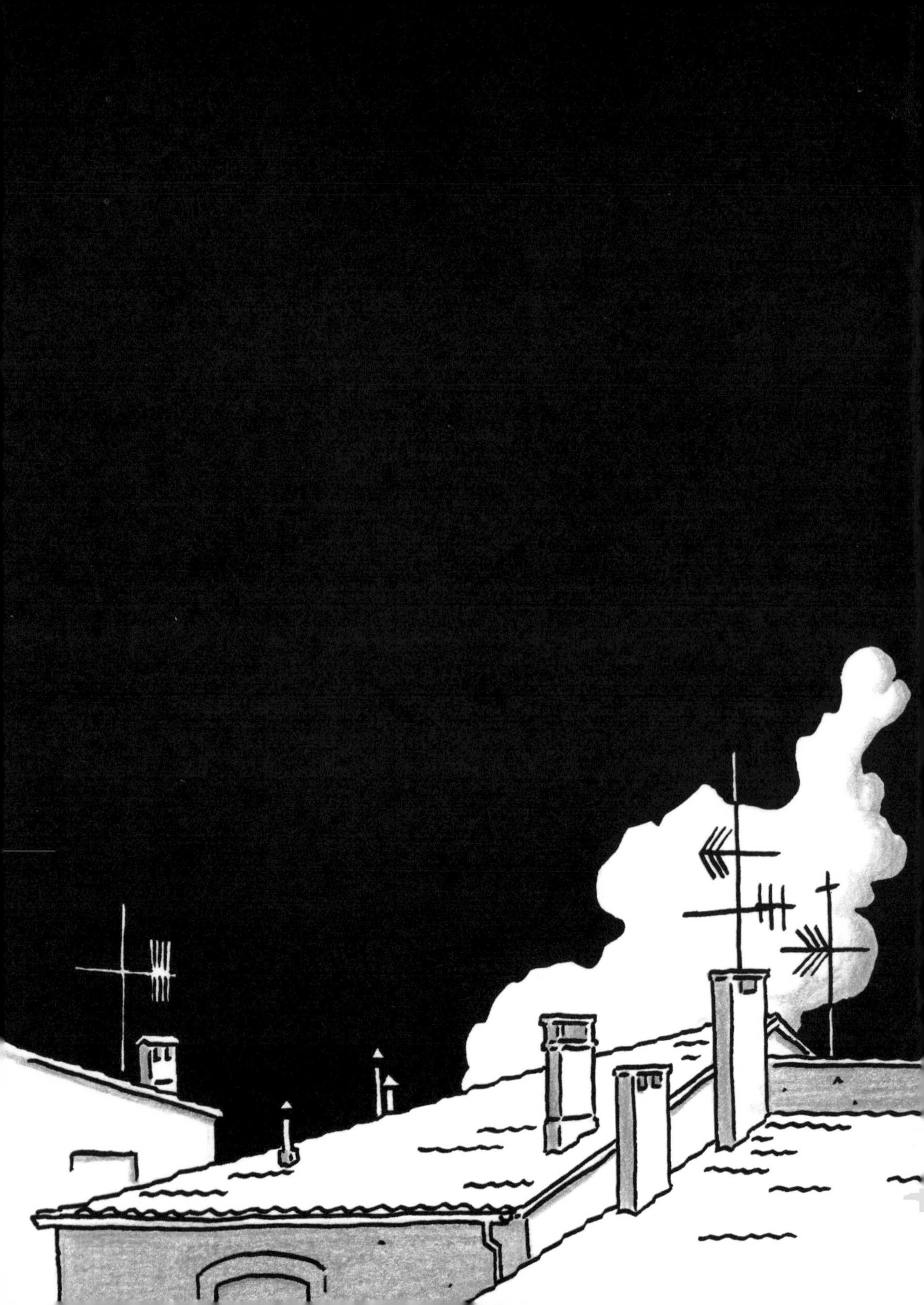

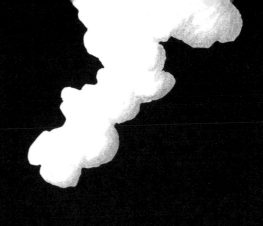

LOST CAT

LOST CAT

by JASON

FANTAGRAPHICS BOOKS

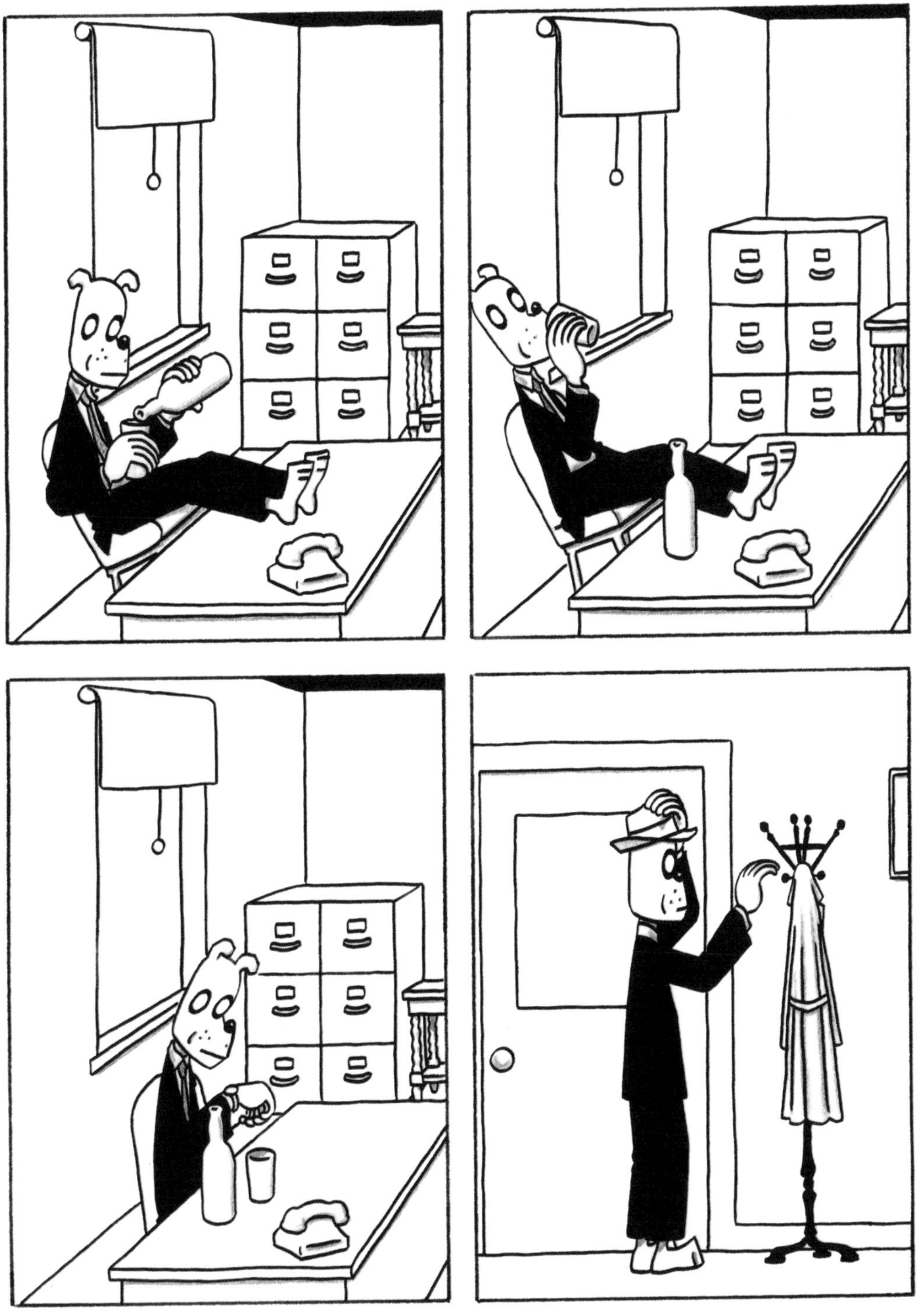

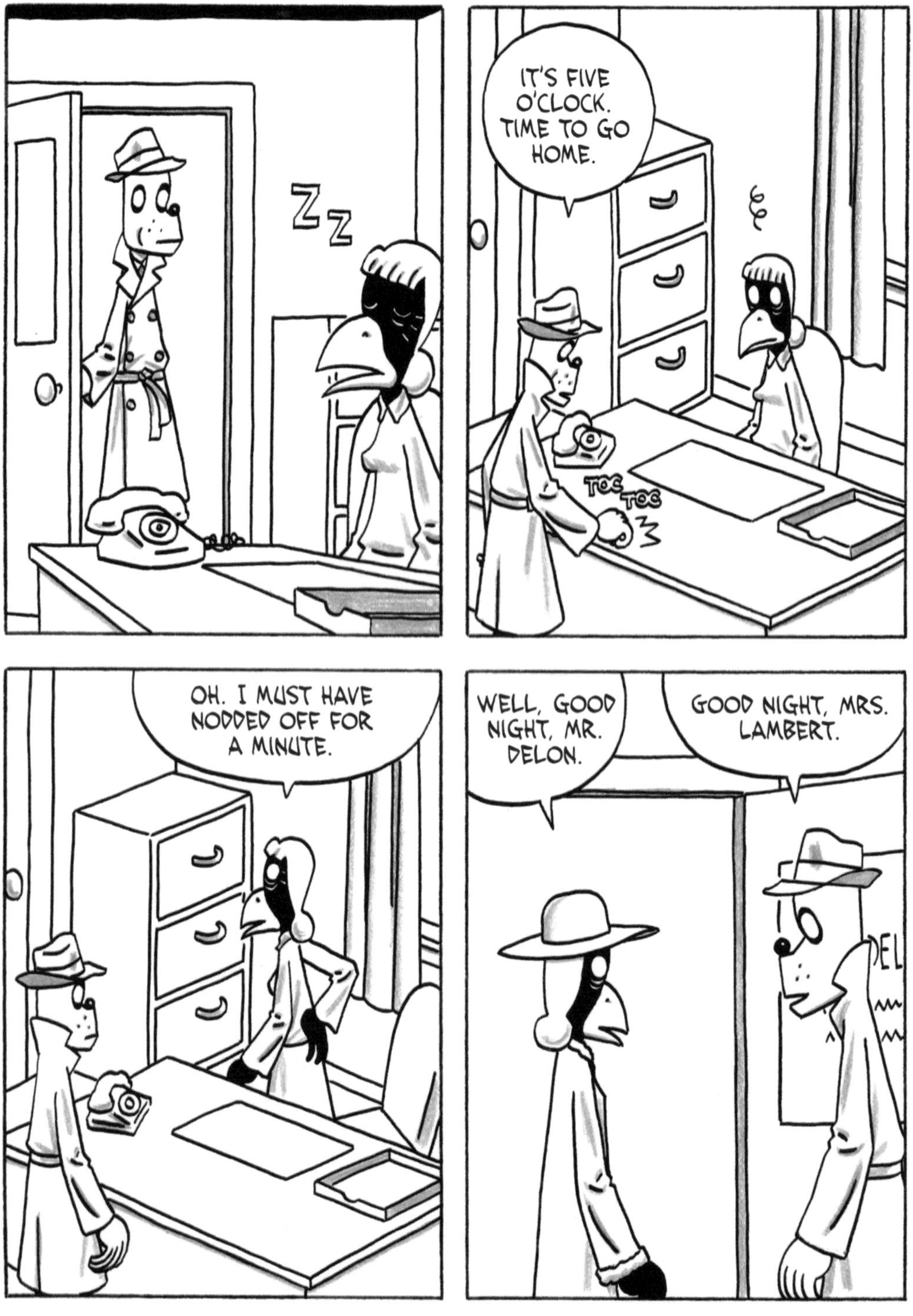

Z Z
IT'S FIVE O'CLOCK. TIME TO GO HOME.
TOC TOC
OH. I MUST HAVE NODDED OFF FOR A MINUTE.
WELL, GOOD NIGHT, MR. DELON.
GOOD NIGHT, MRS. LAMBERT.

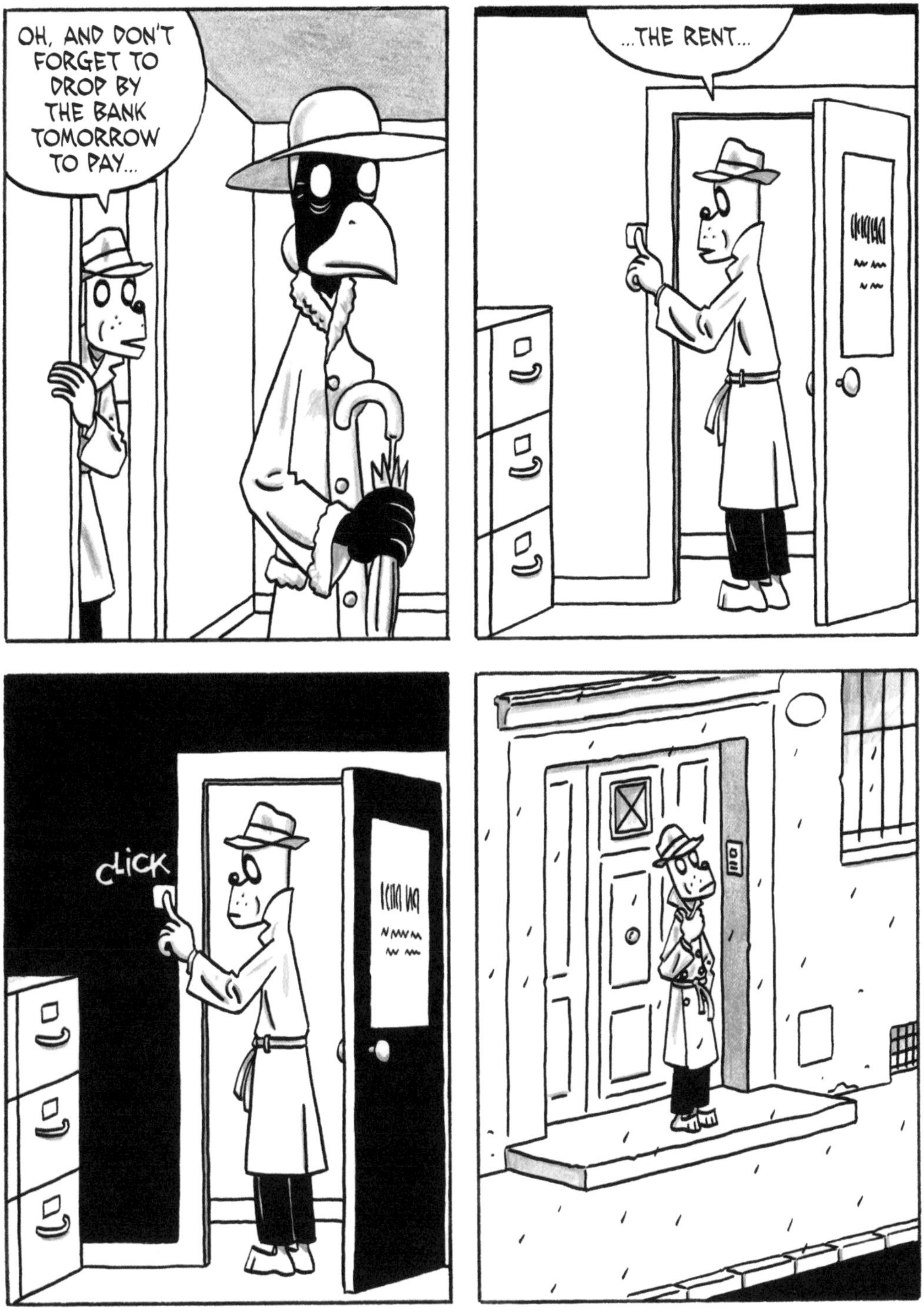
OH, AND DON'T FORGET TO DROP BY THE BANK TOMORROW TO PAY...
...THE RENT...
CLICK

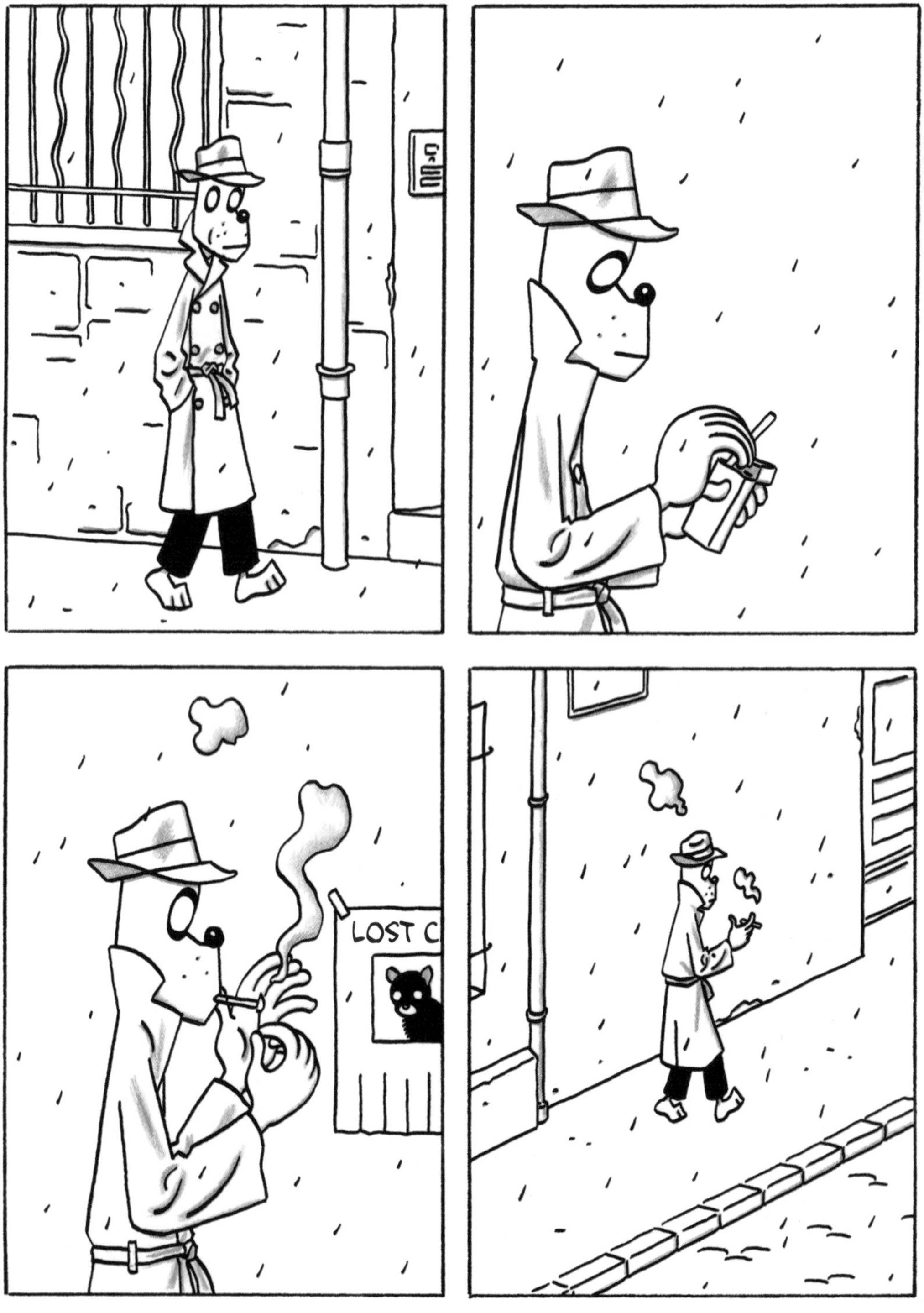
LOST C

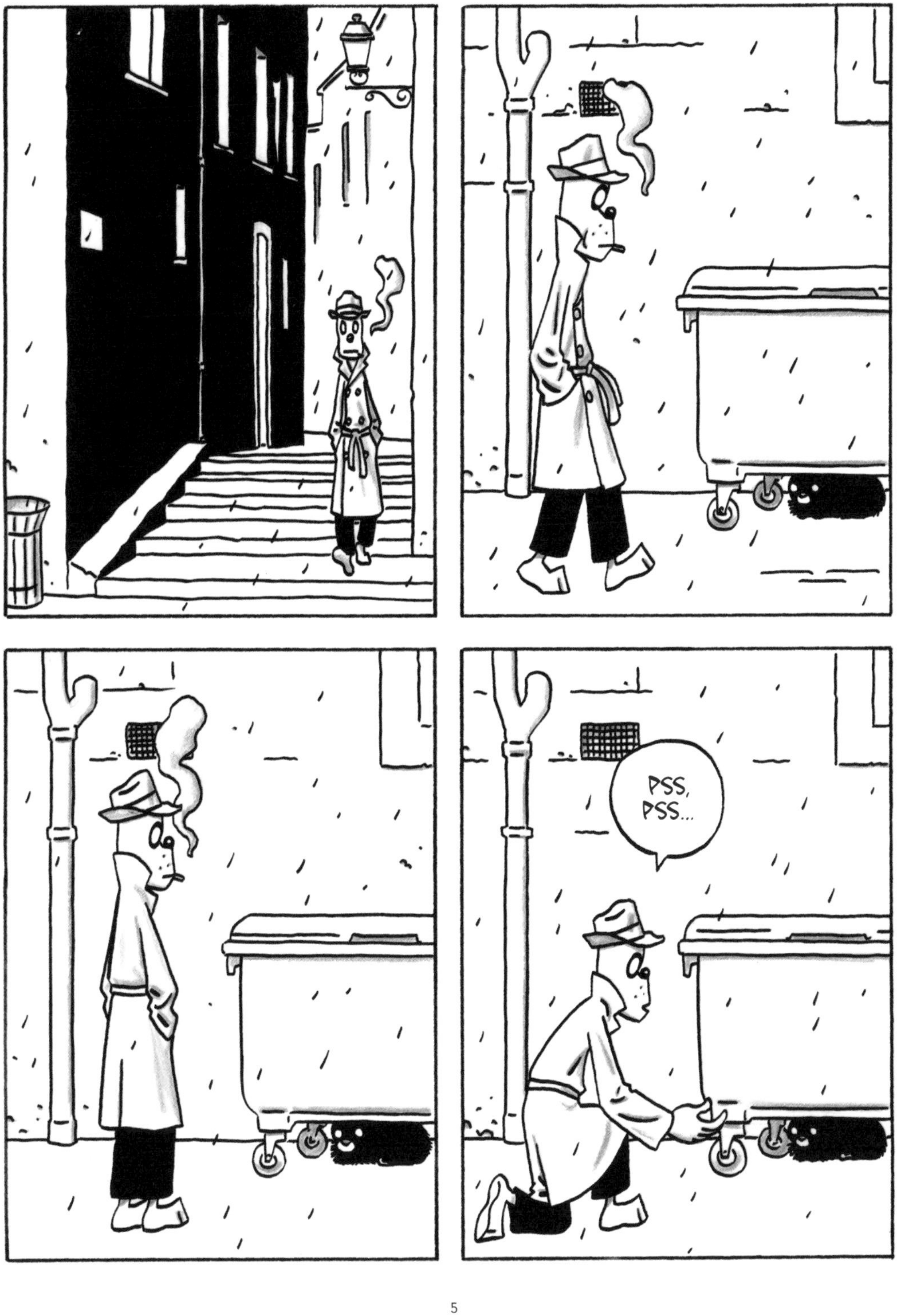
PSS, PSS...

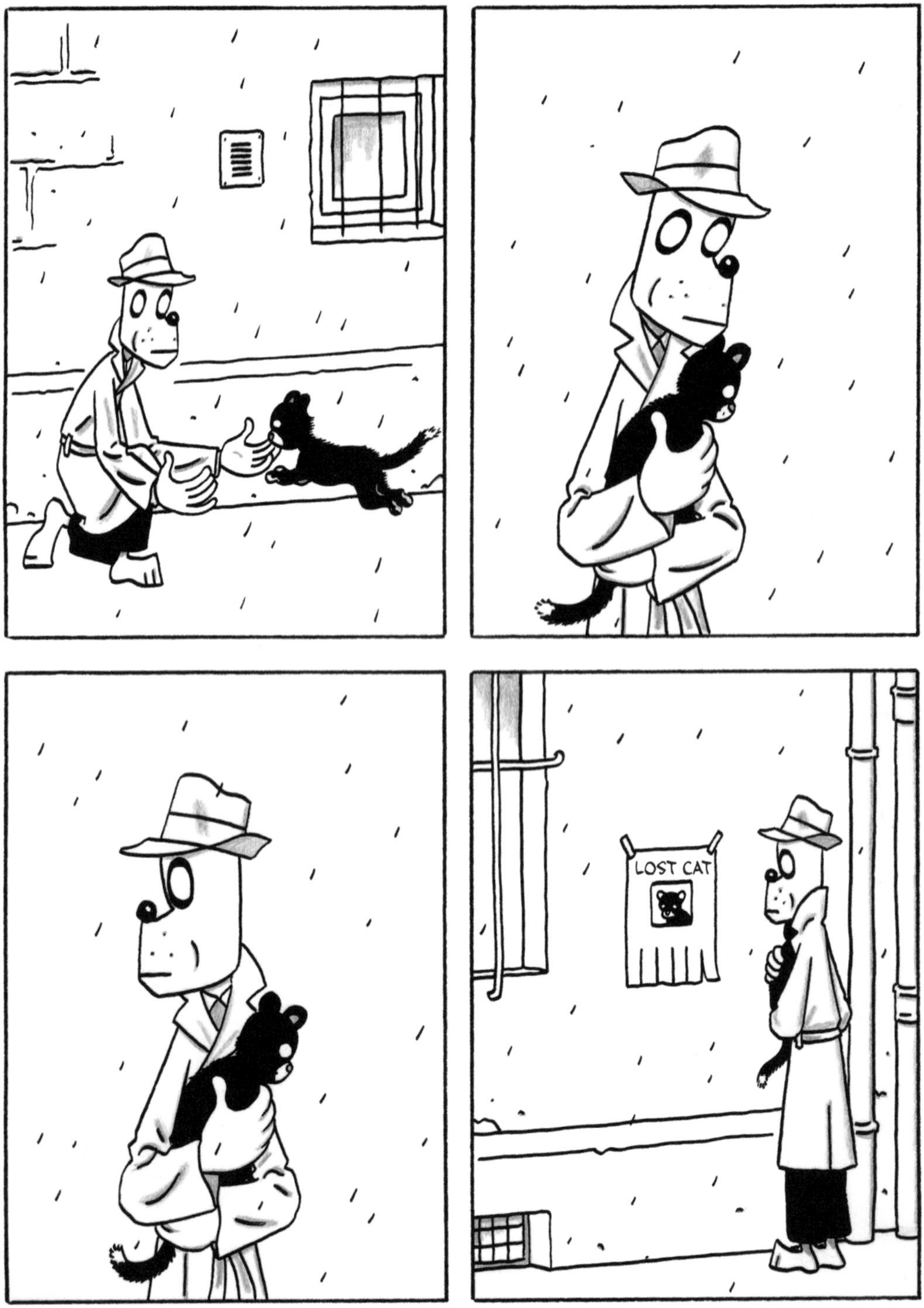
LOST CAT

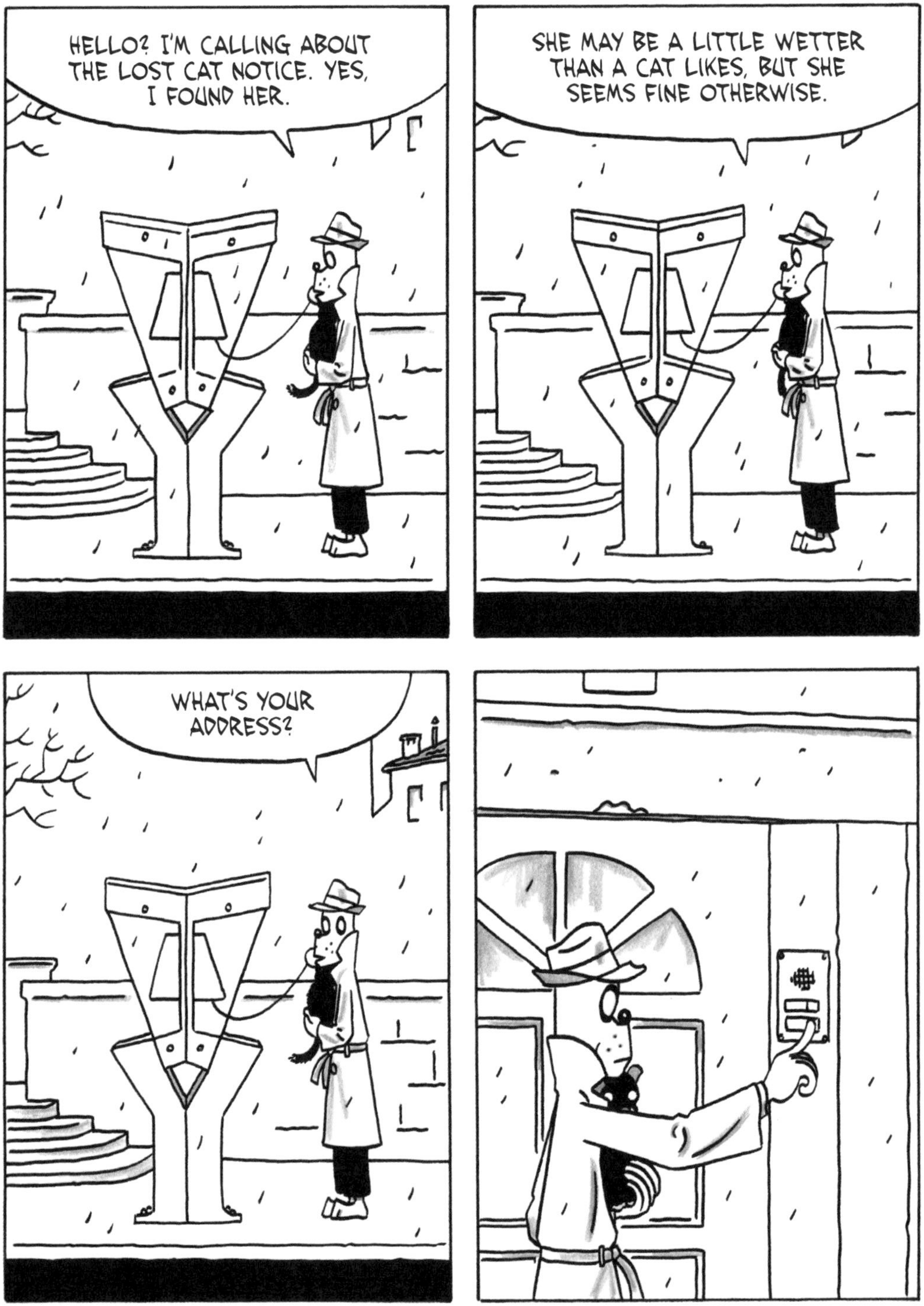
HELLO? I'M CALLING ABOUT THE LOST CAT NOTICE. YES, I FOUND HER.
SHE MAY BE A LITTLE WETTER THAN A CAT LIKES, BUT SHE SEEMS FINE OTHERWISE.
WHAT'S YOUR ADDRESS?

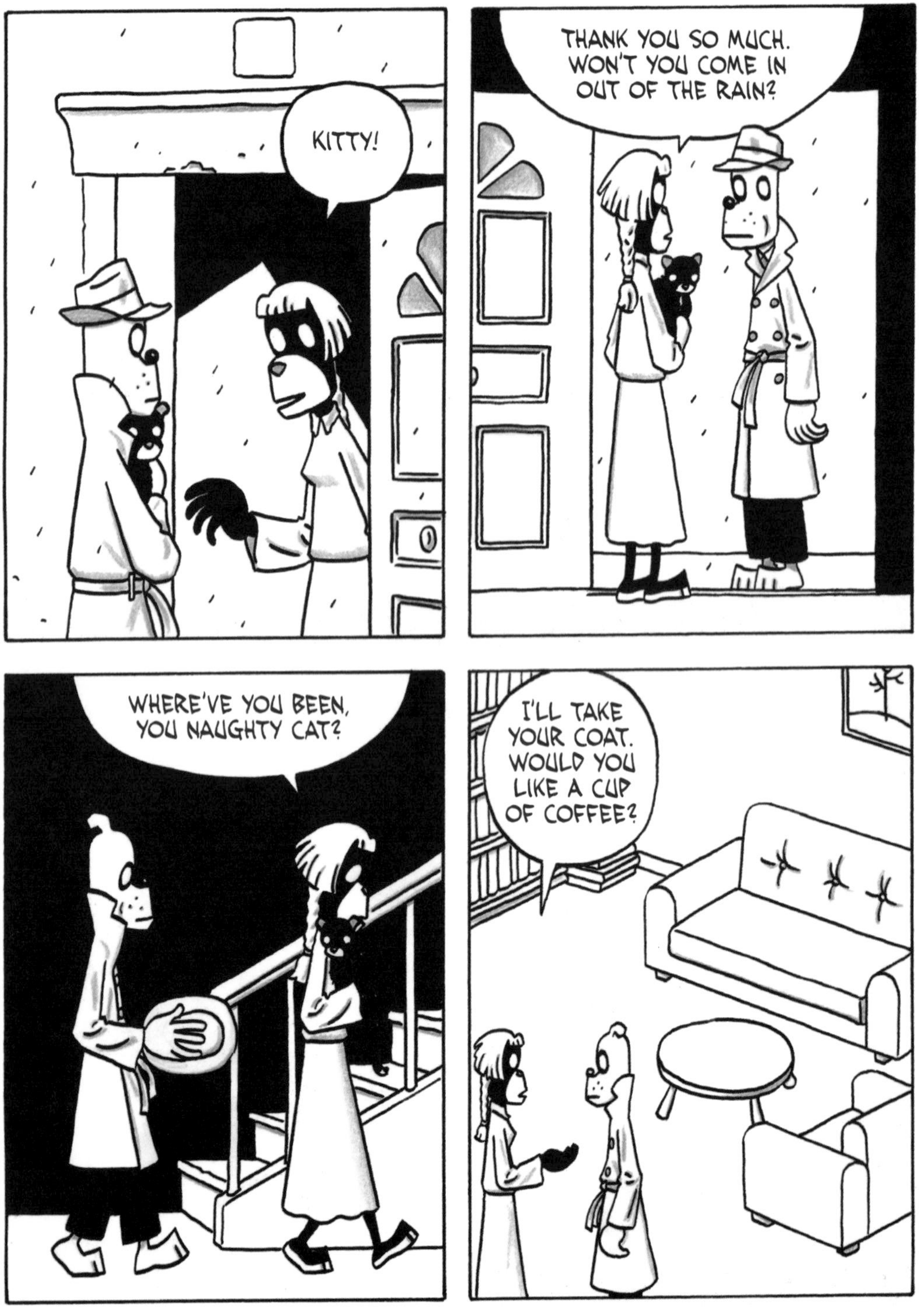
KITTY!
THANK YOU SO MUCH. WON'T YOU COME IN OUT OF THE RAIN?
WHERE'VE YOU BEEN, YOU NAUGHTY CAT?
I'LL TAKE YOUR COAT. WOULD YOU LIKE A CUP OF COFFEE?

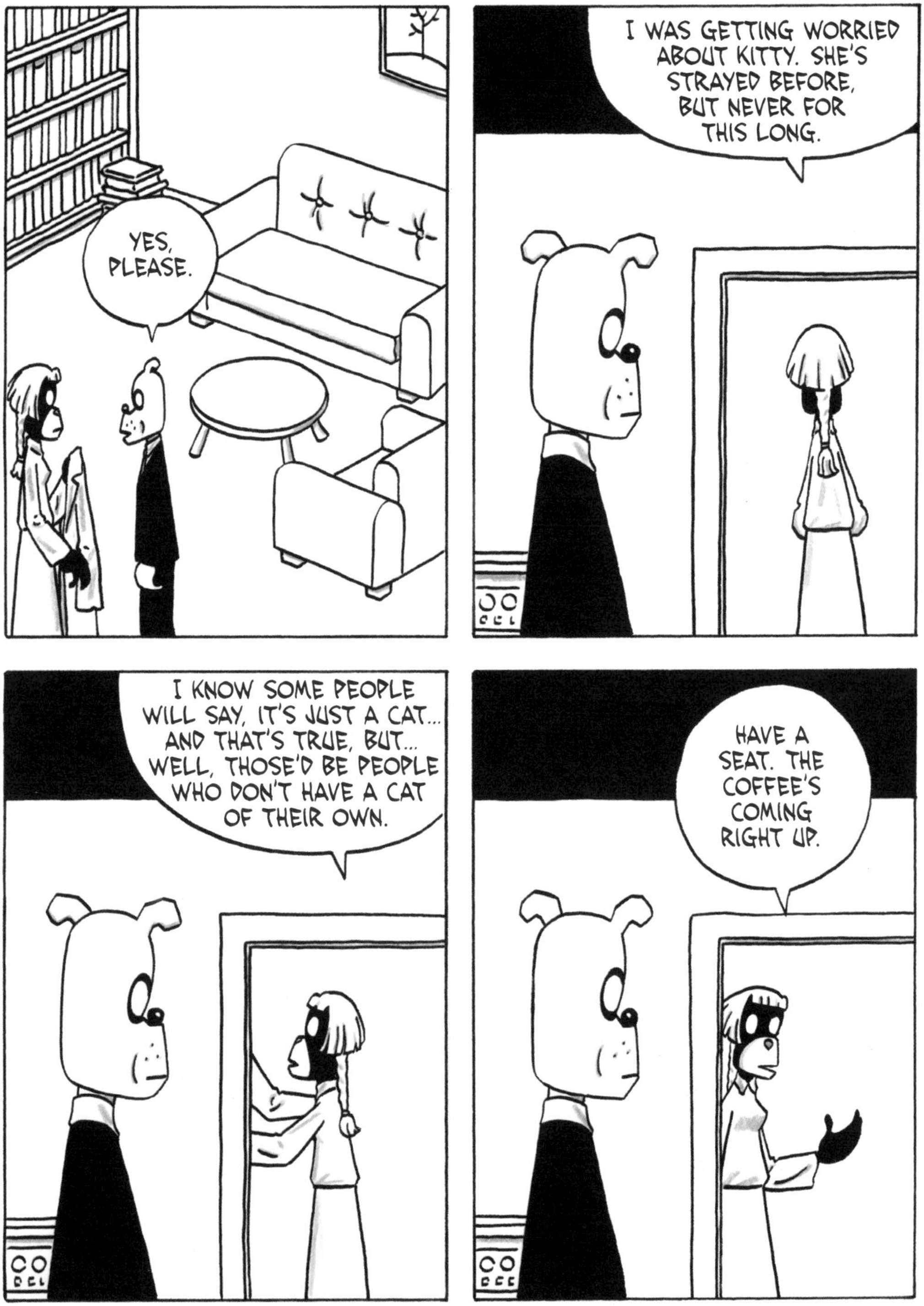
YES, PLEASE.
I WAS GETTING WORRIED ABOUT KITTY. SHE'S STRAYED BEFORE, BUT NEVER FOR THIS LONG.
I KNOW SOME PEOPLE WILL SAY, IT'S JUST A CAT... AND THAT'S TRUE, BUT... WELL, THOSE'D BE PEOPLE WHO DON'T HAVE A CAT OF THEIR OWN.
HAVE A SEAT. THE COFFEE'S COMING RIGHT UP.

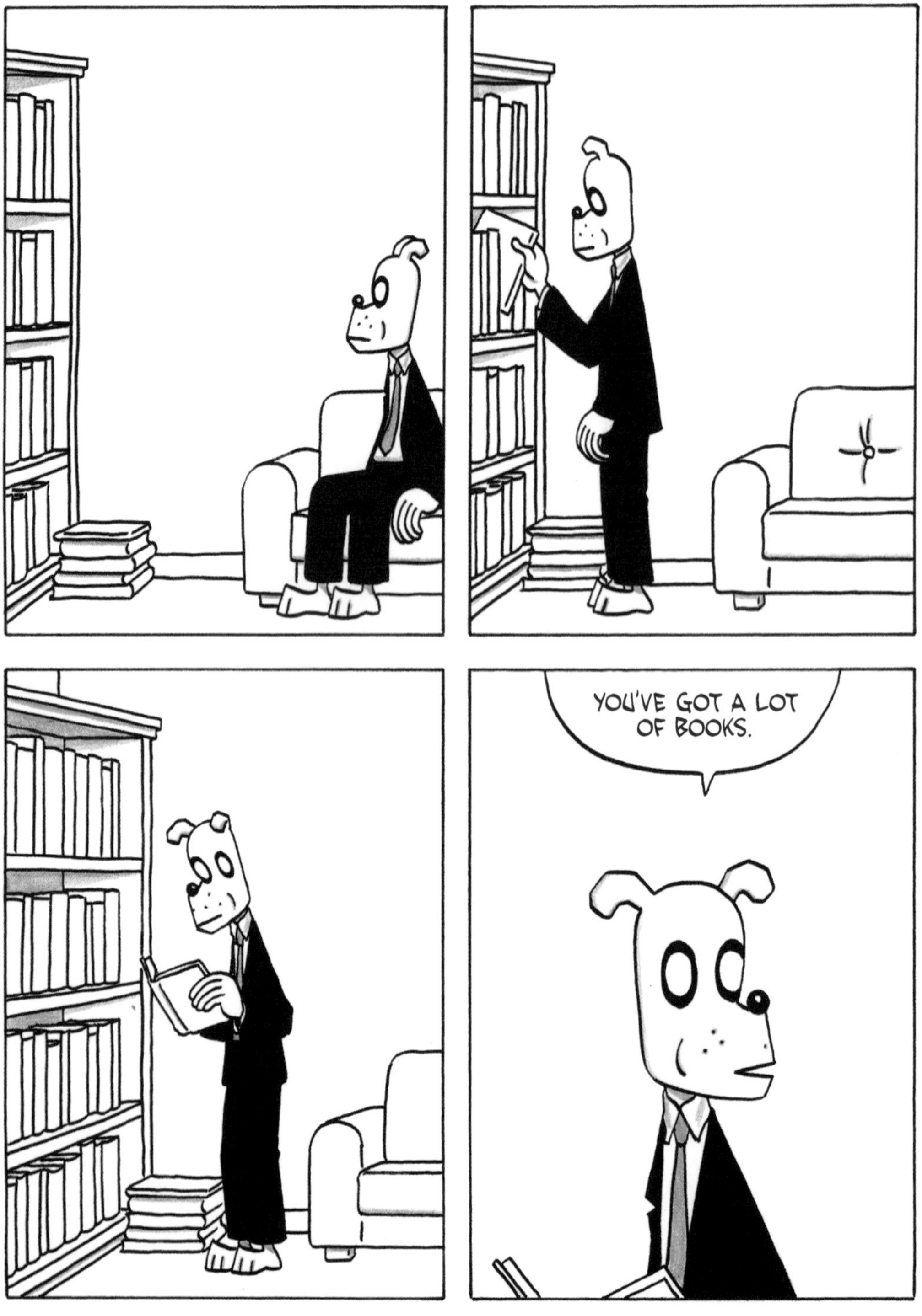
YOU'VE GOT A LOT OF BOOKS.

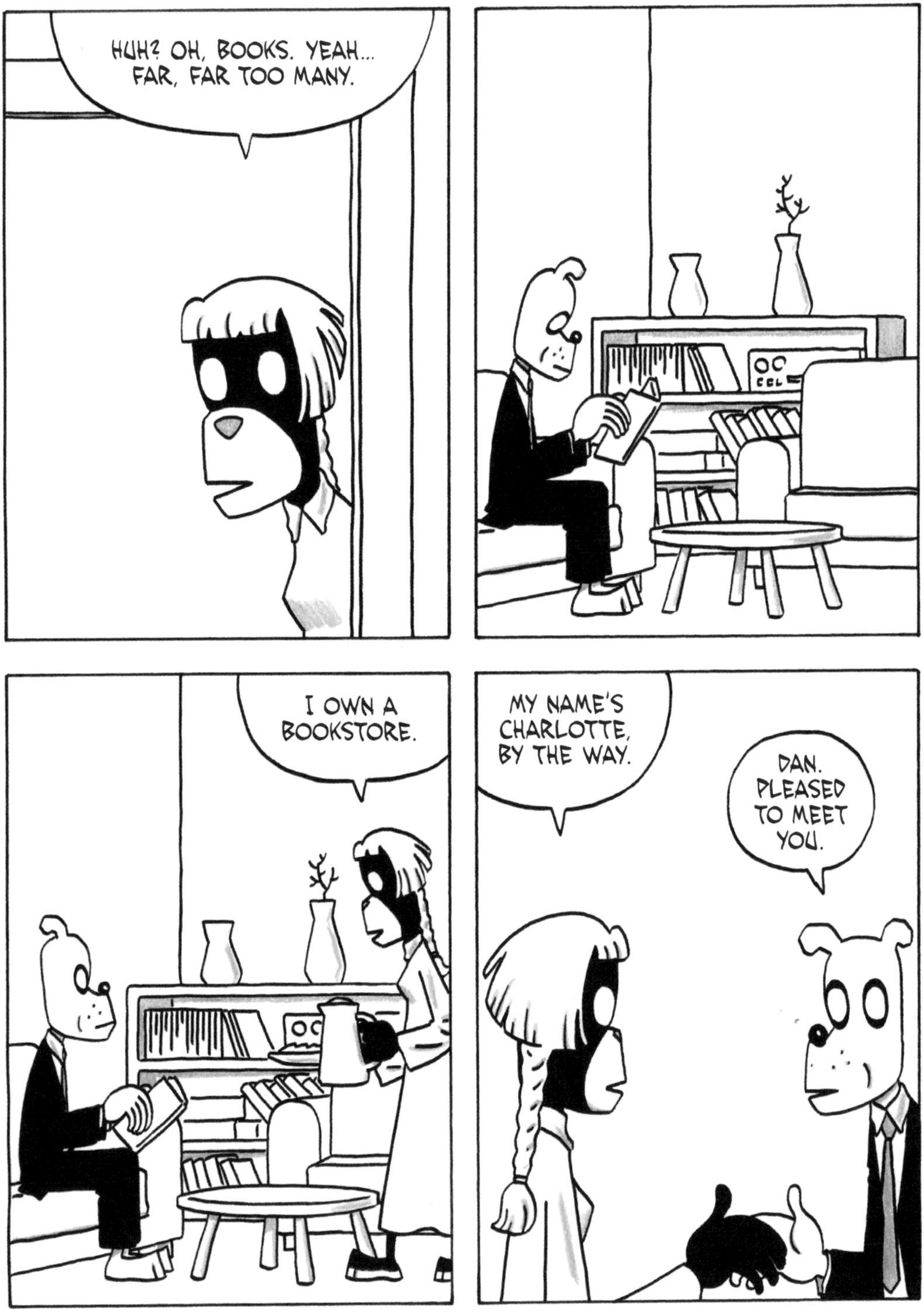
HUH? OH, BOOKS. YEAH... FAR, FAR TOO MANY.
I OWN A BOOKSTORE.
MY NAME'S CHARLOTTE, BY THE WAY.
DAN. PLEASED TO MEET YOU.

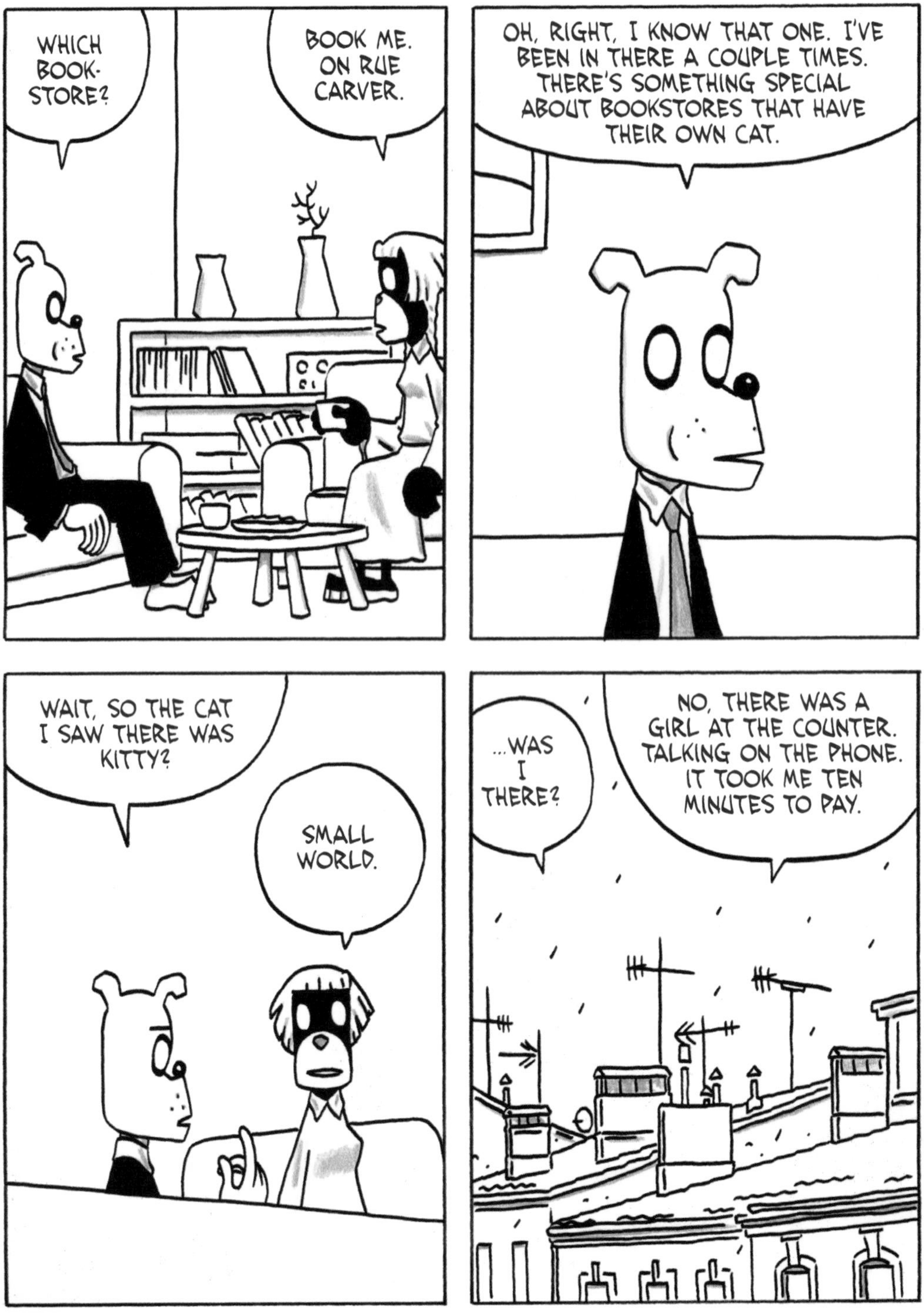
WHICH BOOK-STORE?
BOOK ME. ON RUE CARVER.
OH, RIGHT, I KNOW THAT ONE. I'VE BEEN IN THERE A COUPLE TIMES. THERE'S SOMETHING SPECIAL ABOUT BOOKSTORES THAT HAVE THEIR OWN CAT.
WAIT, SO THE CAT I SAW THERE WAS KITTY?
SMALL WORLD.
...WAS I THERE?
NO, THERE WAS A GIRL AT THE COUNTER. TALKING ON THE PHONE. IT TOOK ME TEN MINUTES TO PAY.

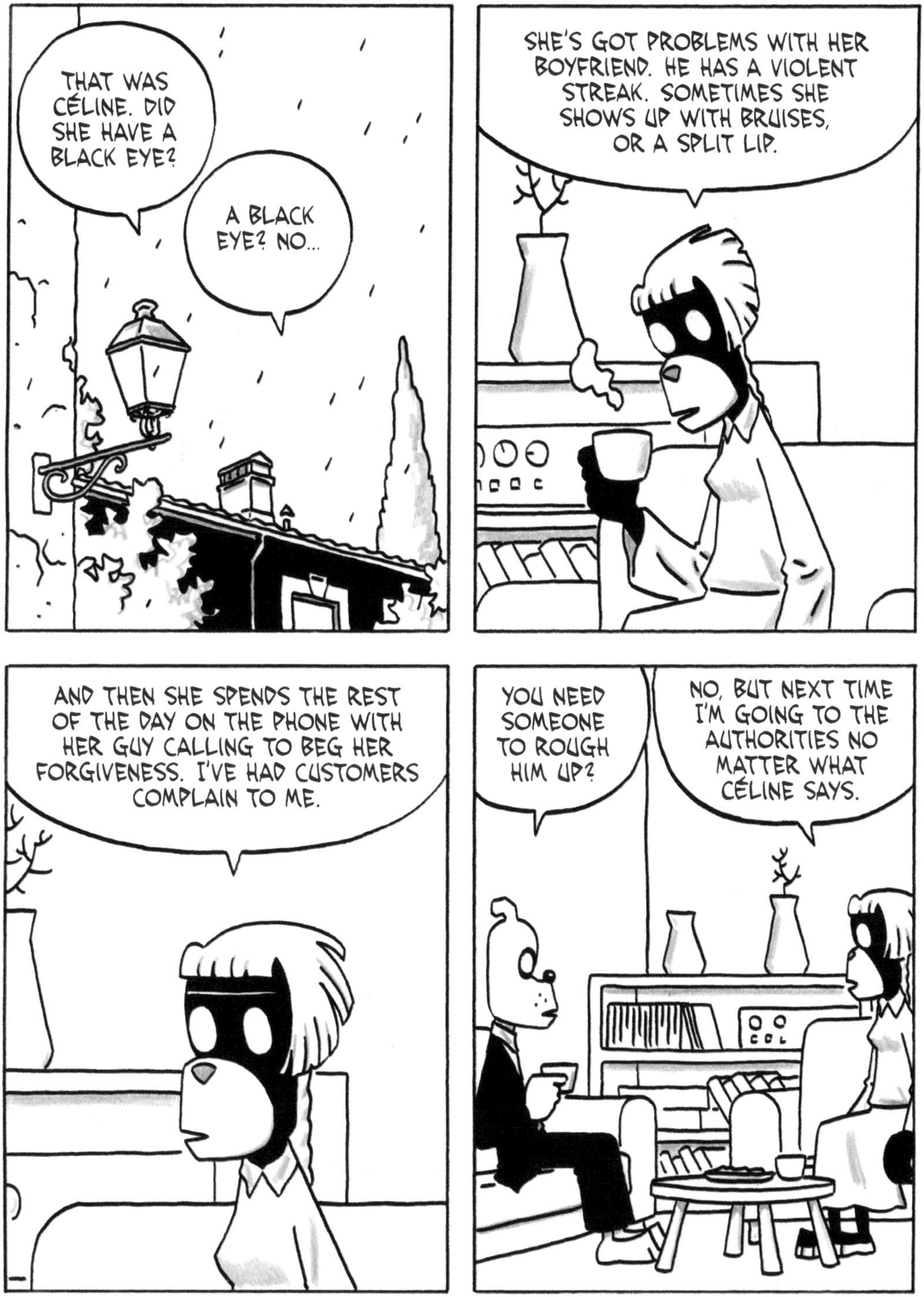
THAT WAS CÉLINE. DID SHE HAVE A BLACK EYE?
A BLACK EYE? NO...
SHE'S GOT PROBLEMS WITH HER BOYFRIEND. HE HAS A VIOLENT STREAK. SOMETIMES SHE SHOWS UP WITH BRUISES, OR A SPLIT LIP.
AND THEN SHE SPENDS THE REST OF THE DAY ON THE PHONE WITH HER GUY CALLING TO BEG HER FORGIVENESS. I'VE HAD CUSTOMERS COMPLAIN TO ME.
YOU NEED SOMEONE TO ROUGH HIM UP?
NO, BUT NEXT TIME I'M GOING TO THE AUTHORITIES NO MATTER WHAT CÉLINE SAYS.

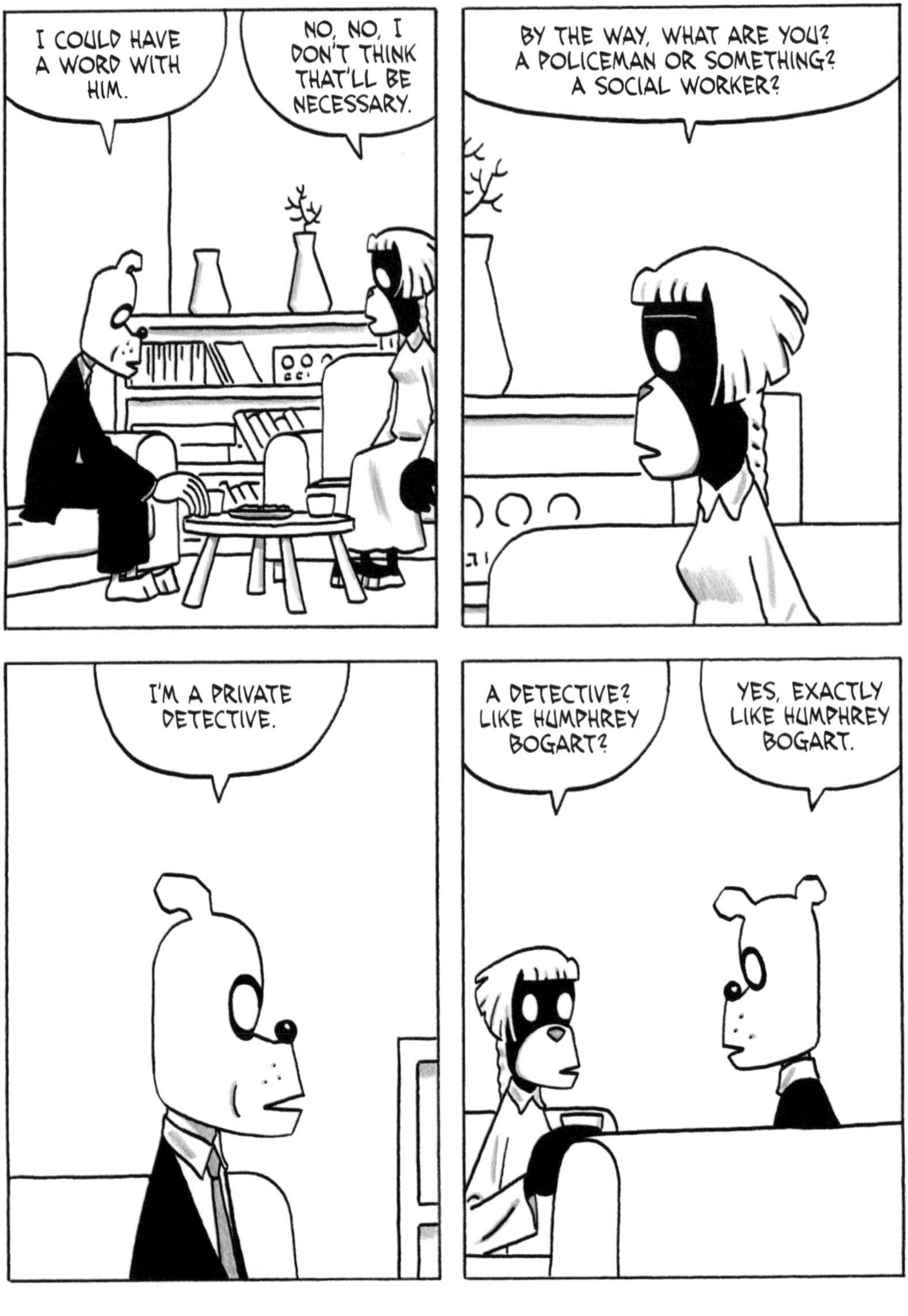
I COULD HAVE A WORD WITH HIM.
NO, NO, I DON'T THINK THAT'LL BE NECESSARY.
BY THE WAY, WHAT ARE YOU? A POLICEMAN OR SOMETHING? A SOCIAL WORKER?
I'M A PRIVATE DETECTIVE.
A DETECTIVE? LIKE HUMPHREY BOGART?
YES, EXACTLY LIKE HUMPHREY BOGART.

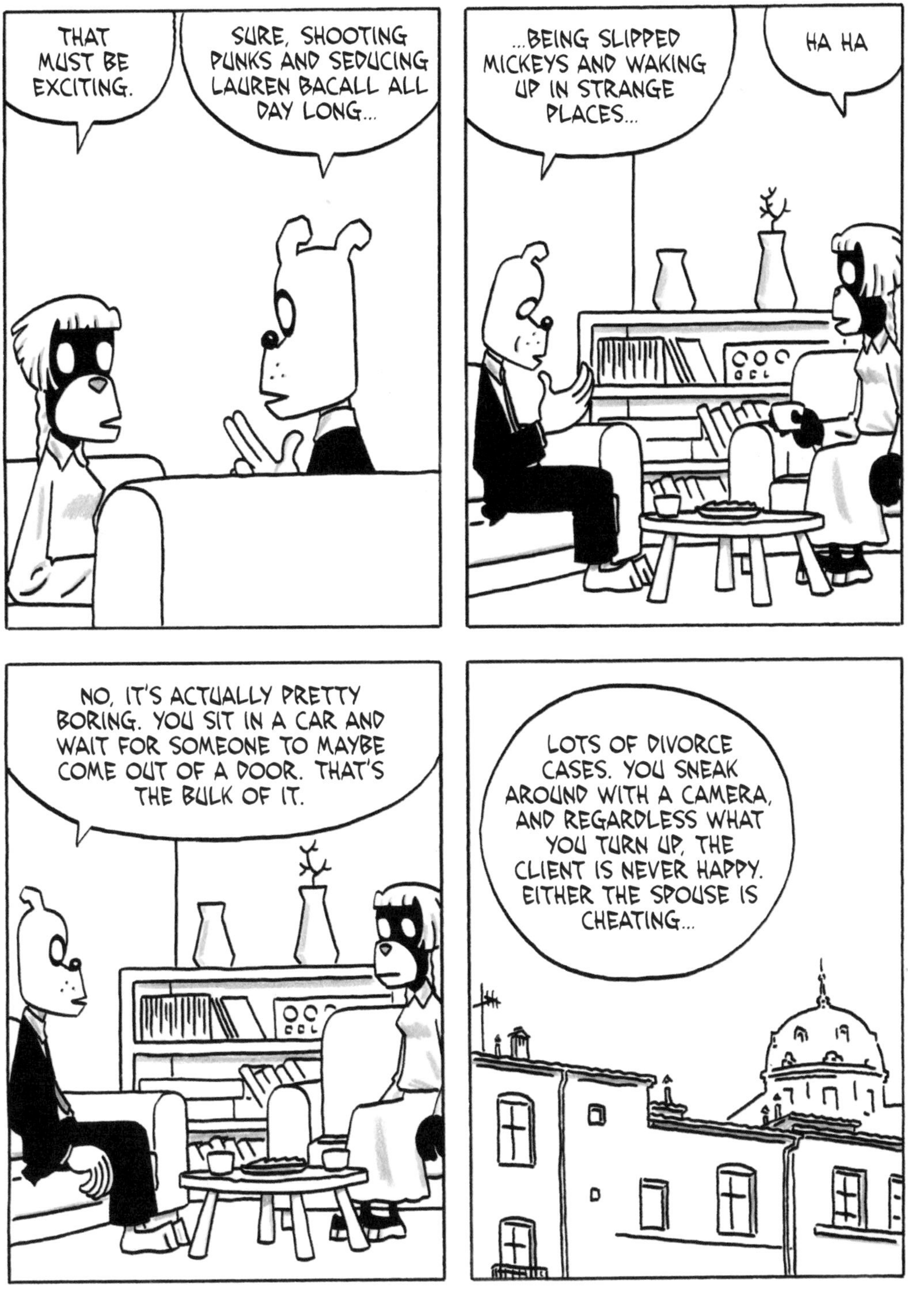
THAT MUST BE EXCITING.
SURE, SHOOTING PUNKS AND SEDUCING LAUREN BACALL ALL DAY LONG...
...BEING SLIPPED MICKEYS AND WAKING UP IN STRANGE PLACES...
HA HA
NO, IT'S ACTUALLY PRETTY BORING. YOU SIT IN A CAR AND WAIT FOR SOMEONE TO MAYBE COME OUT OF A DOOR. THAT'S THE BULK OF IT.
LOTS OF DIVORCE CASES. YOU SNEAK AROUND WITH A CAMERA, AND REGARDLESS WHAT YOU TURN UP, THE CLIENT IS NEVER HAPPY. EITHER THE SPOUSE IS CHEATING...

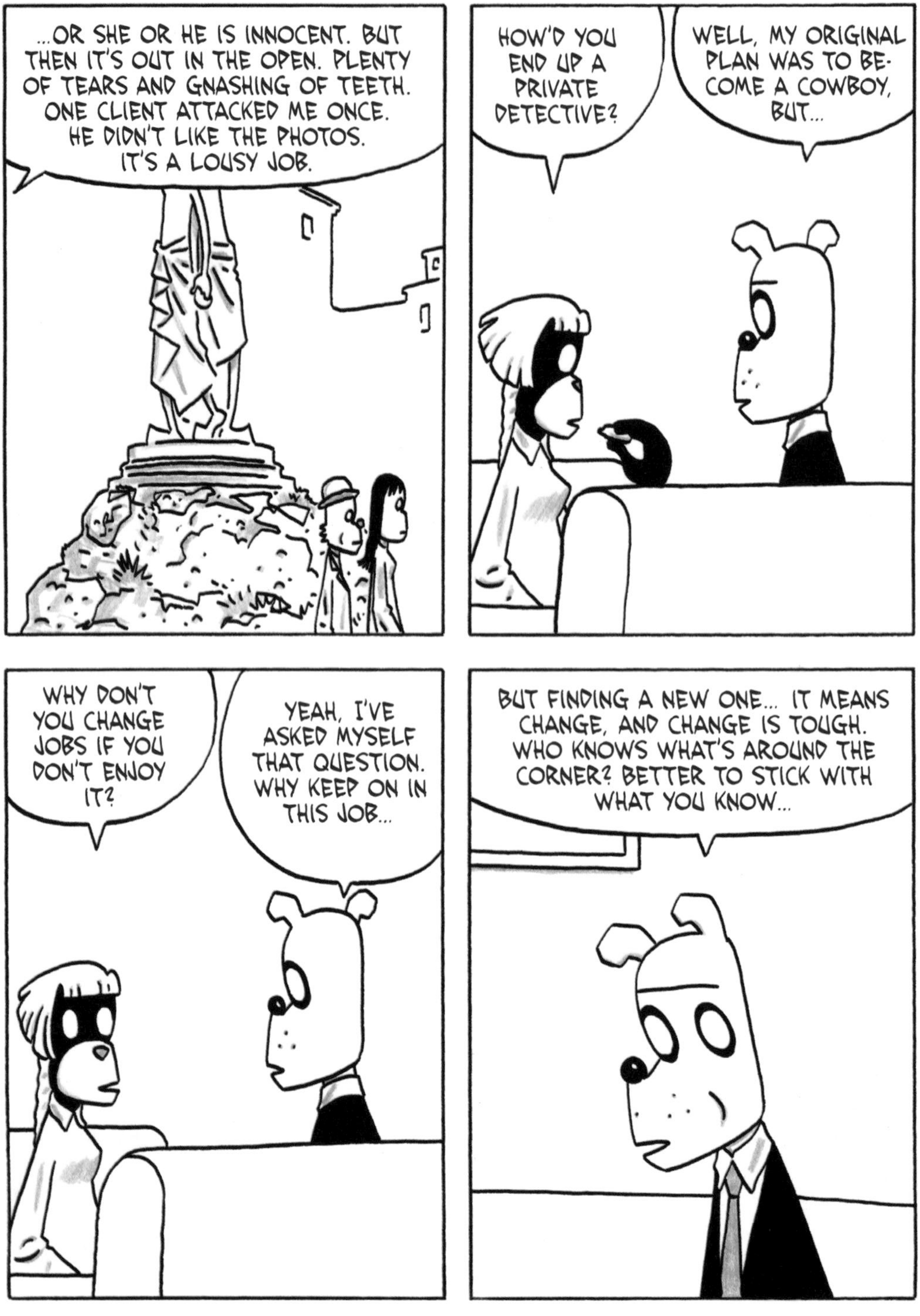
...OR SHE OR HE IS INNOCENT. BUT THEN IT'S OUT IN THE OPEN. PLENTY OF TEARS AND GNASHING OF TEETH. ONE CLIENT ATTACKED ME ONCE. HE DIDN'T LIKE THE PHOTOS. IT'S A LOUSY JOB.
HOW'D YOU END UP A PRIVATE DETECTIVE?
WELL, MY ORIGINAL PLAN WAS TO BE-COME A COWBOY, BUT...
WHY DON'T YOU CHANGE JOBS IF YOU DON'T ENJOY IT?
YEAH, I'VE ASKED MYSELF THAT QUESTION. WHY KEEP ON IN THIS JOB...
BUT FINDING A NEW ONE... IT MEANS CHANGE, AND CHANGE IS TOUGH. WHO KNOWS WHAT'S AROUND THE CORNER? BETTER TO STICK WITH WHAT YOU KNOW...

I KNOW THE FEELING. I FELT THE SAME WAY DURING MY MARRIAGE. YOU HAVE THESE EXPECTATIONS. FAIRY TALES, PROBABLY.

YOU END UP WAITING TOO LONG, HOPING THINGS'LL GET BETTER, AND EVENTUALLY, AFTER THE BREAKUP, YOU REALIZE YOU SHOULD'VE DONE IT EARLIER. YOU LOSE YEARS, TIME YOU'LL NEVER GET BACK.

ARE YOU MARRIED? OR HAVE YOU GONE THROUGH...

A DIVORCE? YES.

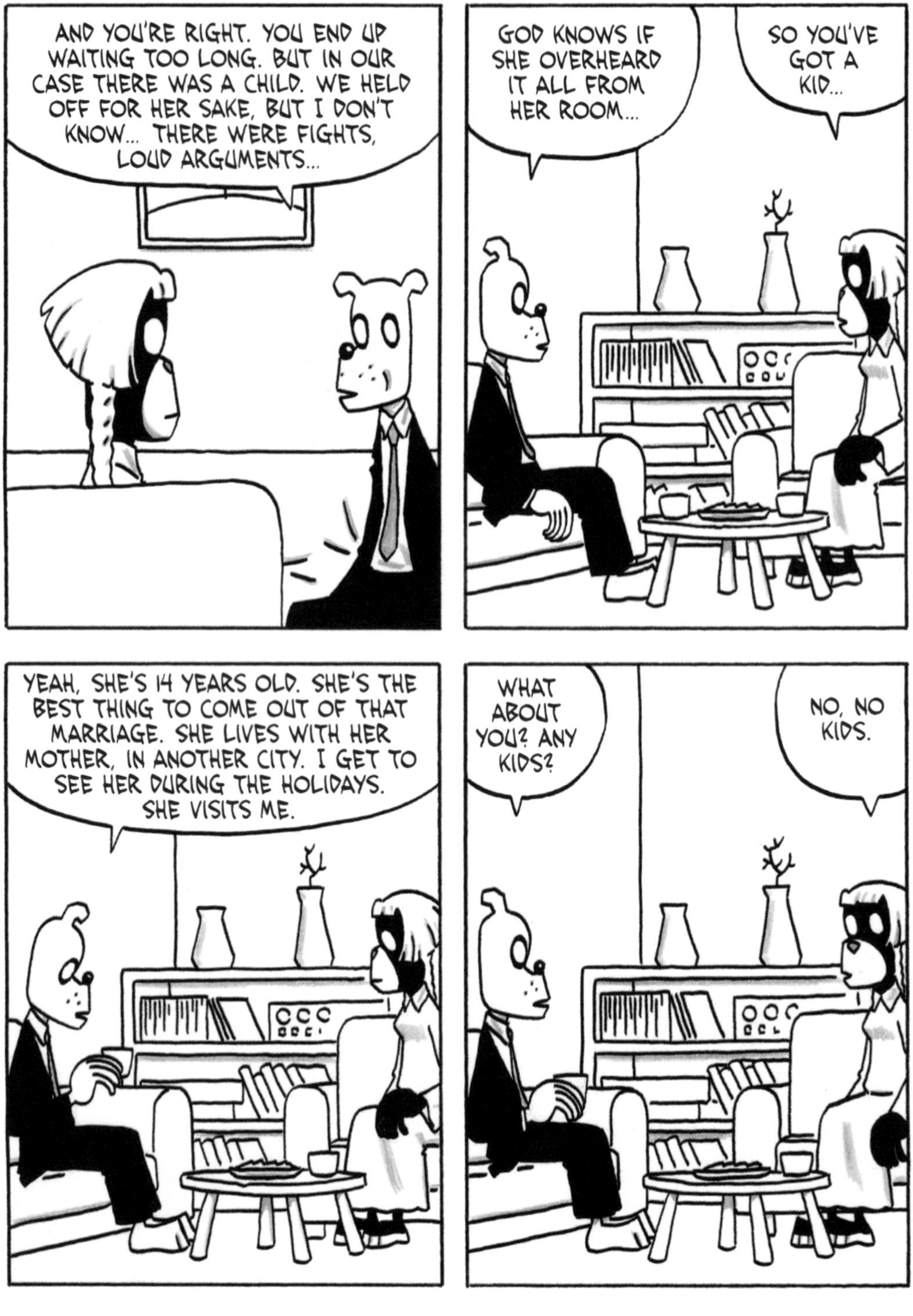
AND YOU'RE RIGHT. YOU END UP WAITING TOO LONG. BUT IN OUR CASE THERE WAS A CHILD. WE HELD OFF FOR HER SAKE, BUT I DON'T KNOW... THERE WERE FIGHTS, LOUD ARGUMENTS...
GOD KNOWS IF SHE OVERHEARD IT ALL FROM HER ROOM...
SO YOU'VE GOT A KID...
YEAH, SHE'S 14 YEARS OLD. SHE'S THE BEST THING TO COME OUT OF THAT MARRIAGE. SHE LIVES WITH HER MOTHER, IN ANOTHER CITY. I GET TO SEE HER DURING THE HOLIDAYS. SHE VISITS ME.
WHAT ABOUT YOU? ANY KIDS?
NO, NO KIDS.

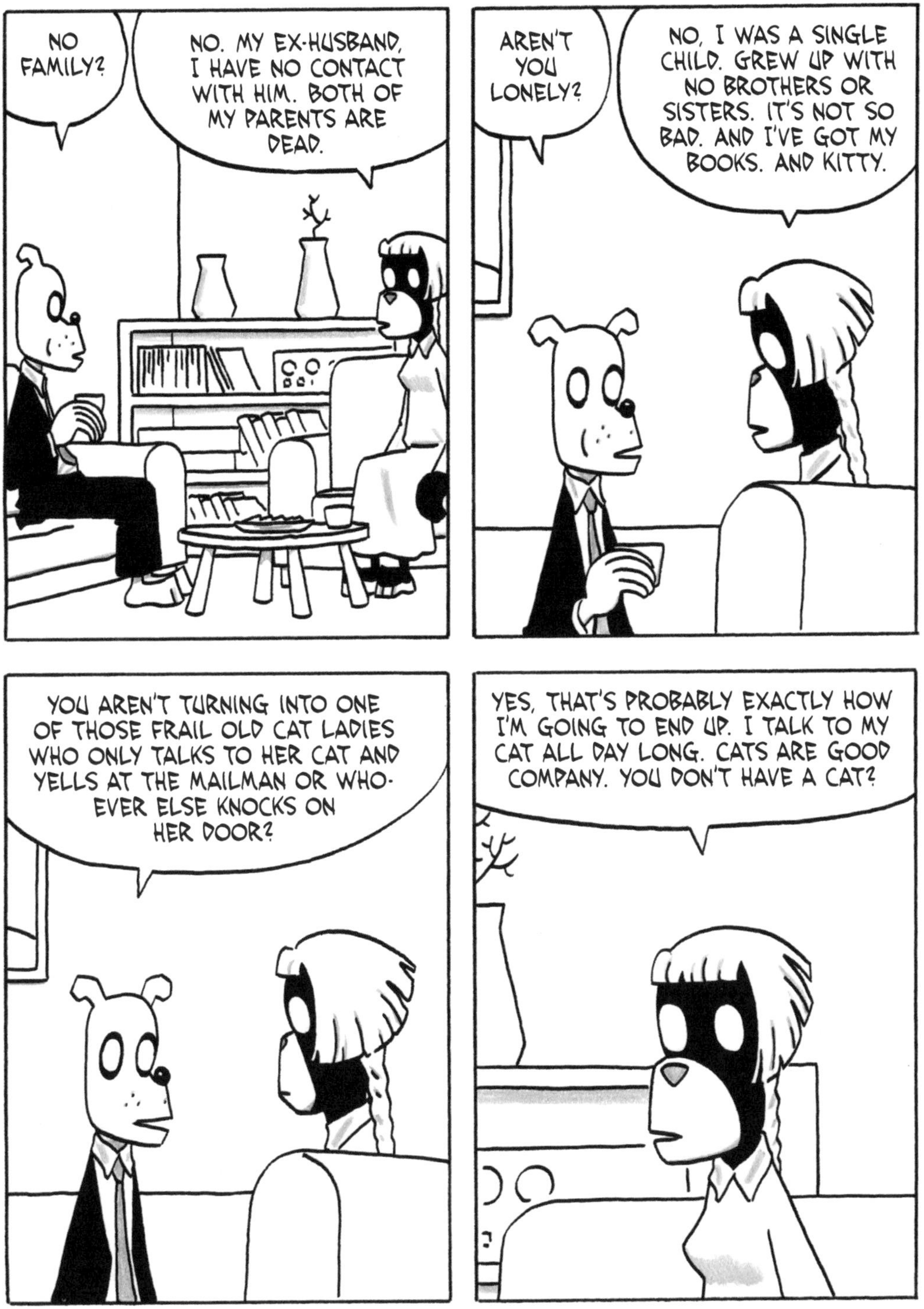
NO FAMILY?
NO. MY EX-HUSBAND, I HAVE NO CONTACT WITH HIM. BOTH OF MY PARENTS ARE DEAD.
AREN'T YOU LONELY?
NO, I WAS A SINGLE CHILD. GREW UP WITH NO BROTHERS OR SISTERS. IT'S NOT SO BAD. AND I'VE GOT MY BOOKS. AND KITTY.
YOU AREN'T TURNING INTO ONE OF THOSE FRAIL OLD CAT LADIES WHO ONLY TALKS TO HER CAT AND YELLS AT THE MAILMAN OR WHO-EVER ELSE KNOCKS ON HER DOOR?
YES, THAT'S PROBABLY EXACTLY HOW I'M GOING TO END UP. I TALK TO MY CAT ALL DAY LONG. CATS ARE GOOD COMPANY. YOU DON'T HAVE A CAT?

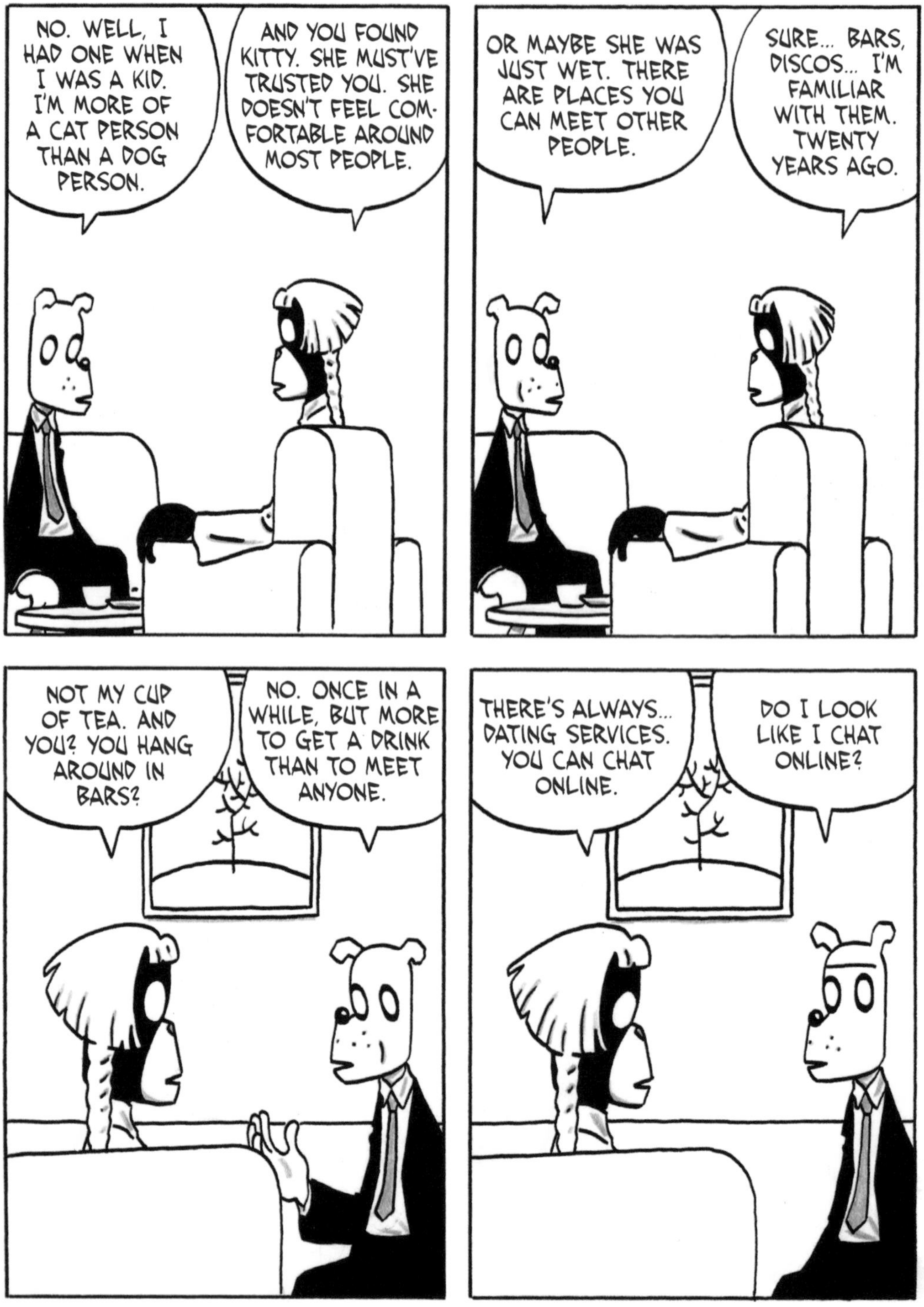
NO. WELL, I HAD ONE WHEN I WAS A KID. I'M MORE OF A CAT PERSON THAN A DOG PERSON.
AND YOU FOUND KITTY. SHE MUST'VE TRUSTED YOU. SHE DOESN'T FEEL COM-FORTABLE AROUND MOST PEOPLE.
OR MAYBE SHE WAS JUST WET. THERE ARE PLACES YOU CAN MEET OTHER PEOPLE.
SURE... BARS, DISCOS... I'M FAMILIAR WITH THEM. TWENTY YEARS AGO.
NOT MY CUP OF TEA. AND YOU? YOU HANG AROUND IN BARS?
NO. ONCE IN A WHILE, BUT MORE TO GET A DRINK THAN TO MEET ANYONE.
THERE'S ALWAYS... DATING SERVICES. YOU CAN CHAT ONLINE.
DO I LOOK LIKE I CHAT ONLINE?

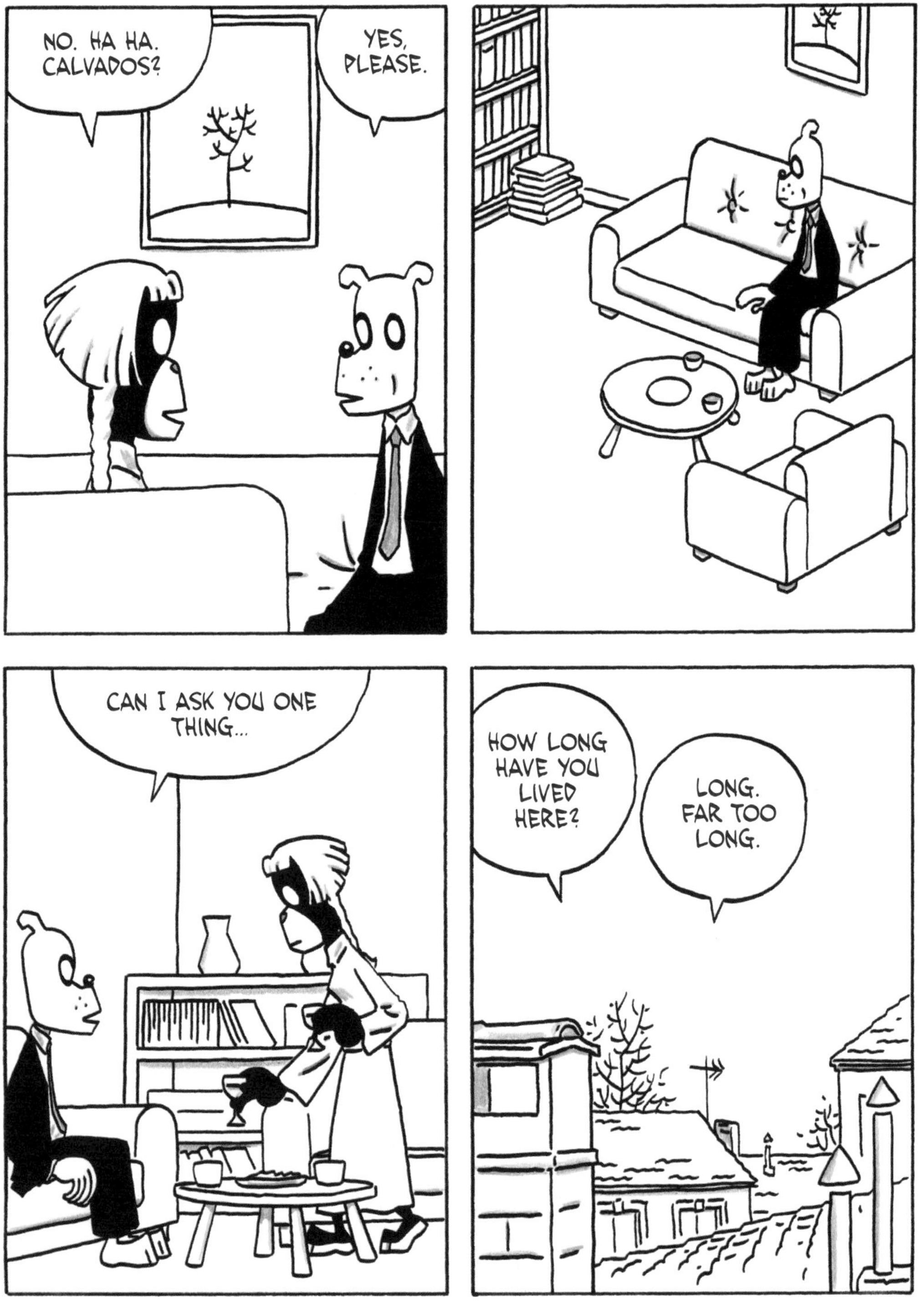
NO. HA HA. CALVADOS?
YES, PLEASE.
CAN I ASK YOU ONE THING...
HOW LONG HAVE YOU LIVED HERE?
LONG. FAR TOO LONG.

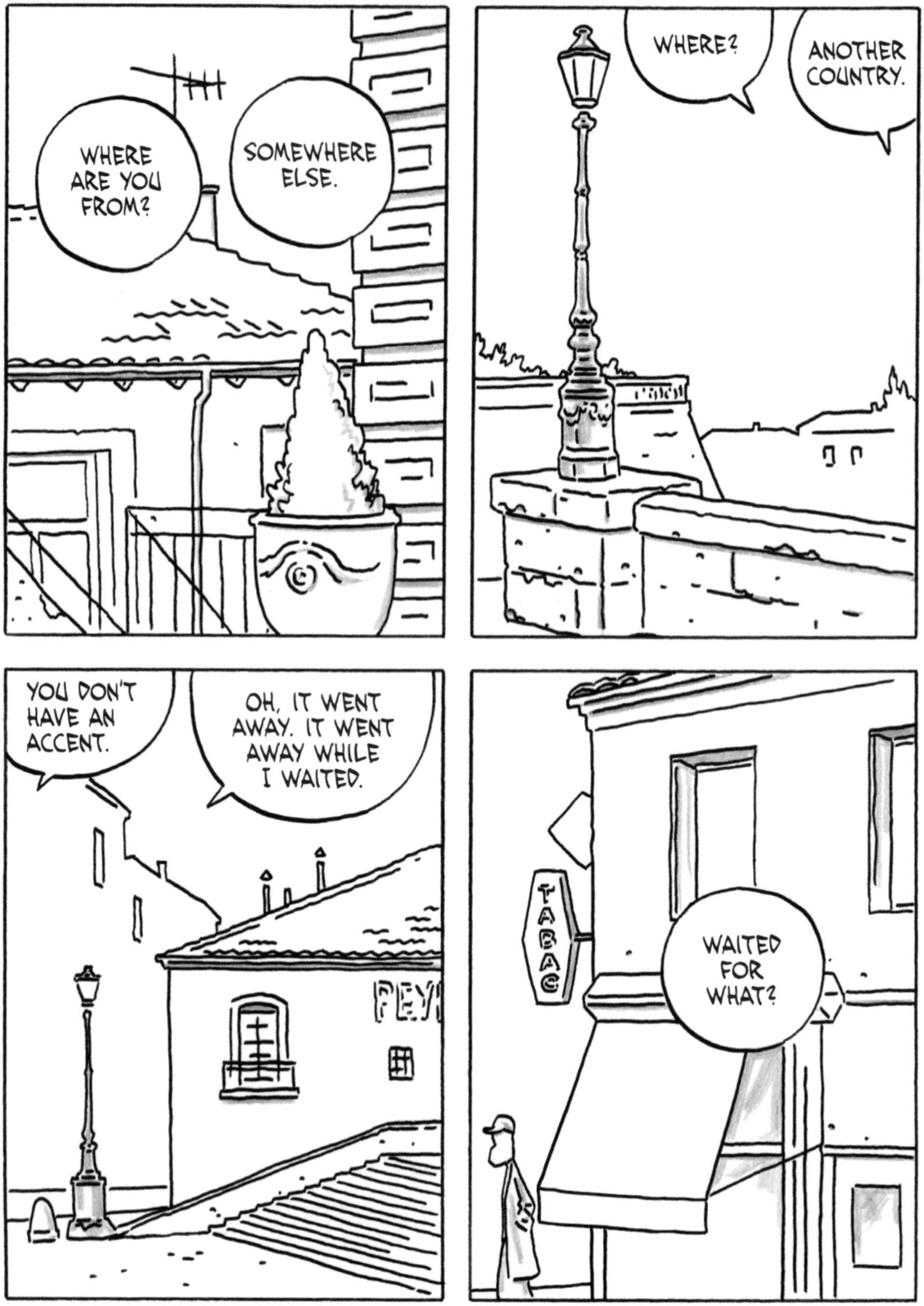
WHERE ARE YOU FROM?
SOMEWHERE ELSE.
WHERE?
ANOTHER COUNTRY.
YOU DON'T HAVE AN ACCENT.
OH, IT WENT AWAY. IT WENT AWAY WHILE I WAITED.
TABAC
WAITED FOR WHAT?

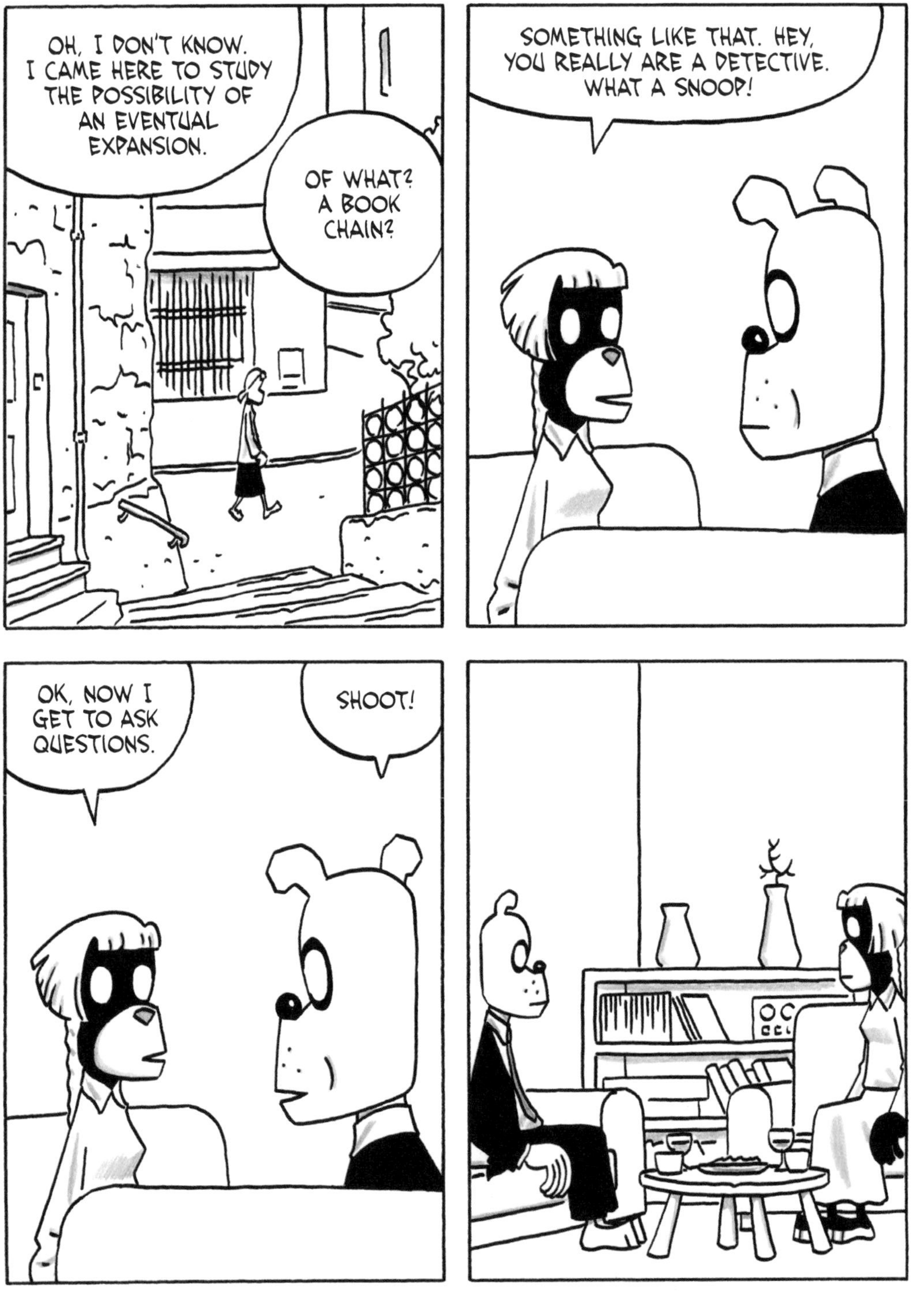
OH, I DON'T KNOW. I CAME HERE TO STUDY THE POSSIBILITY OF AN EVENTUAL EXPANSION.
OF WHAT? A BOOK CHAIN?
SOMETHING LIKE THAT. HEY, YOU REALLY ARE A DETECTIVE. WHAT A SNOOP!
OK, NOW I GET TO ASK QUESTIONS.
SHOOT!

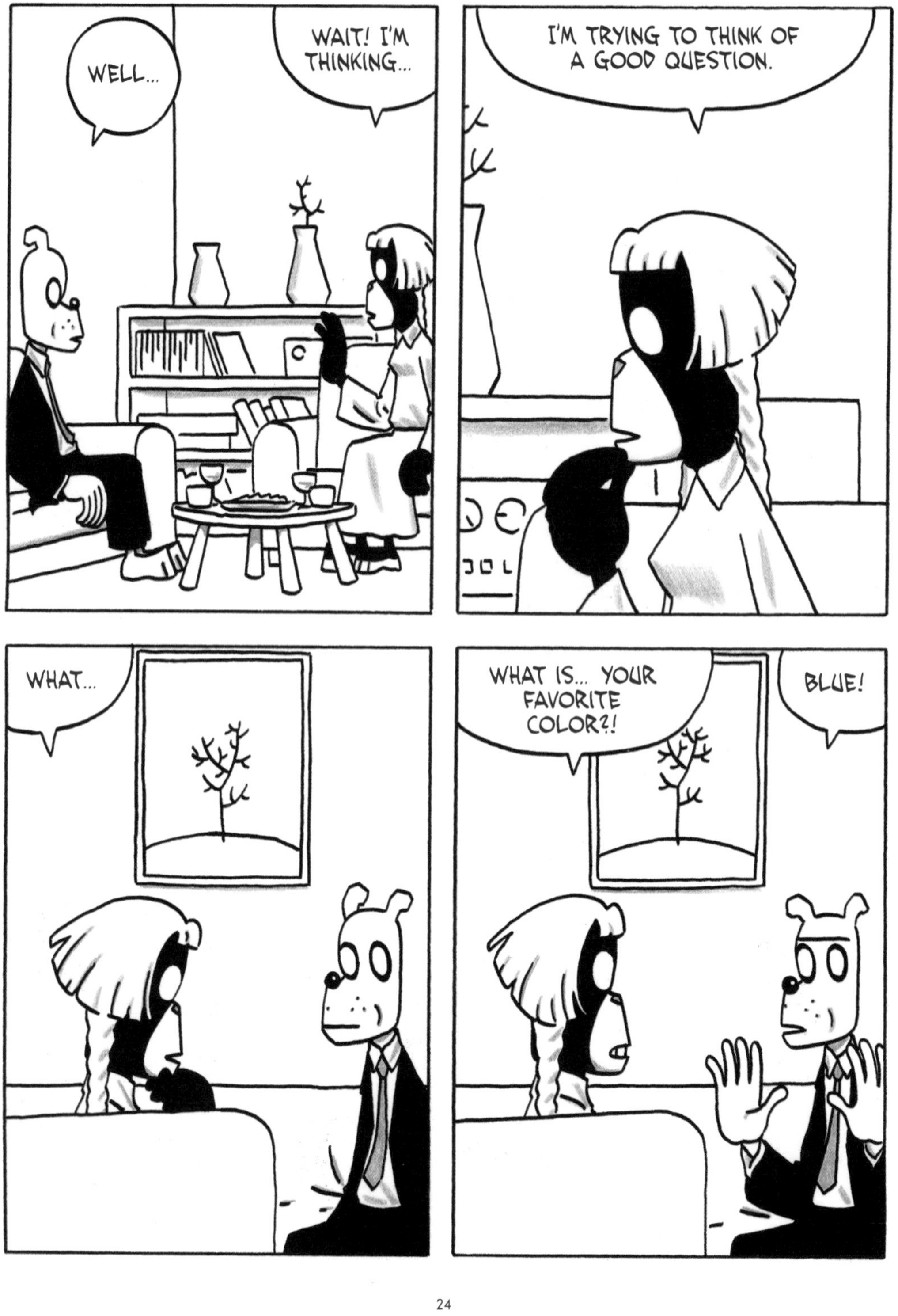
WELL...
WAIT! I'M THINKING...
I'M TRYING TO THINK OF A GOOD QUESTION.
WHAT...
WHAT IS... YOUR FAVORITE COLOR?!
BLUE!

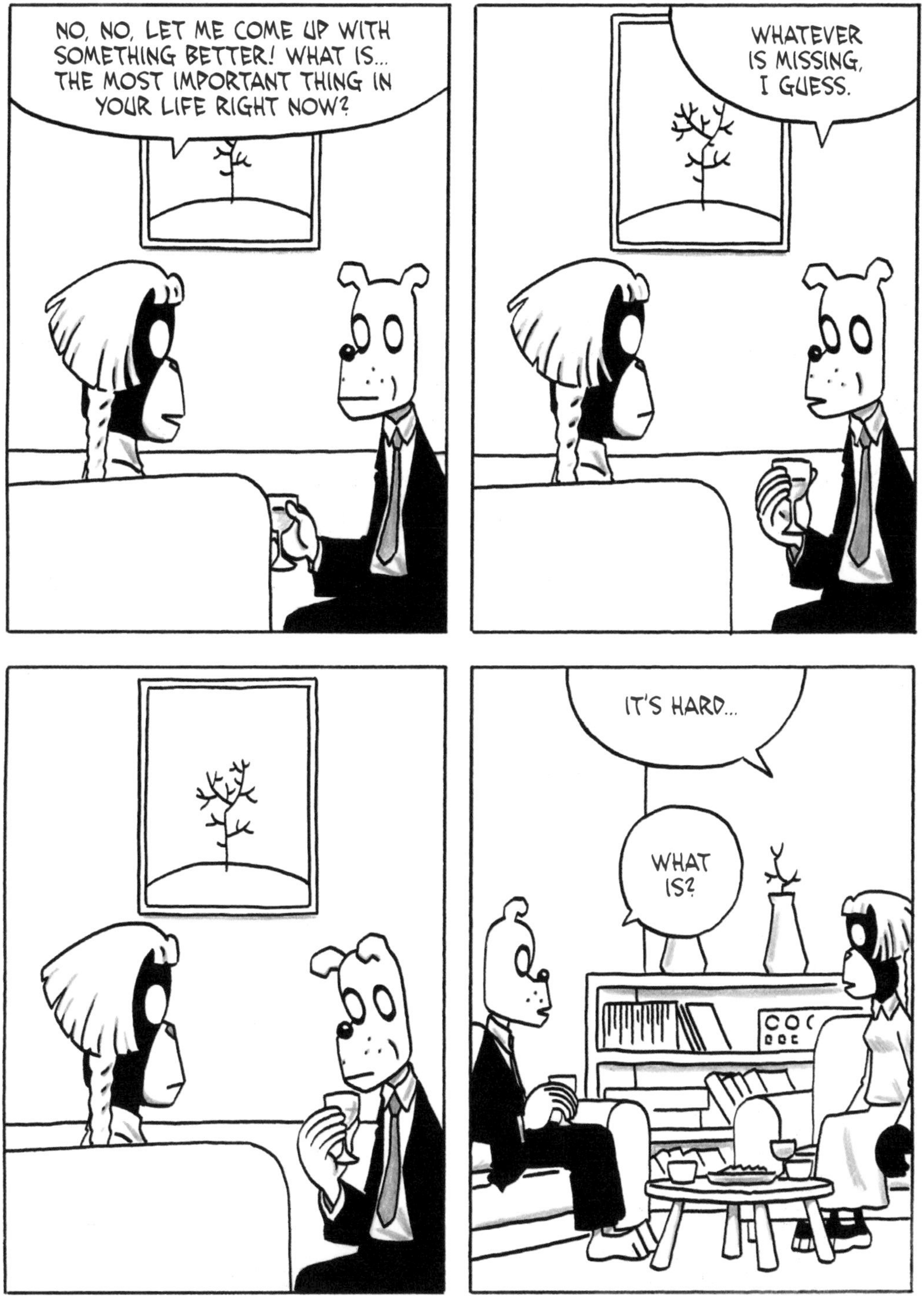
NO, NO, LET ME COME UP WITH SOMETHING BETTER! WHAT IS... THE MOST IMPORTANT THING IN YOUR LIFE RIGHT NOW?
WHATEVER IS MISSING, I GUESS.
IT'S HARD...
WHAT IS?

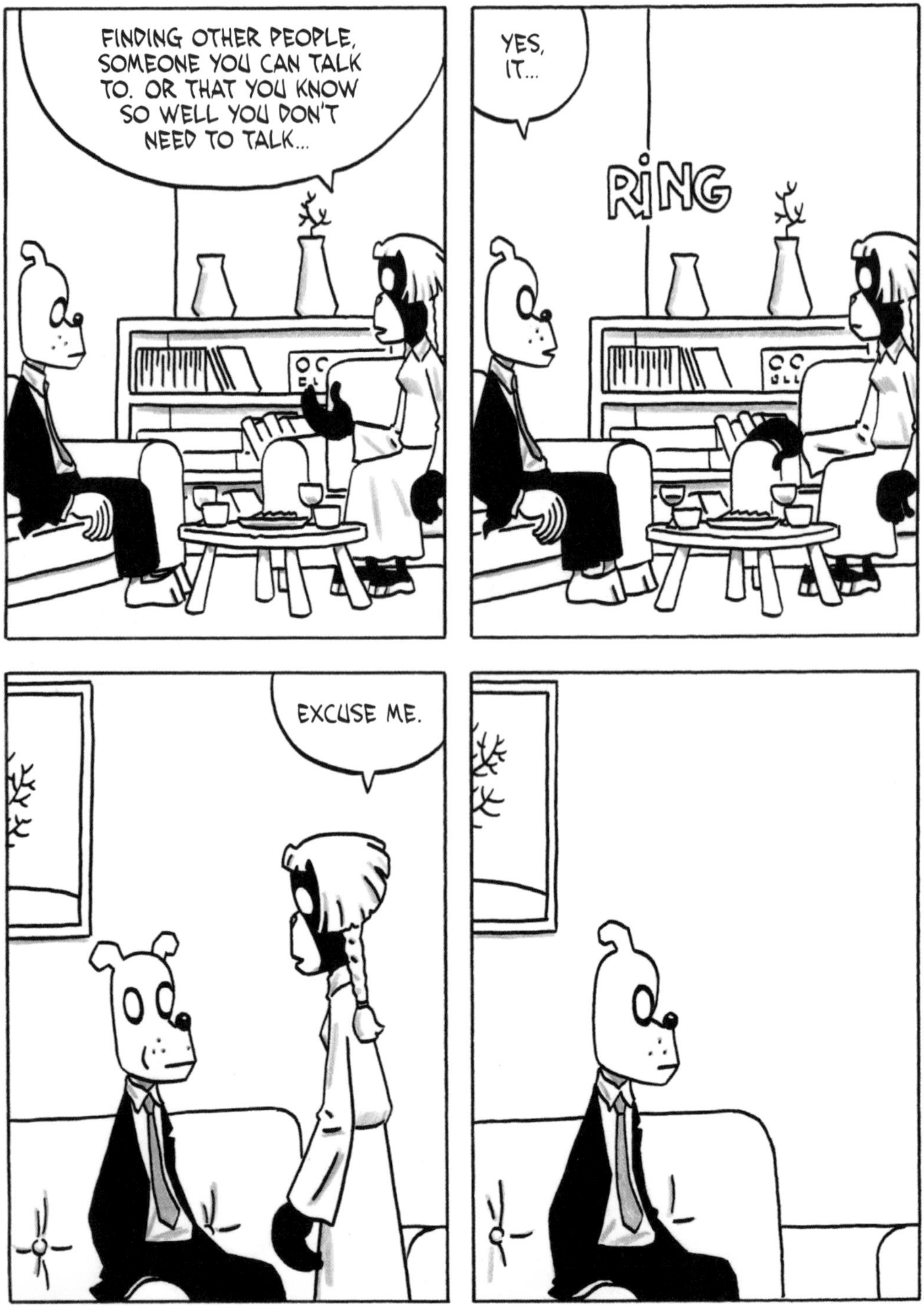
FINDING OTHER PEOPLE, SOMEONE YOU CAN TALK TO. OR THAT YOU KNOW SO WELL YOU DON'T NEED TO TALK...
YES, IT...
RING
EXCUSE ME.

DETECTIVE

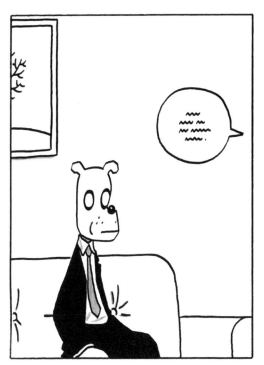

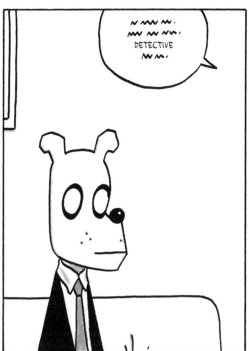

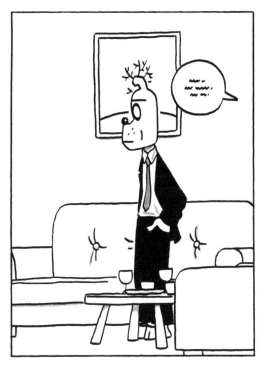

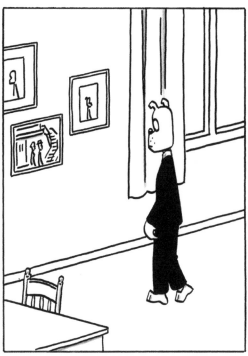

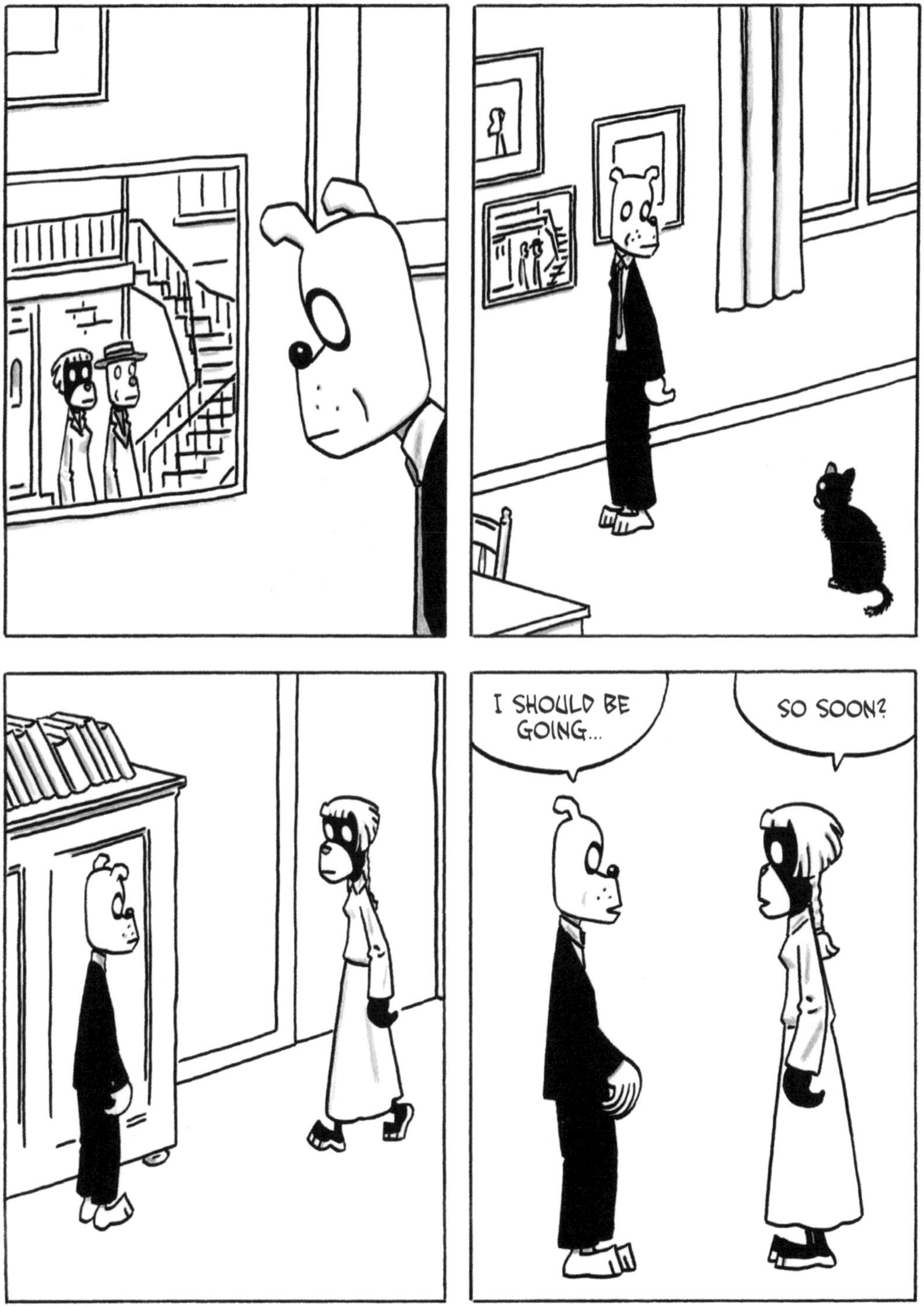
I SHOULD BE GOING...
SO SOON?

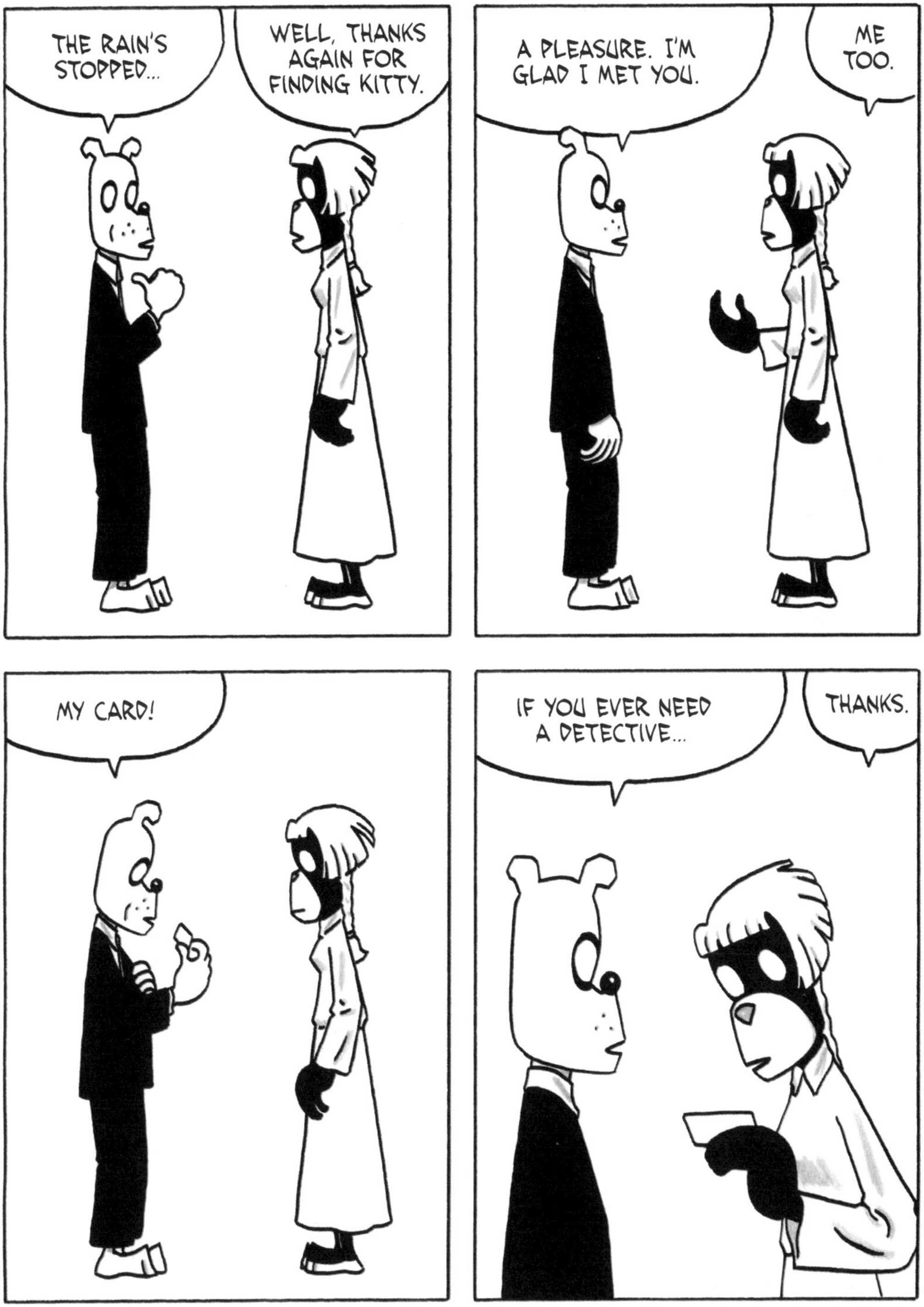
THE RAIN'S STOPPED...
WELL, THANKS AGAIN FOR FINDING KITTY.
A PLEASURE. I'M GLAD I MET YOU.
ME TOO.
MY CARD!
IF YOU EVER NEED A DETECTIVE...
THANKS.

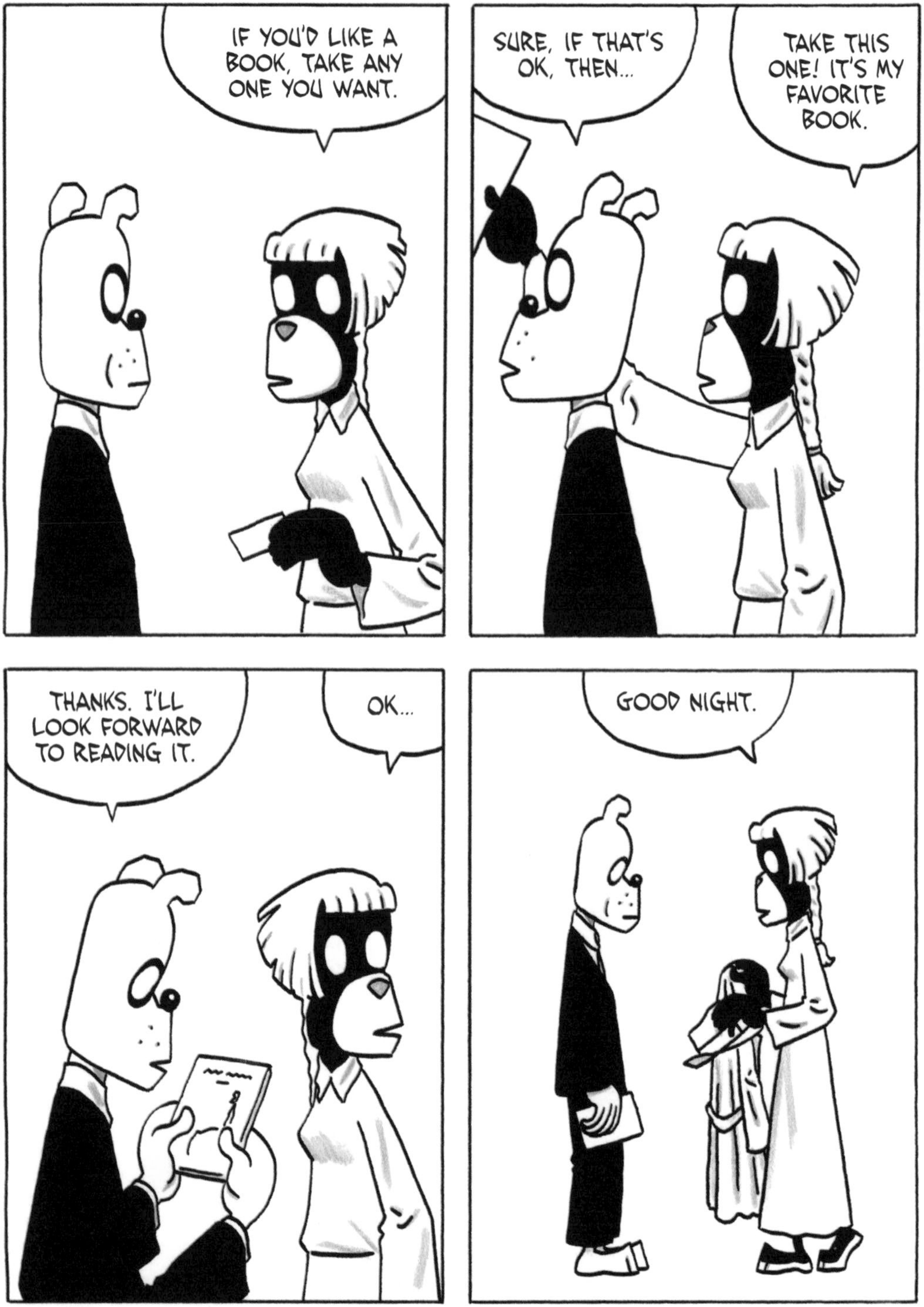
IF YOU'D LIKE A BOOK, TAKE ANY ONE YOU WANT.
SURE, IF THAT'S OK, THEN...
TAKE THIS ONE! IT'S MY FAVORITE BOOK.
THANKS. I'LL LOOK FORWARD TO READING IT.
OK...
GOOD NIGHT.

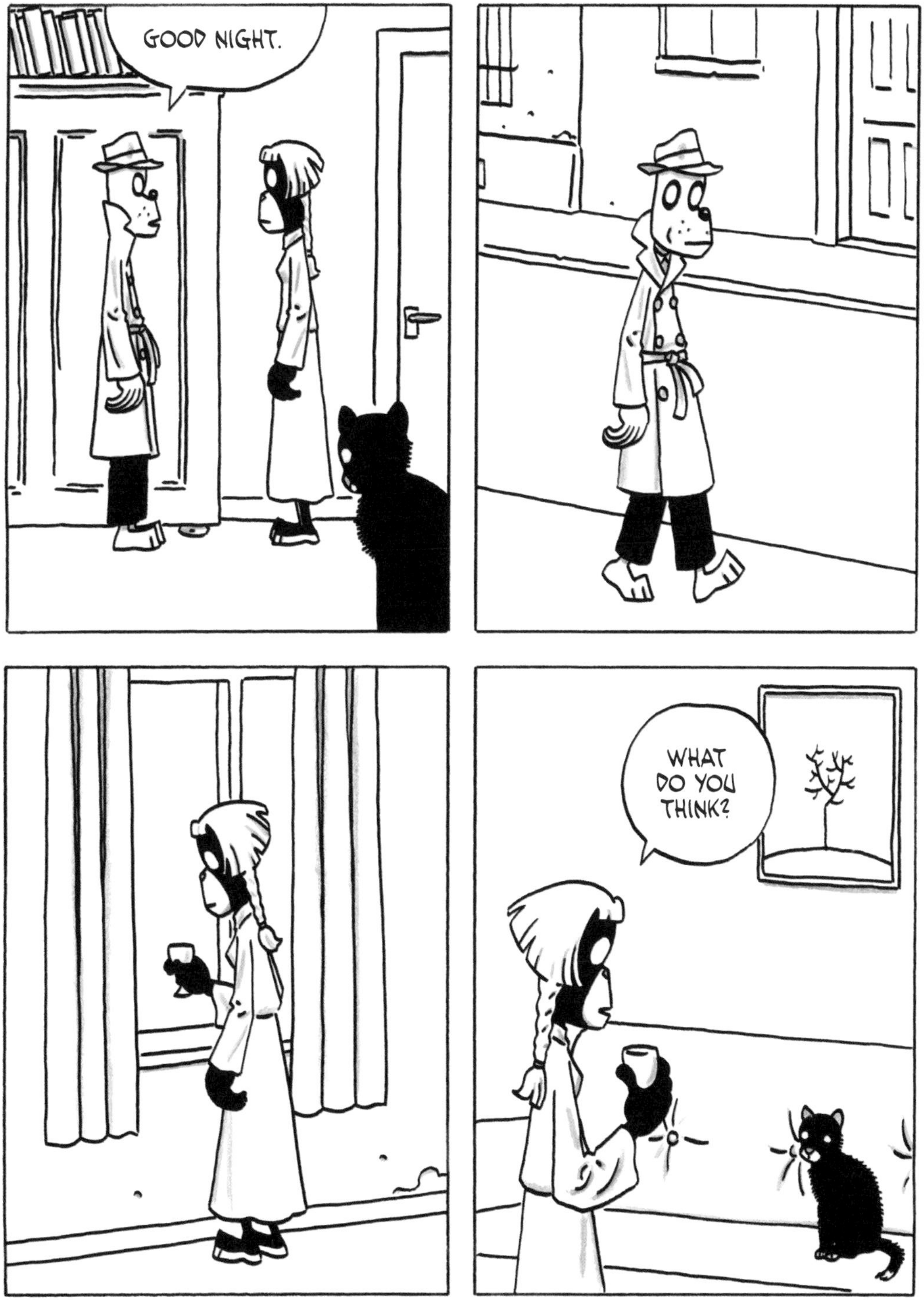
GOOD NIGHT.
WHAT DO YOU THINK?

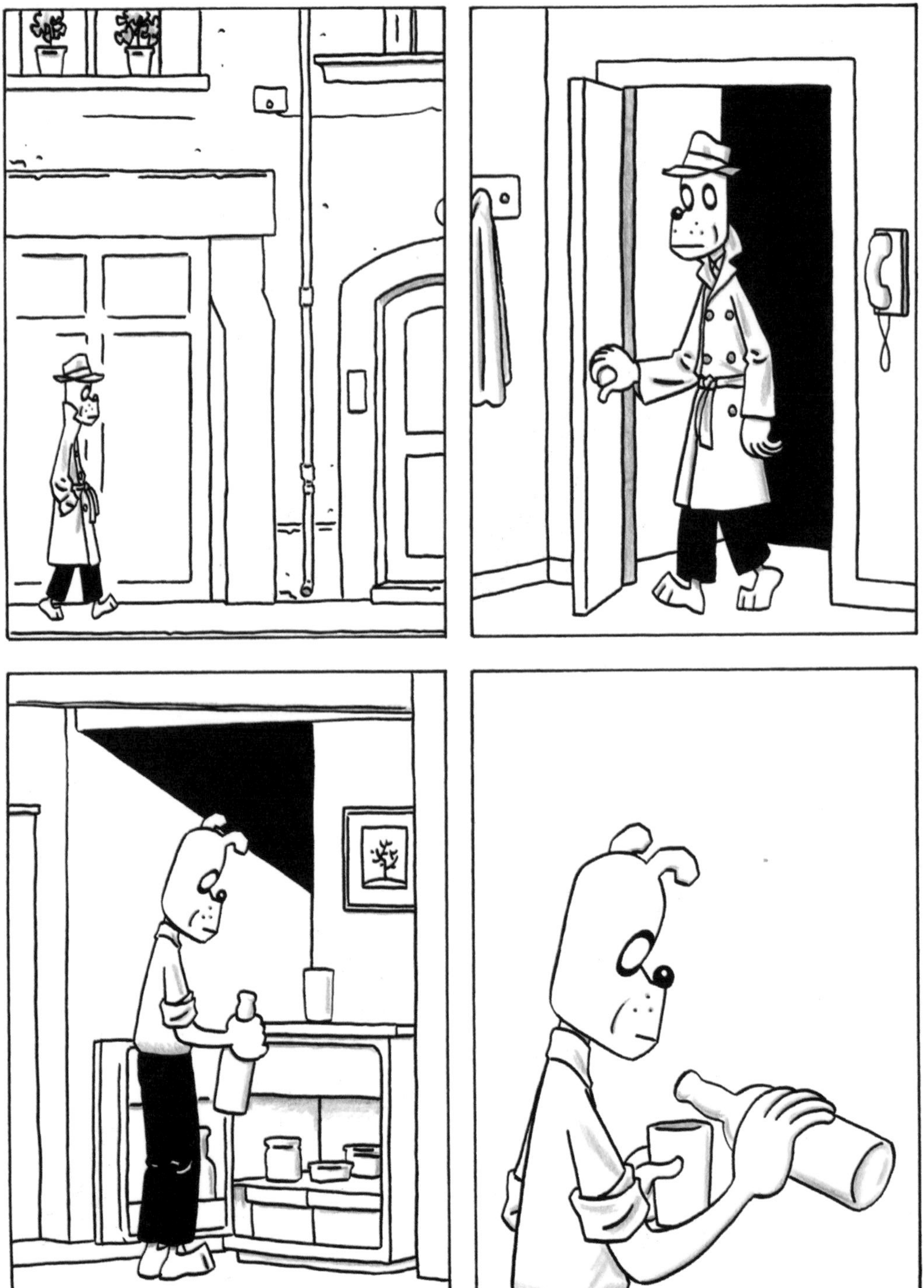

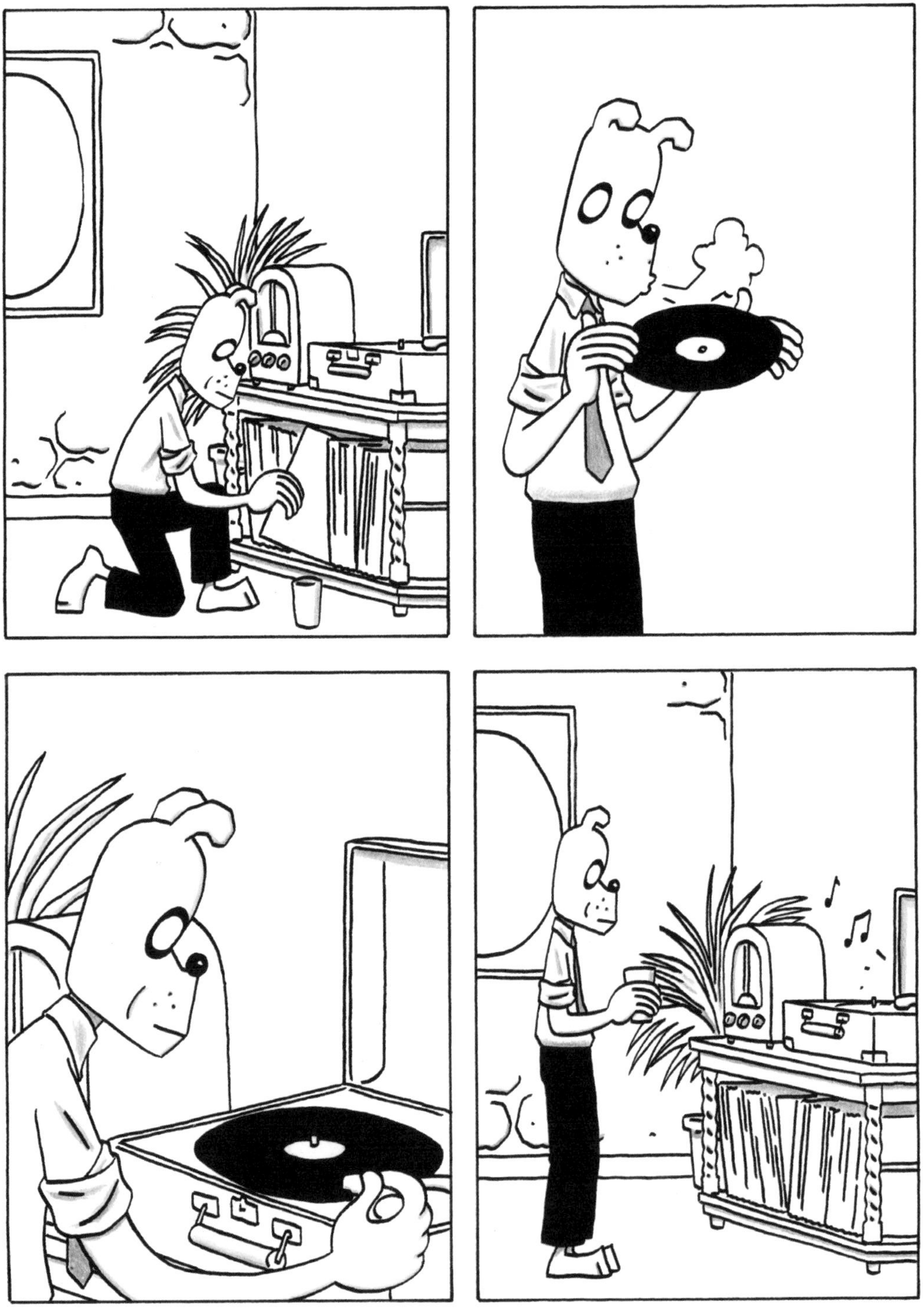

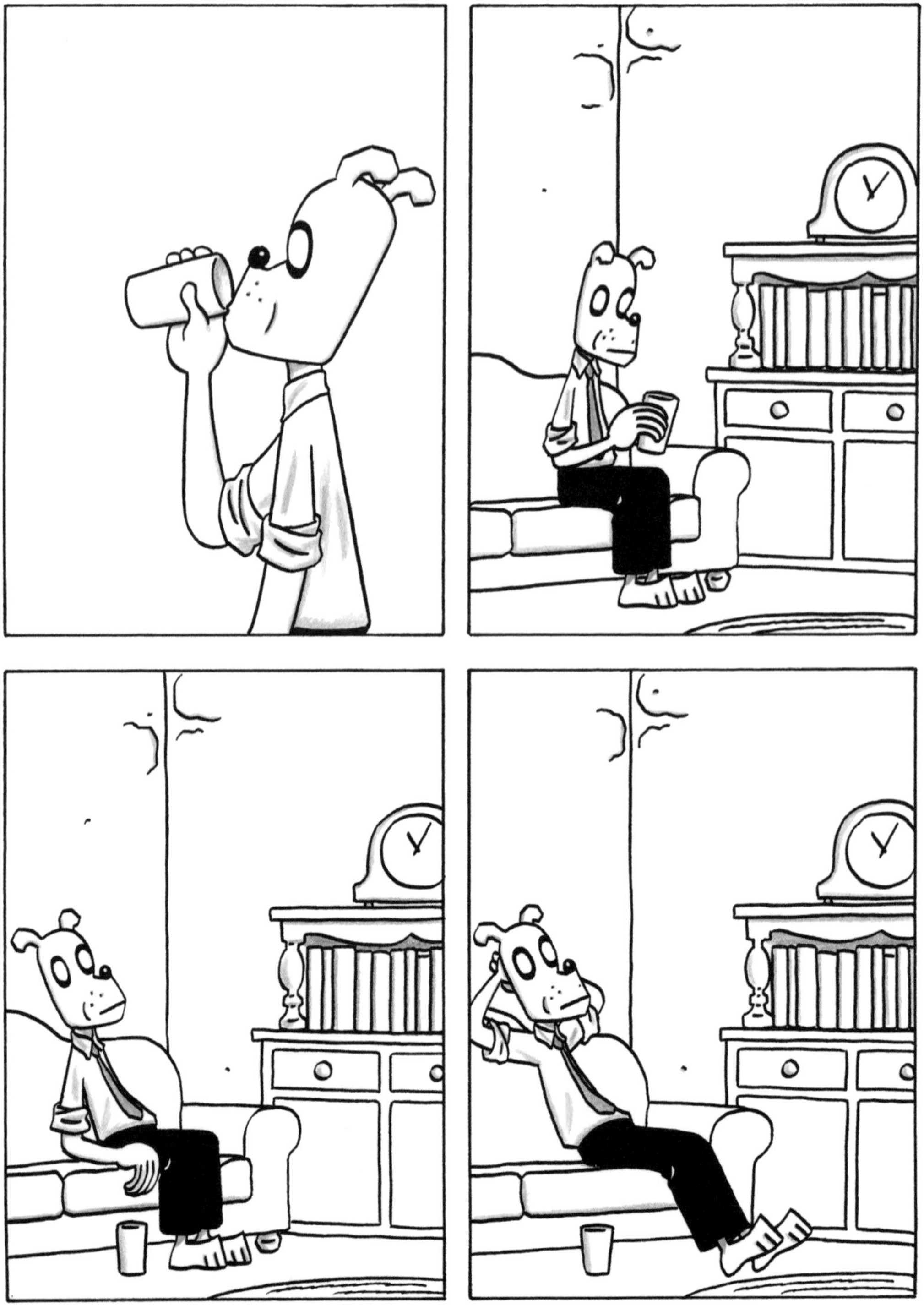

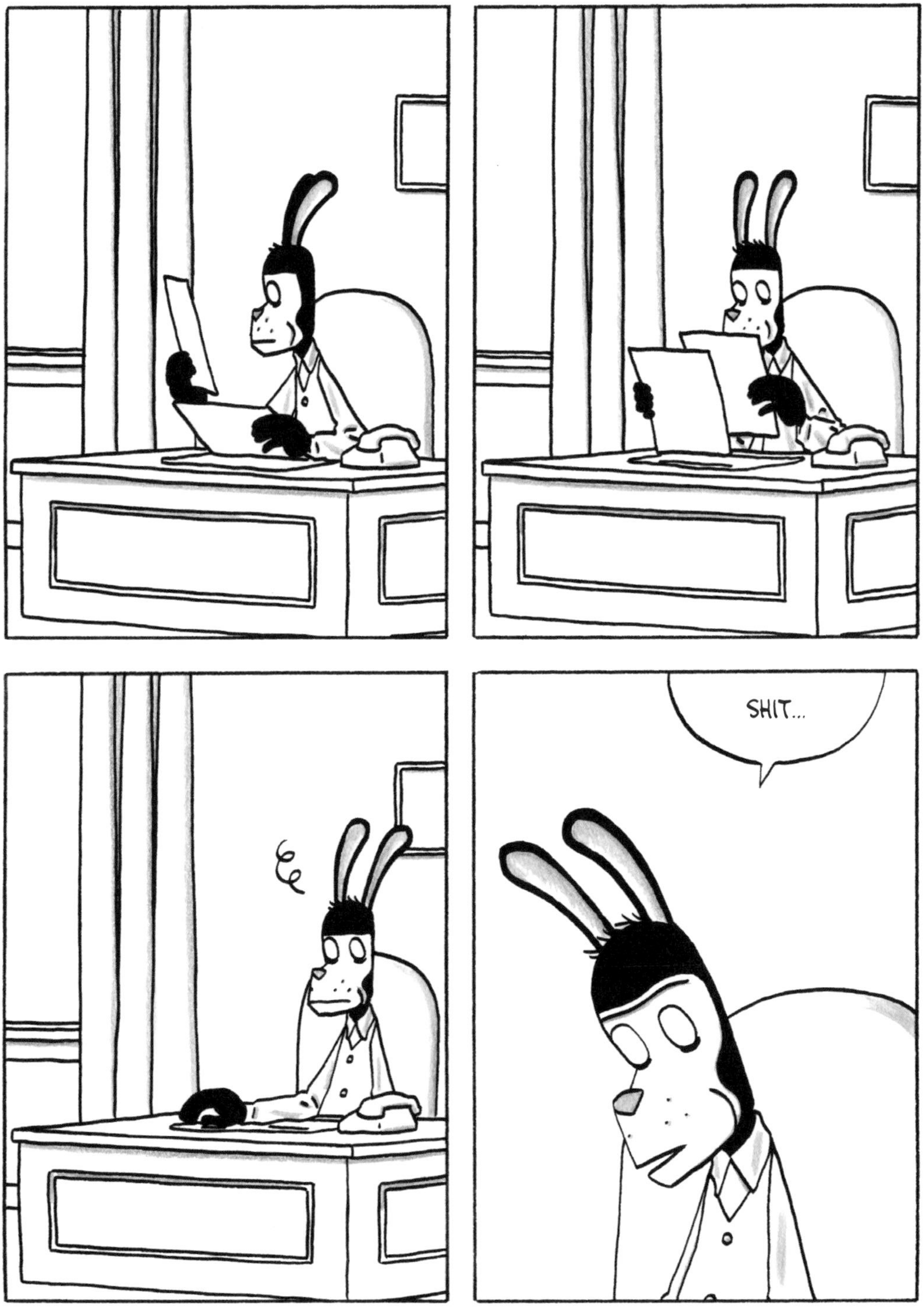
SHIT...

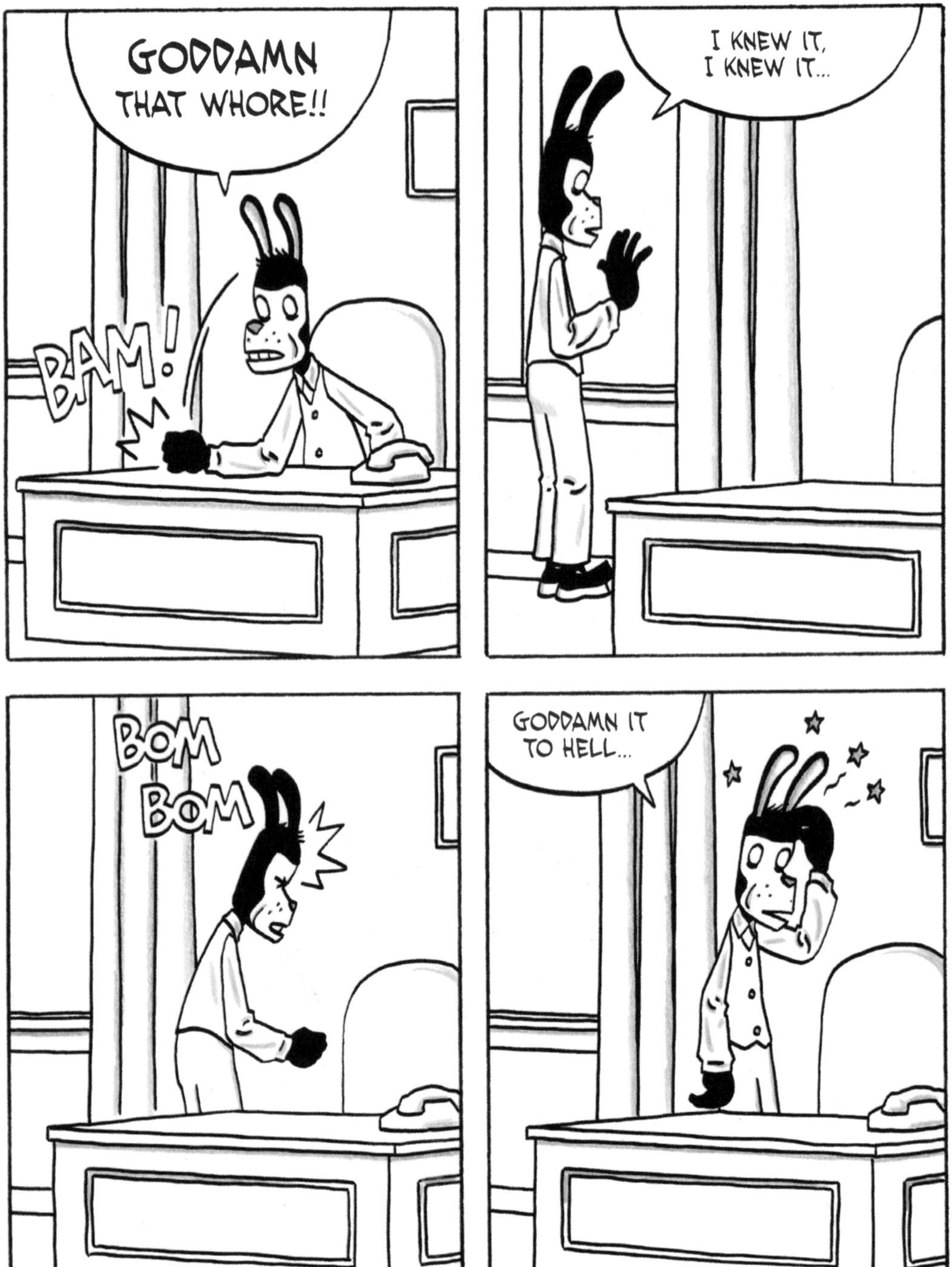
GODDAMN THAT WHORE!!
BAM!
I KNEW IT, I KNEW IT...
BOM
BOM
GODDAMN IT TO HELL...

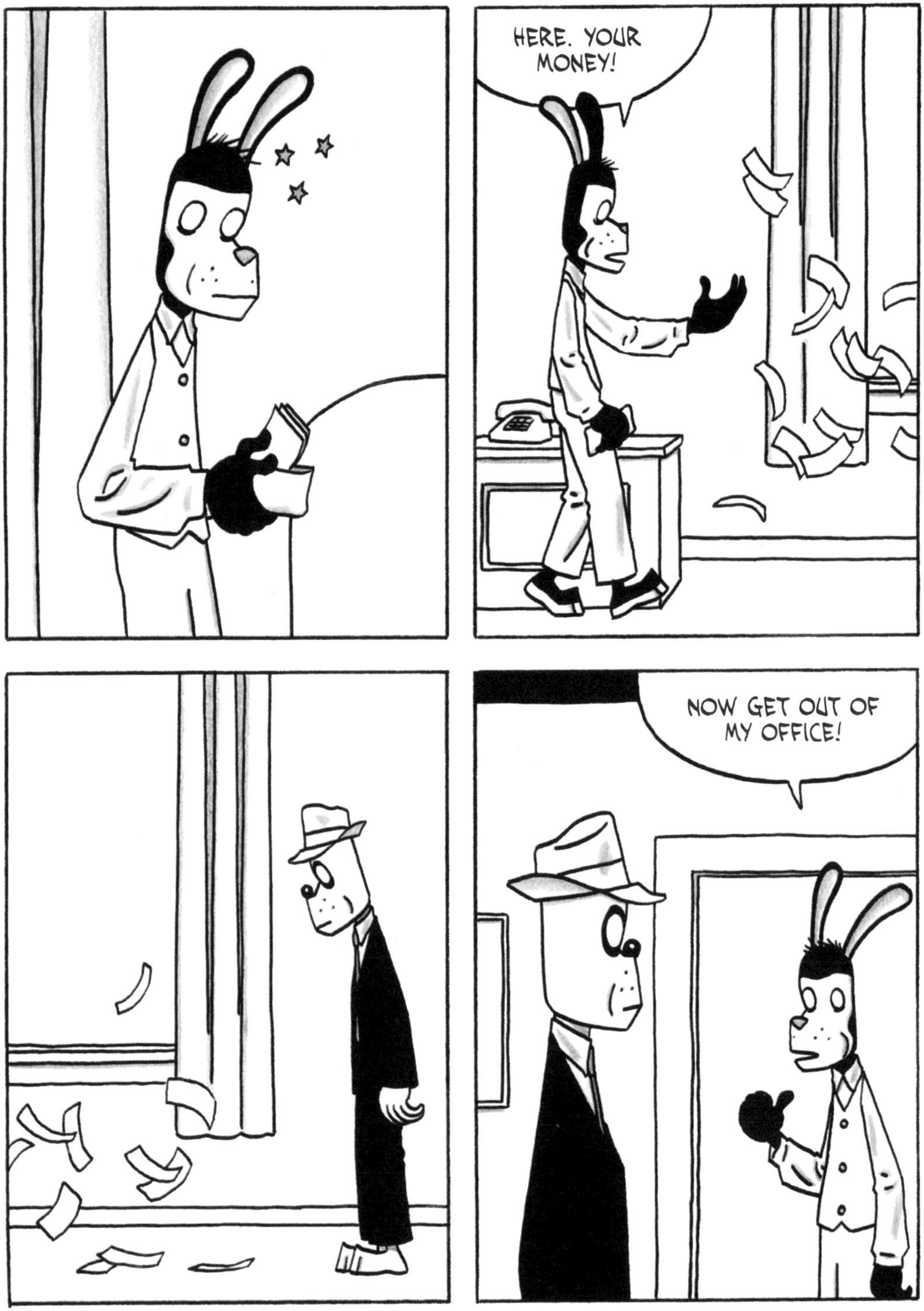
HERE. YOUR MONEY!
NOW GET OUT OF MY OFFICE!

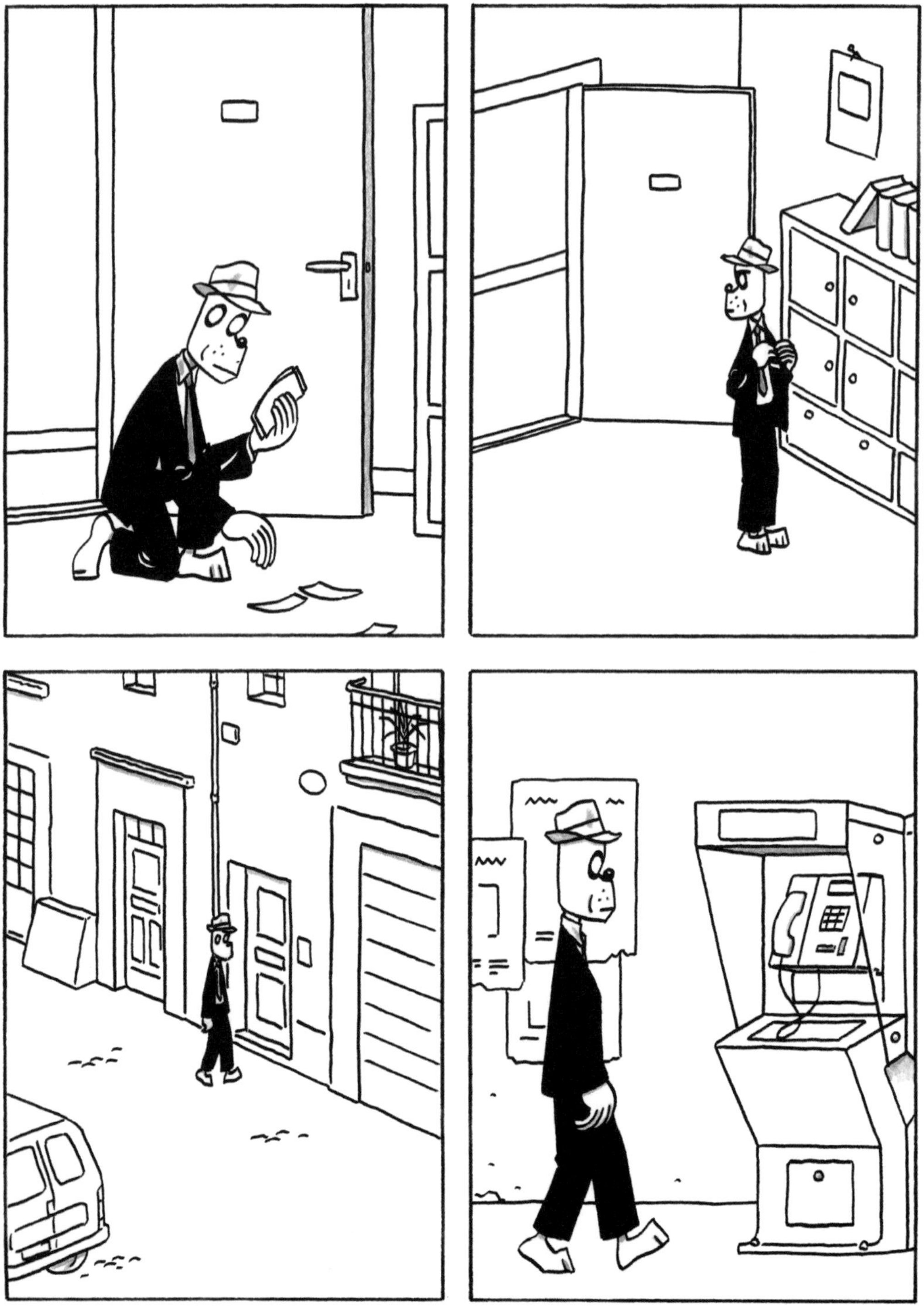

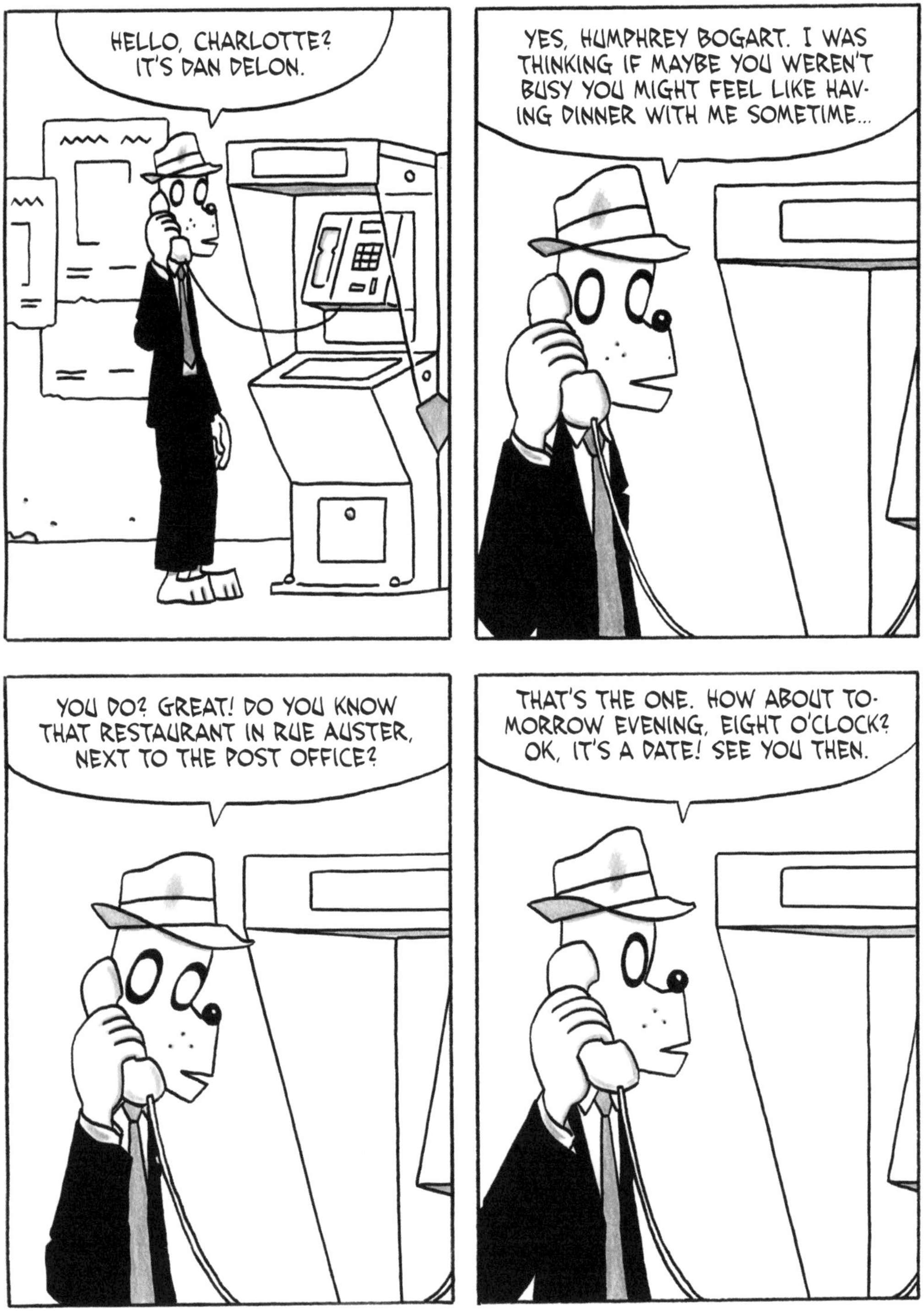
HELLO, CHARLOTTE? IT'S DAN DELON.
YES, HUMPHREY BOGART. I WAS THINKING IF MAYBE YOU WEREN'T BUSY YOU MIGHT FEEL LIKE HAV-ING DINNER WITH ME SOMETIME...
YOU DO? GREAT! DO YOU KNOW THAT RESTAURANT IN RUE AUSTER, NEXT TO THE POST OFFICE?
THAT'S THE ONE. HOW ABOUT TO-MORROW EVENING, EIGHT O'CLOCK? OK, IT'S A DATE! SEE YOU THEN.

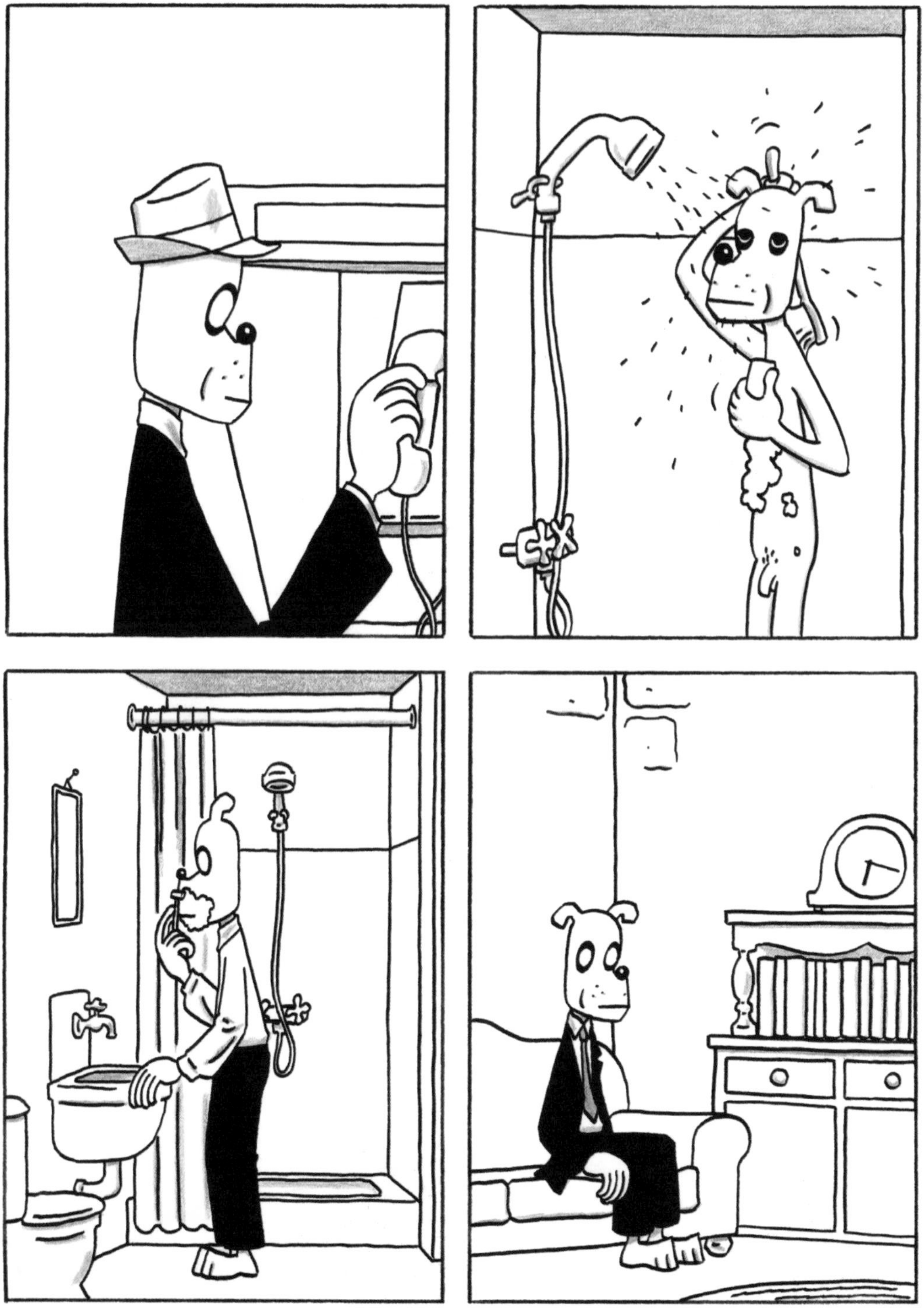

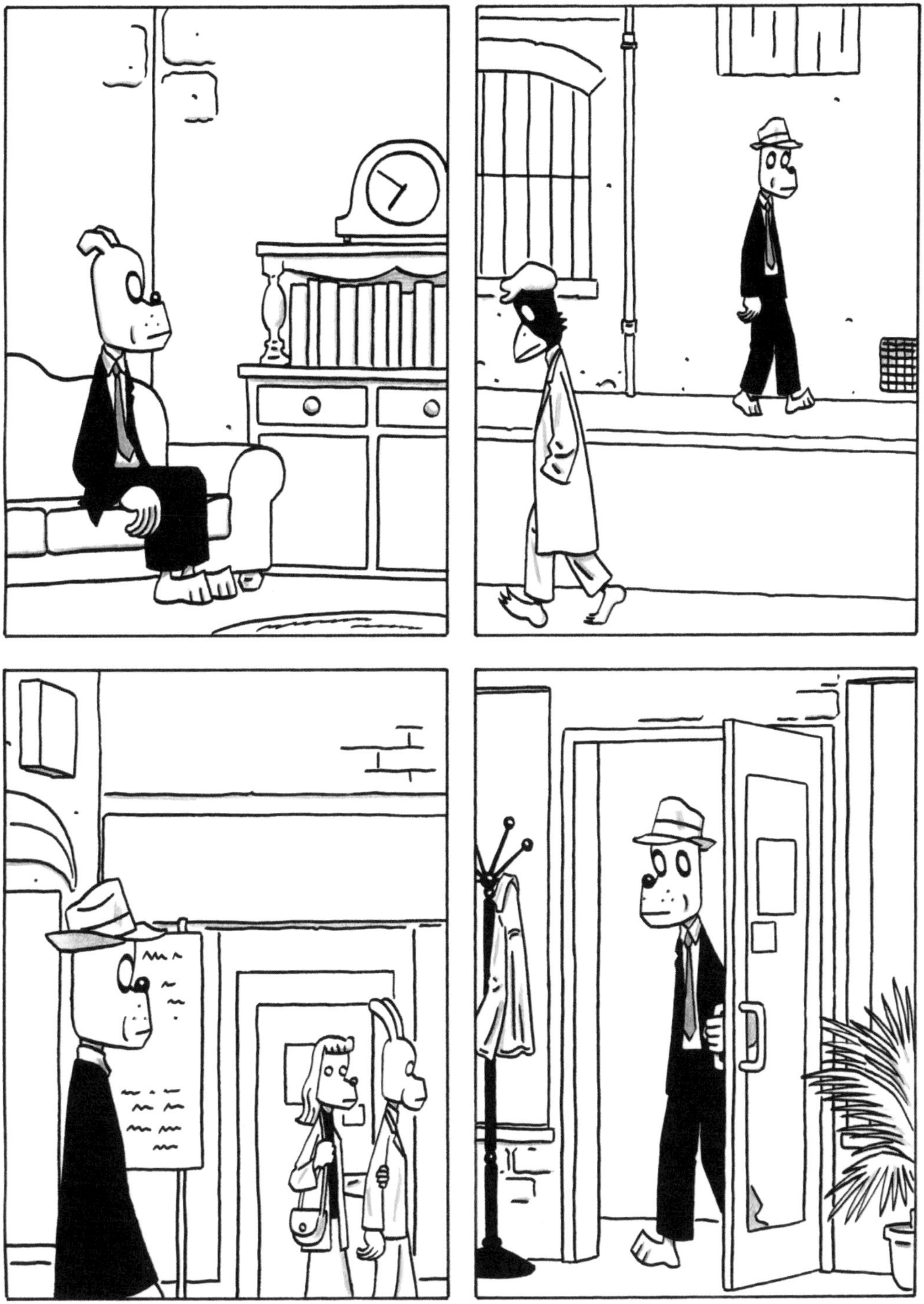

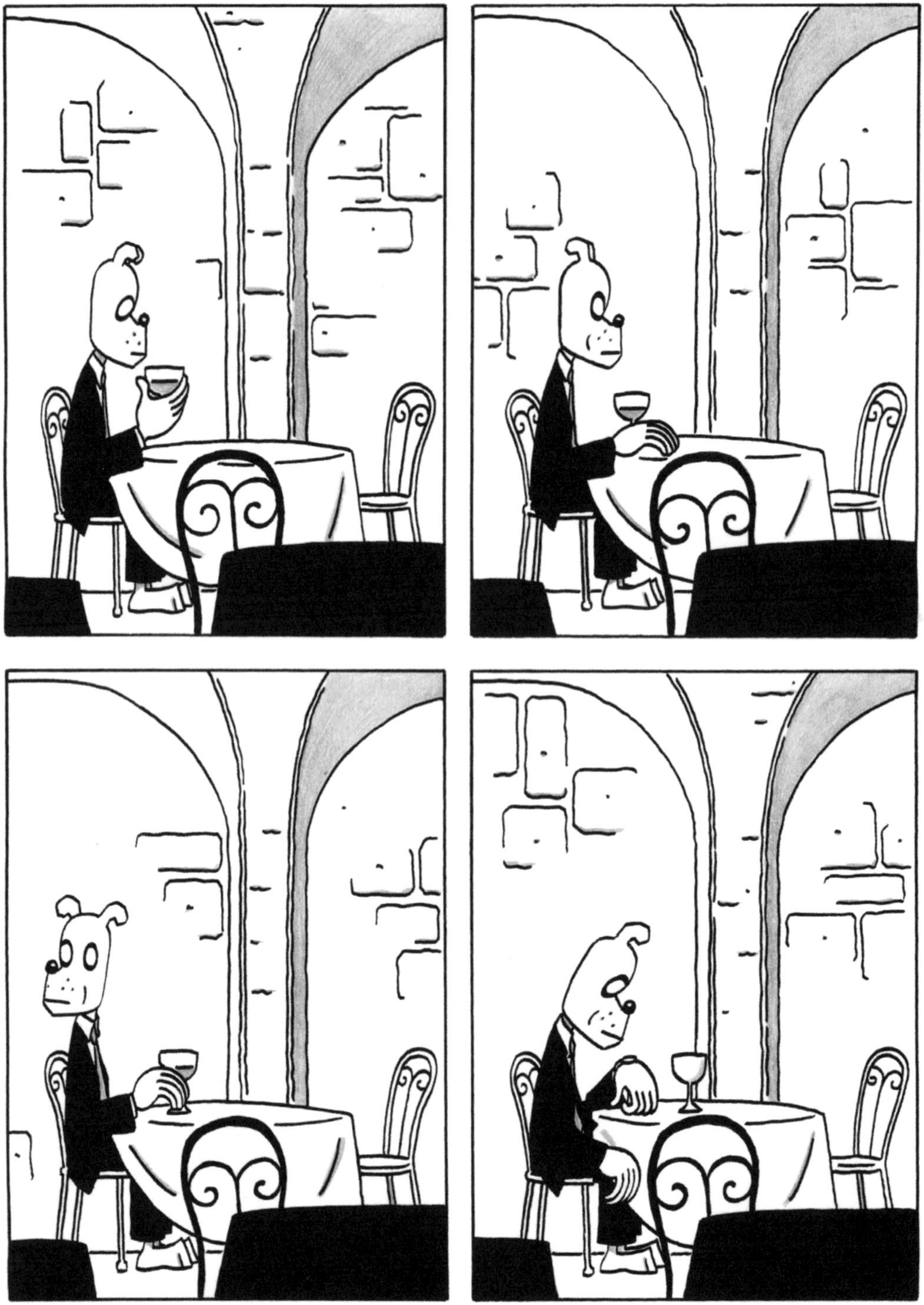

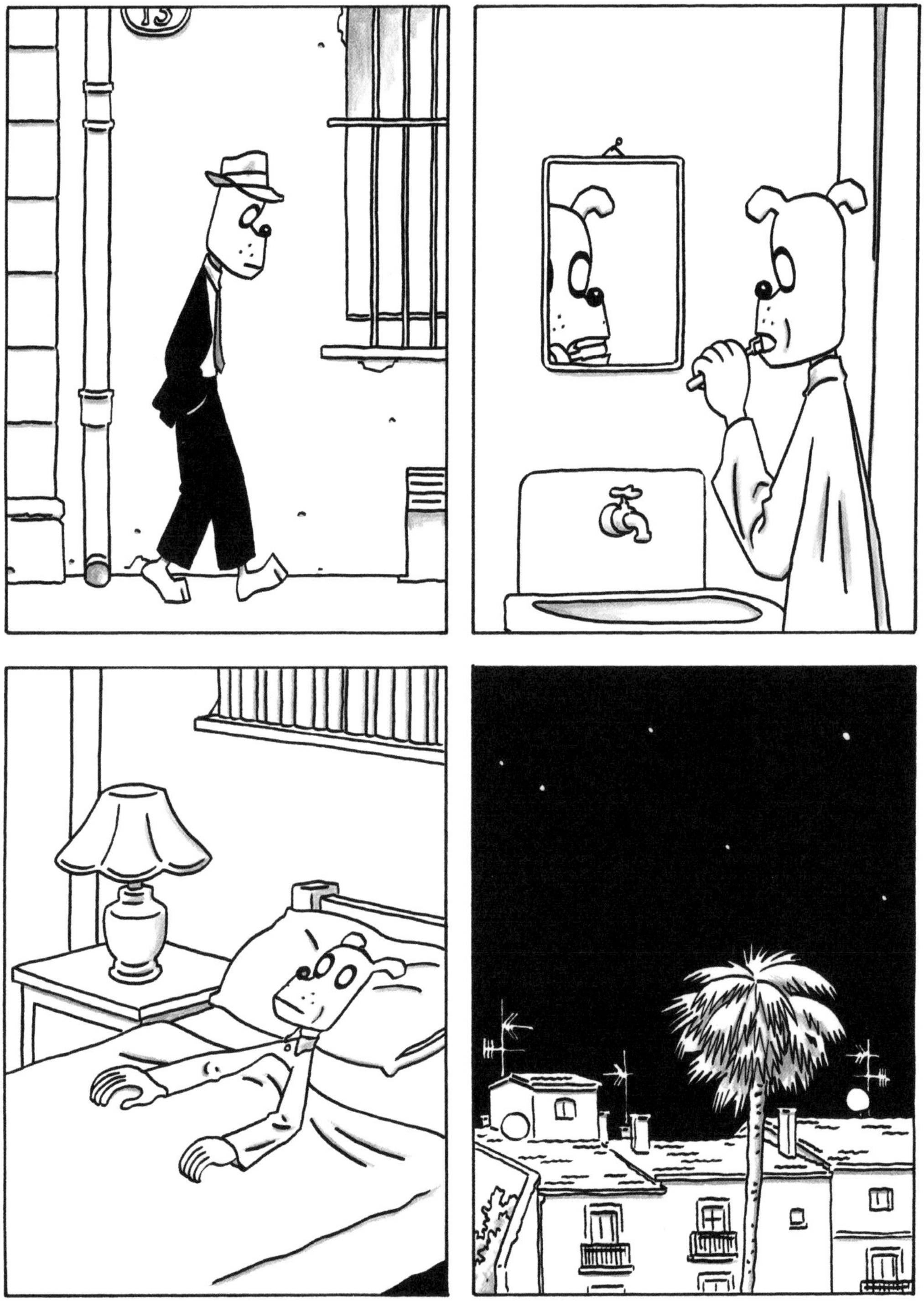
13

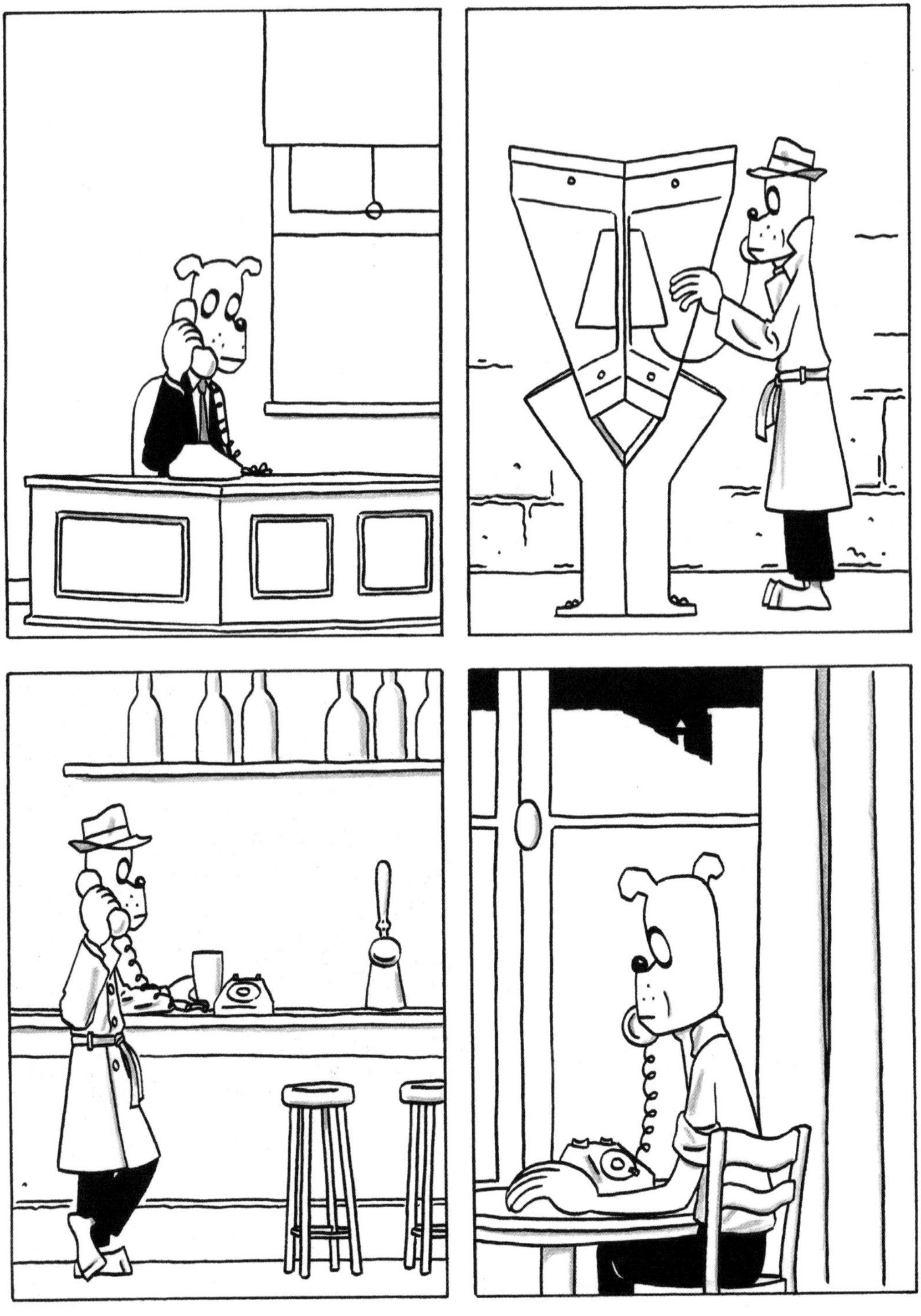

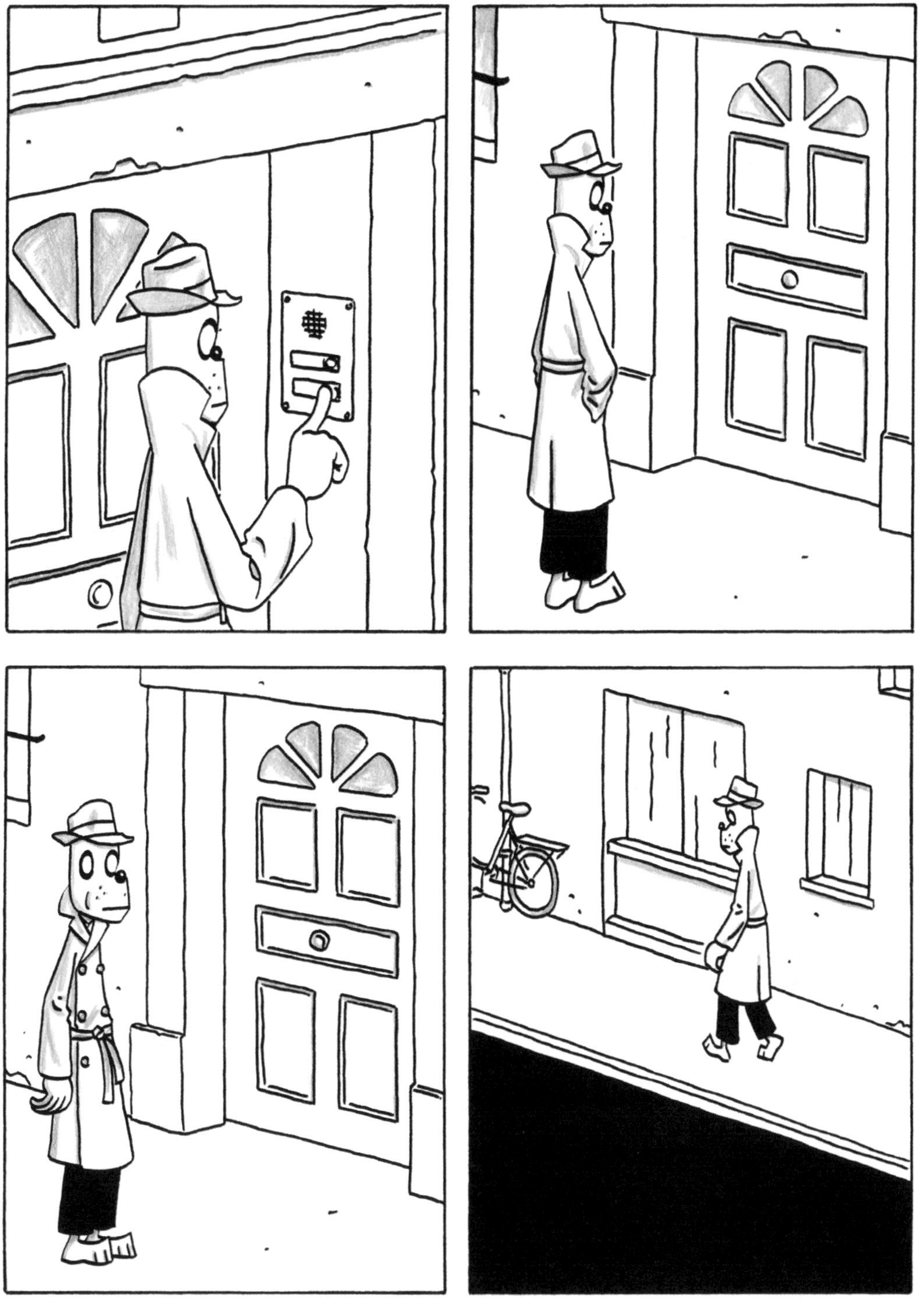

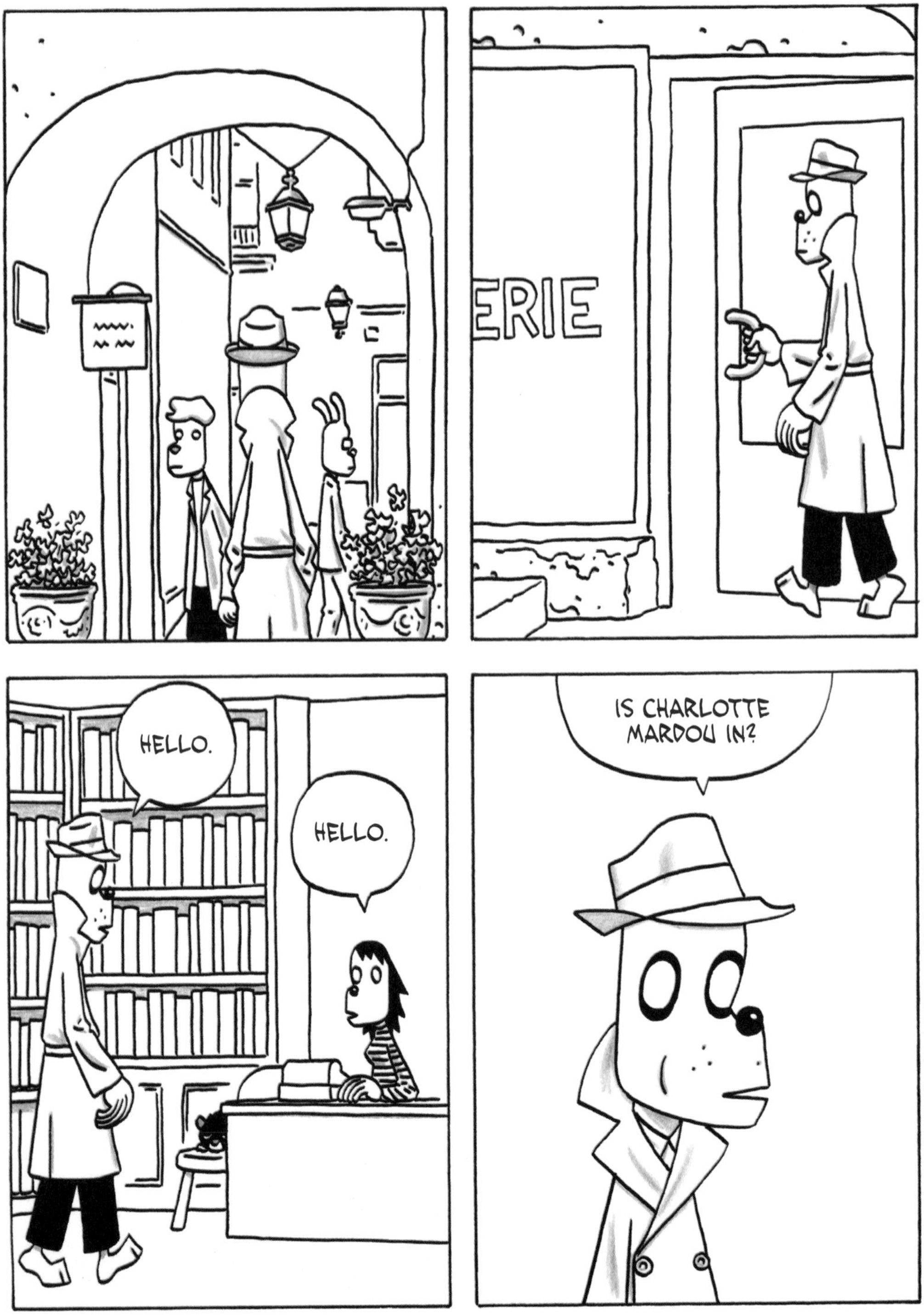
ERIE
HELLO.
HELLO.
IS CHARLOTTE MARDOU IN?

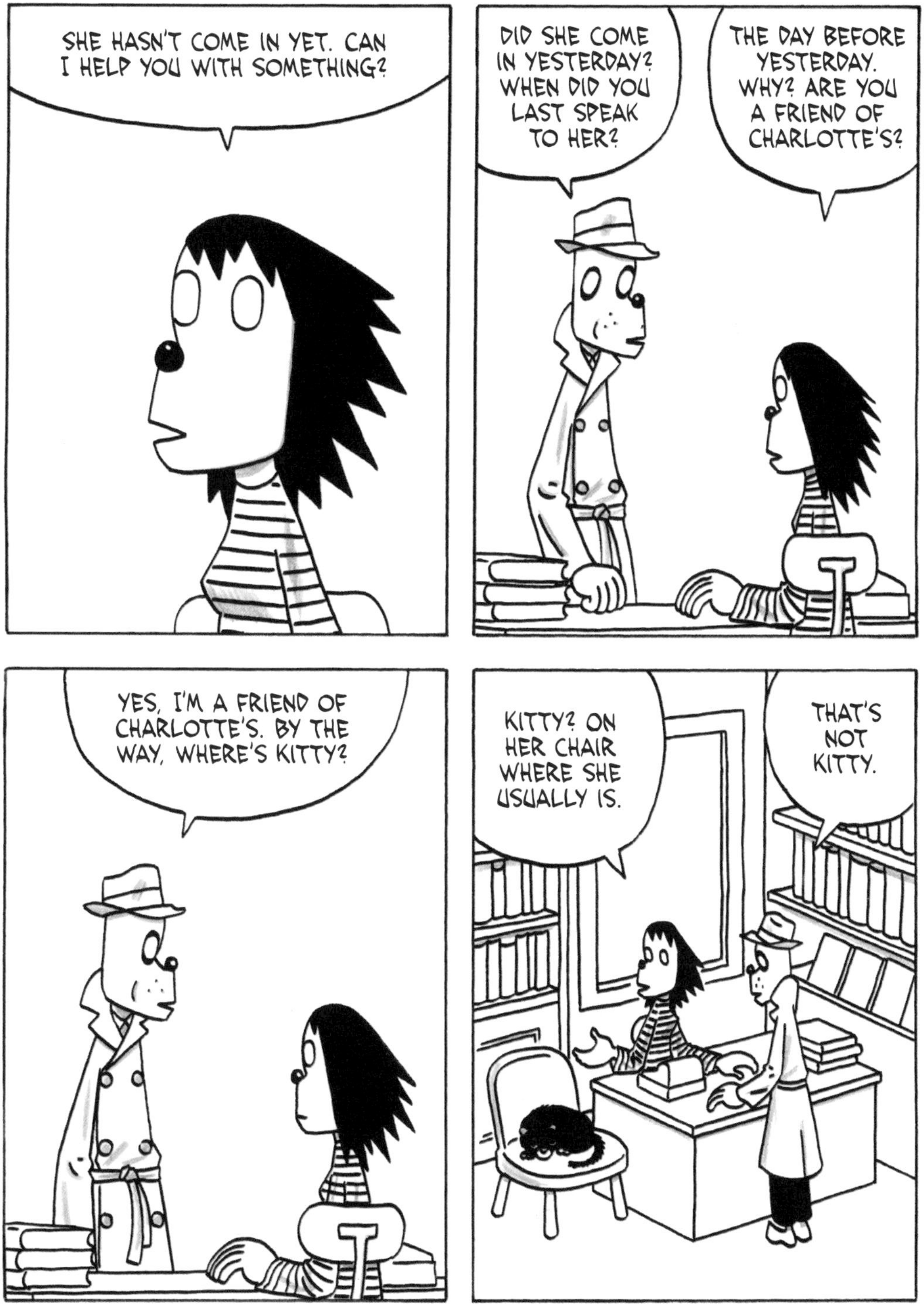
SHE HASN'T COME IN YET. CAN I HELP YOU WITH SOMETHING?
DID SHE COME IN YESTERDAY? WHEN DID YOU LAST SPEAK TO HER?
THE DAY BEFORE YESTERDAY. WHY? ARE YOU A FRIEND OF CHARLOTTE'S?
YES, I'M A FRIEND OF CHARLOTTE'S. BY THE WAY, WHERE'S KITTY?
KITTY? ON HER CHAIR WHERE SHE USUALLY IS.
THAT'S NOT KITTY.

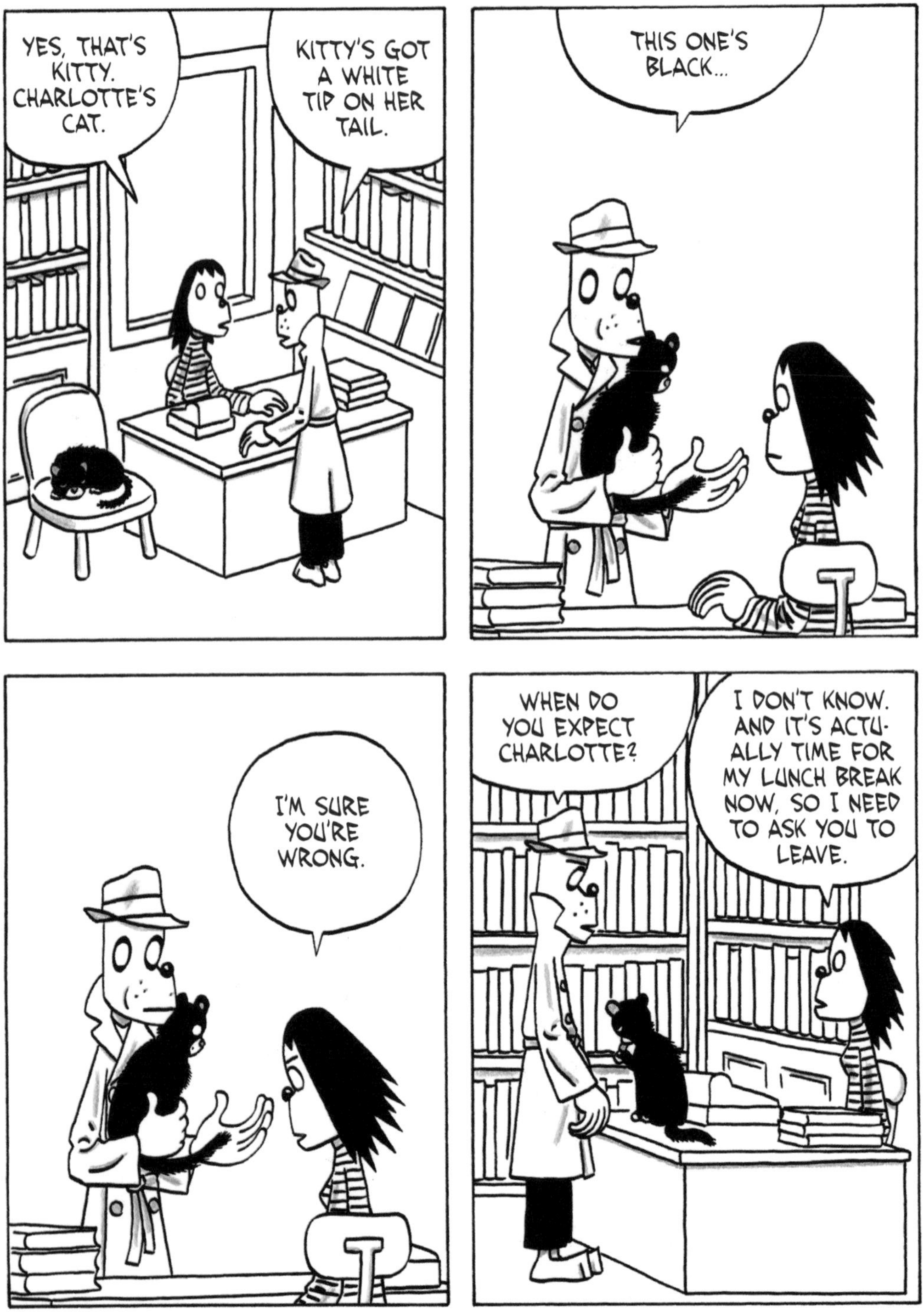
YES, THAT'S KITTY. CHARLOTTE'S CAT.
KITTY'S GOT A WHITE TIP ON HER TAIL.
THIS ONE'S BLACK...
I'M SURE YOU'RE WRONG.
WHEN DO YOU EXPECT CHARLOTTE?
I DON'T KNOW. AND IT'S ACTU-ALLY TIME FOR MY LUNCH BREAK NOW, SO I NEED TO ASK YOU TO LEAVE.

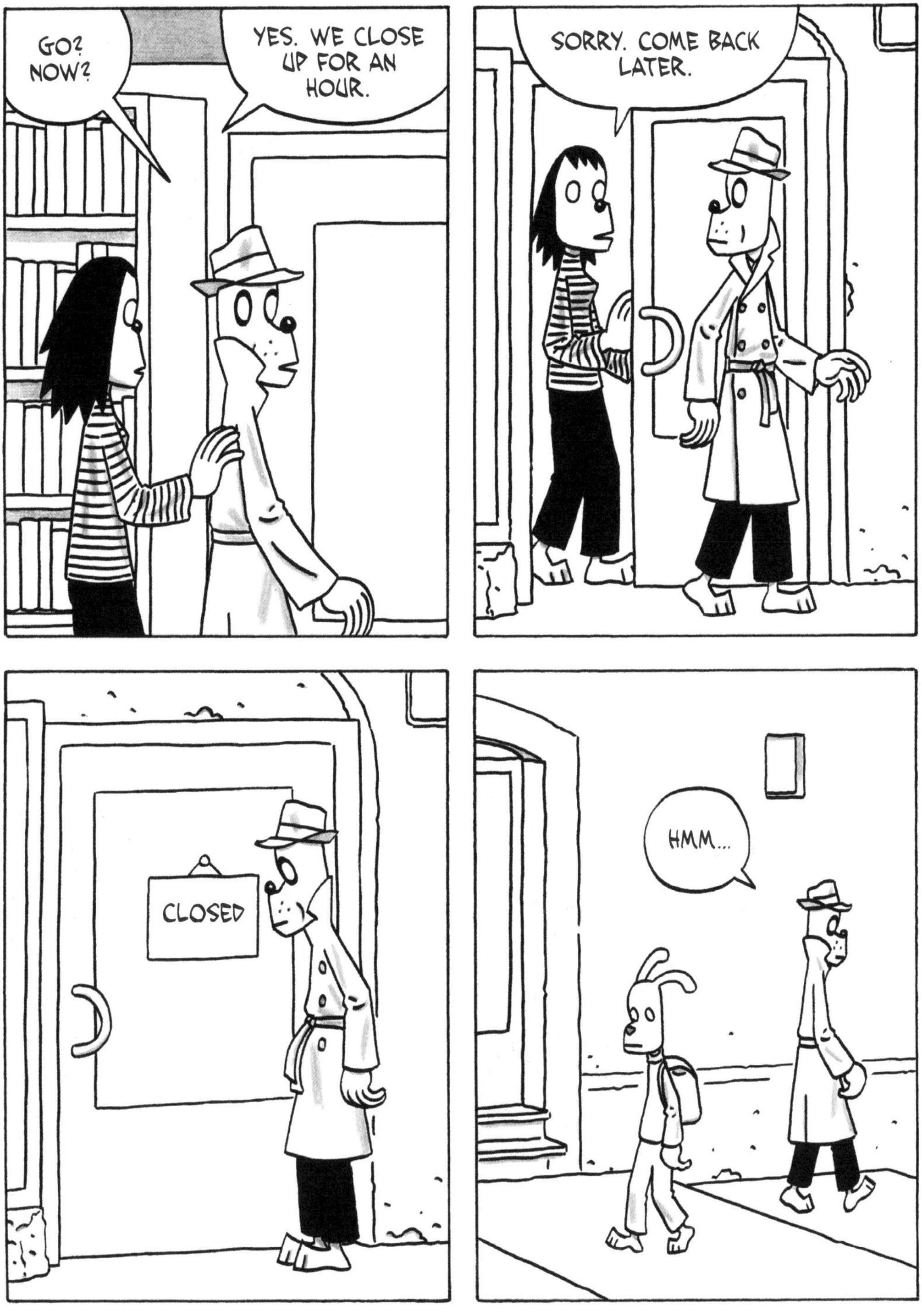
GO? NOW?
YES. WE CLOSE UP FOR AN HOUR.
SORRY. COME BACK LATER.
CLOSED
HMM...

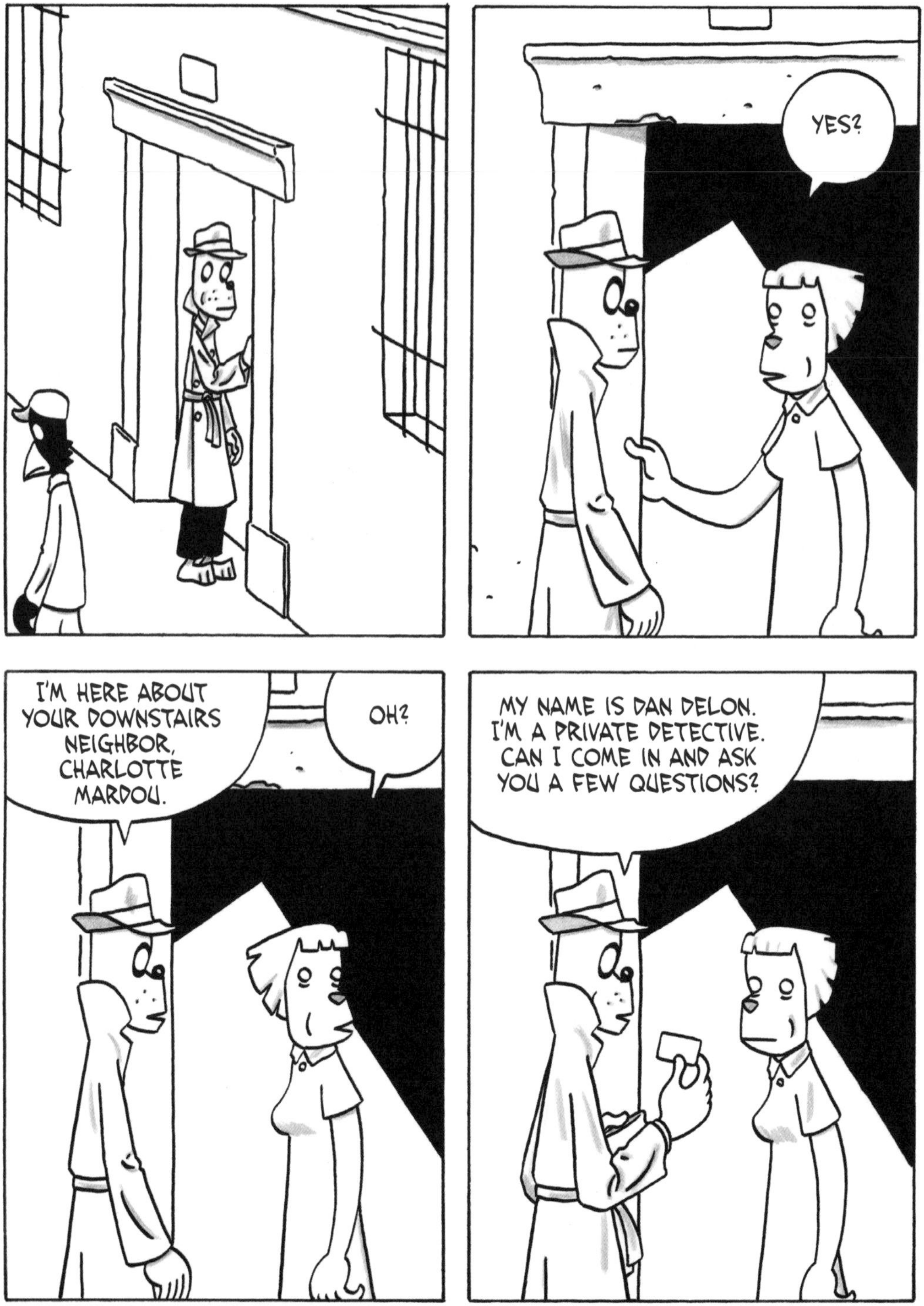
YES?
I'M HERE ABOUT YOUR DOWNSTAIRS NEIGHBOR, CHARLOTTE MARDOU.
OH?
MY NAME IS DAN DELON. I'M A PRIVATE DETECTIVE. CAN I COME IN AND ASK YOU A FEW QUESTIONS?

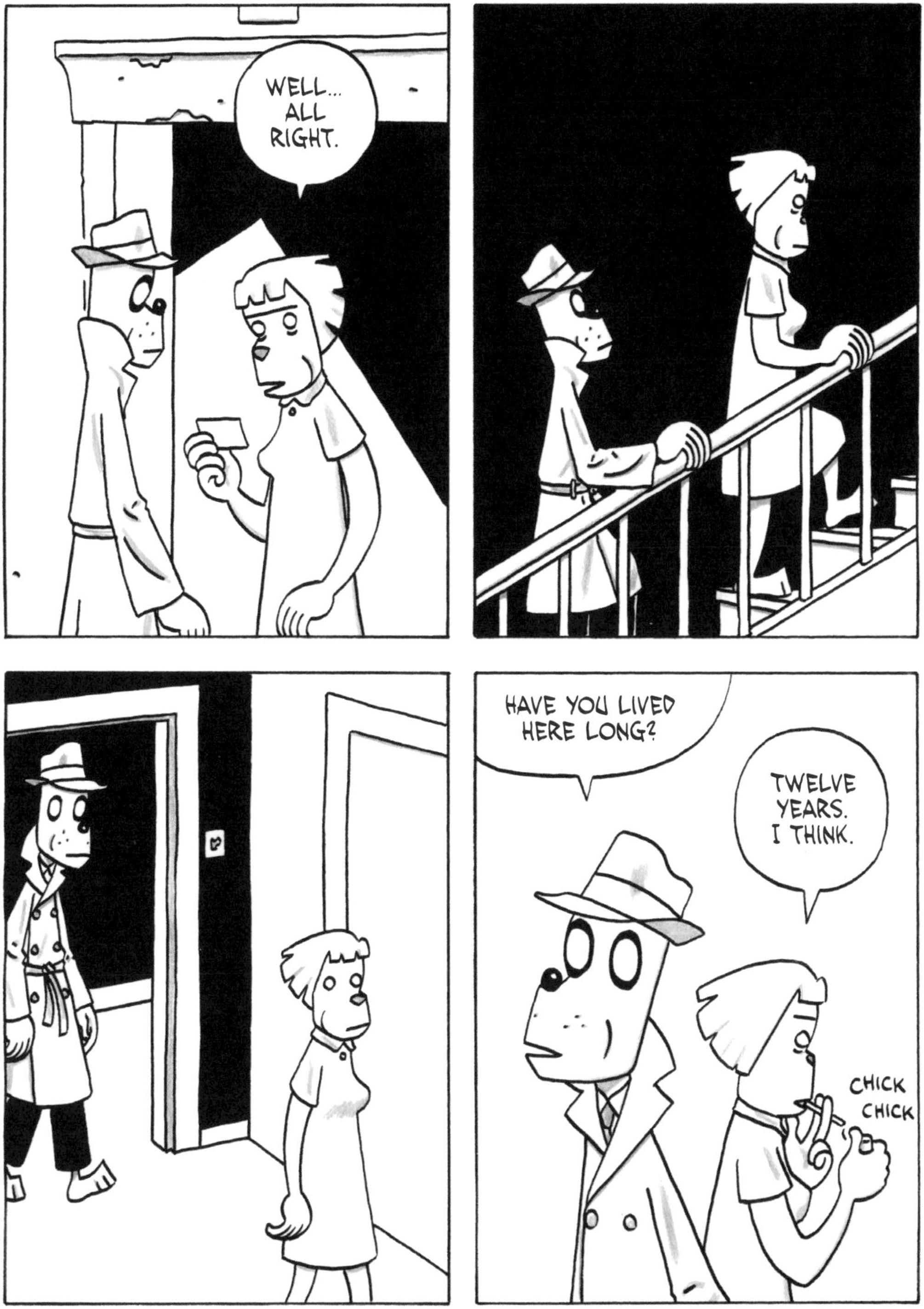
WELL... ALL RIGHT.
HAVE YOU LIVED HERE LONG?
TWELVE YEARS. I THINK.
CHICK CHICK

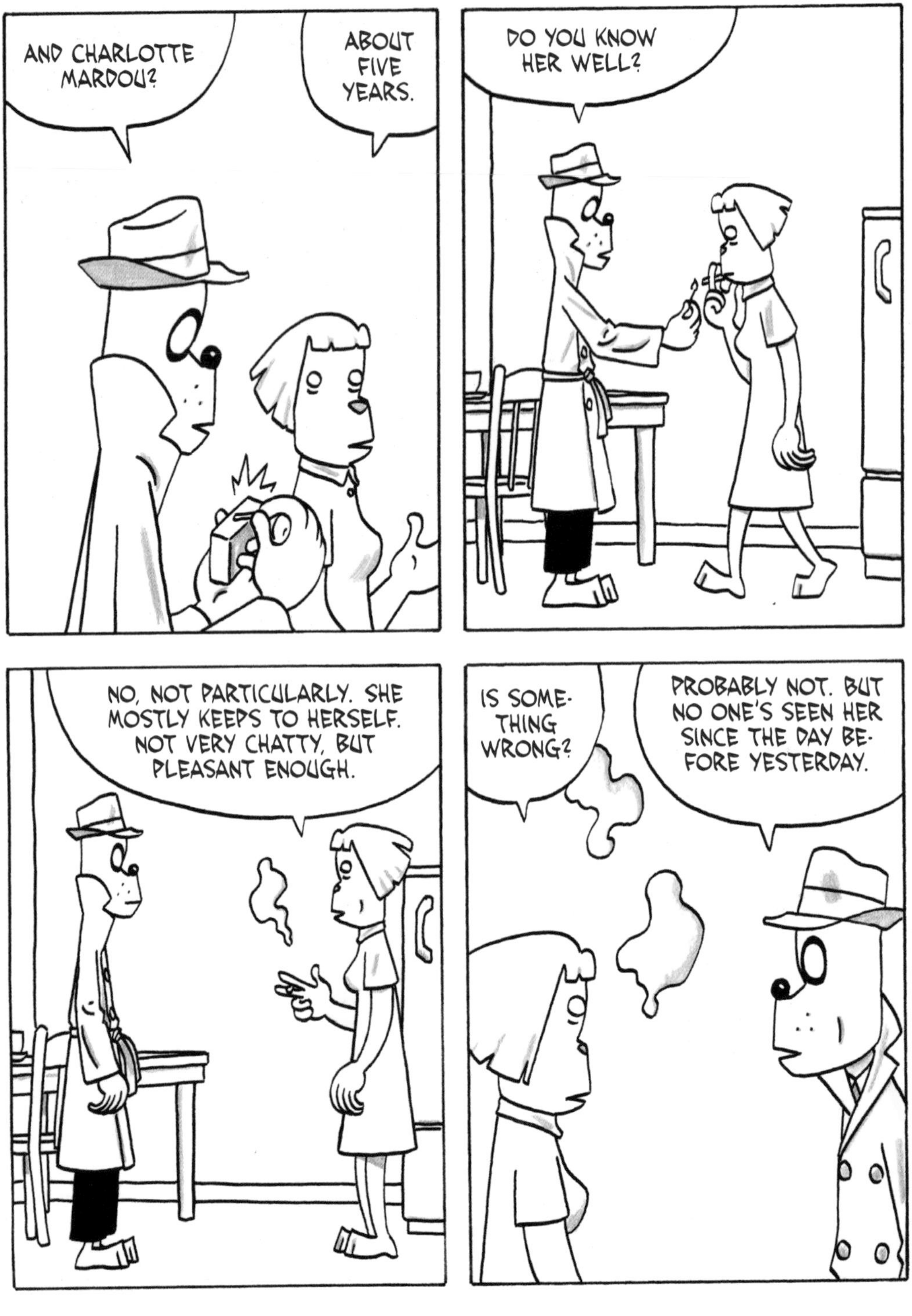
AND CHARLOTTE MARDOU?
ABOUT FIVE YEARS.
DO YOU KNOW HER WELL?
NO, NOT PARTICULARLY. SHE MOSTLY KEEPS TO HERSELF. NOT VERY CHATTY, BUT PLEASANT ENOUGH.
IS SOME-THING WRONG?
PROBABLY NOT. BUT NO ONE'S SEEN HER SINCE THE DAY BE-FORE YESTERDAY.

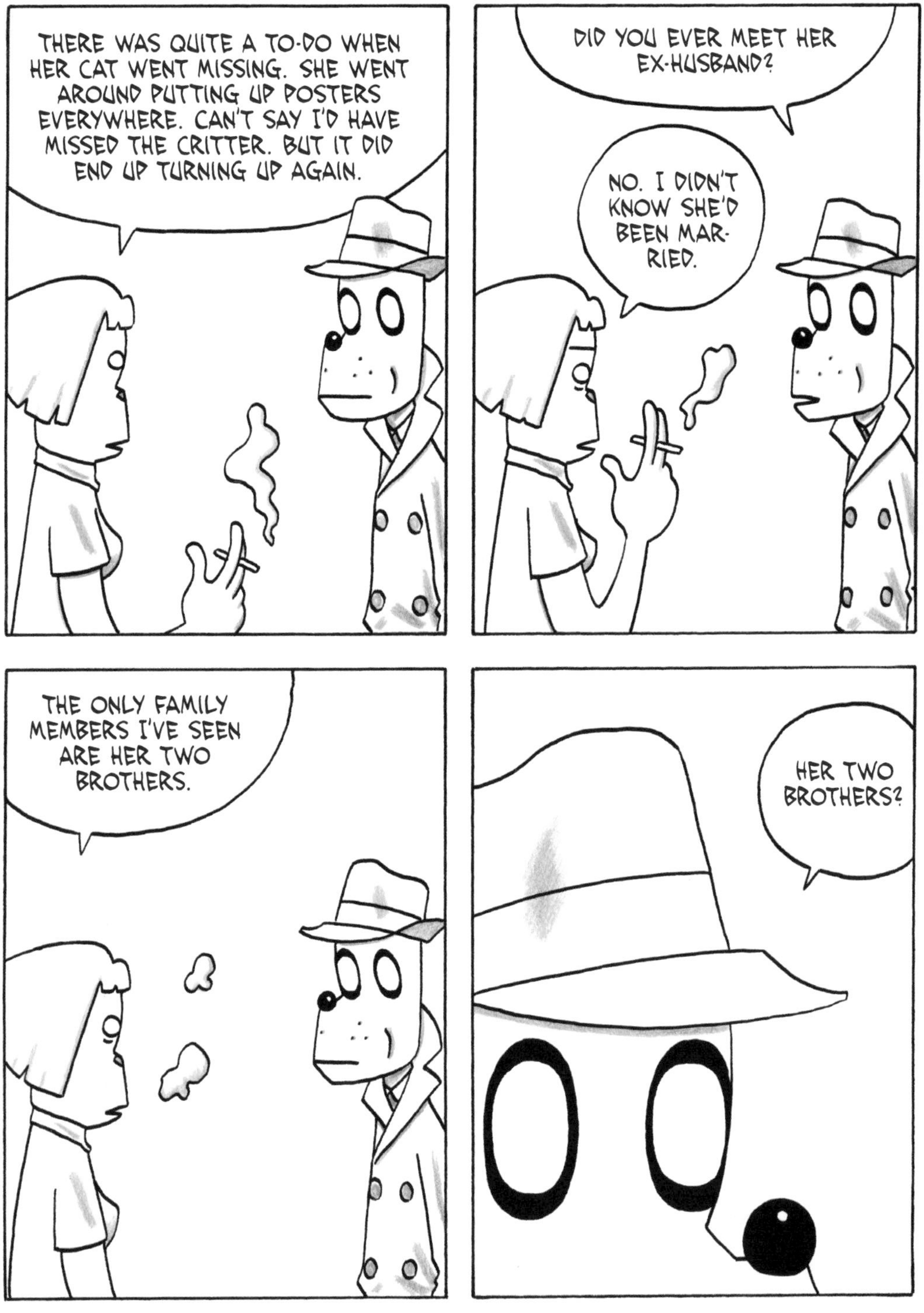
THERE WAS QUITE A TO-DO WHEN HER CAT WENT MISSING. SHE WENT AROUND PUTTING UP POSTERS EVERYWHERE. CAN'T SAY I'D HAVE MISSED THE CRITTER. BUT IT DID END UP TURNING UP AGAIN.
DID YOU EVER MEET HER EX-HUSBAND?
NO. I DIDN'T KNOW SHE'D BEEN MAR-RIED.
THE ONLY FAMILY MEMBERS I'VE SEEN ARE HER TWO BROTHERS.
HER TWO BROTHERS?

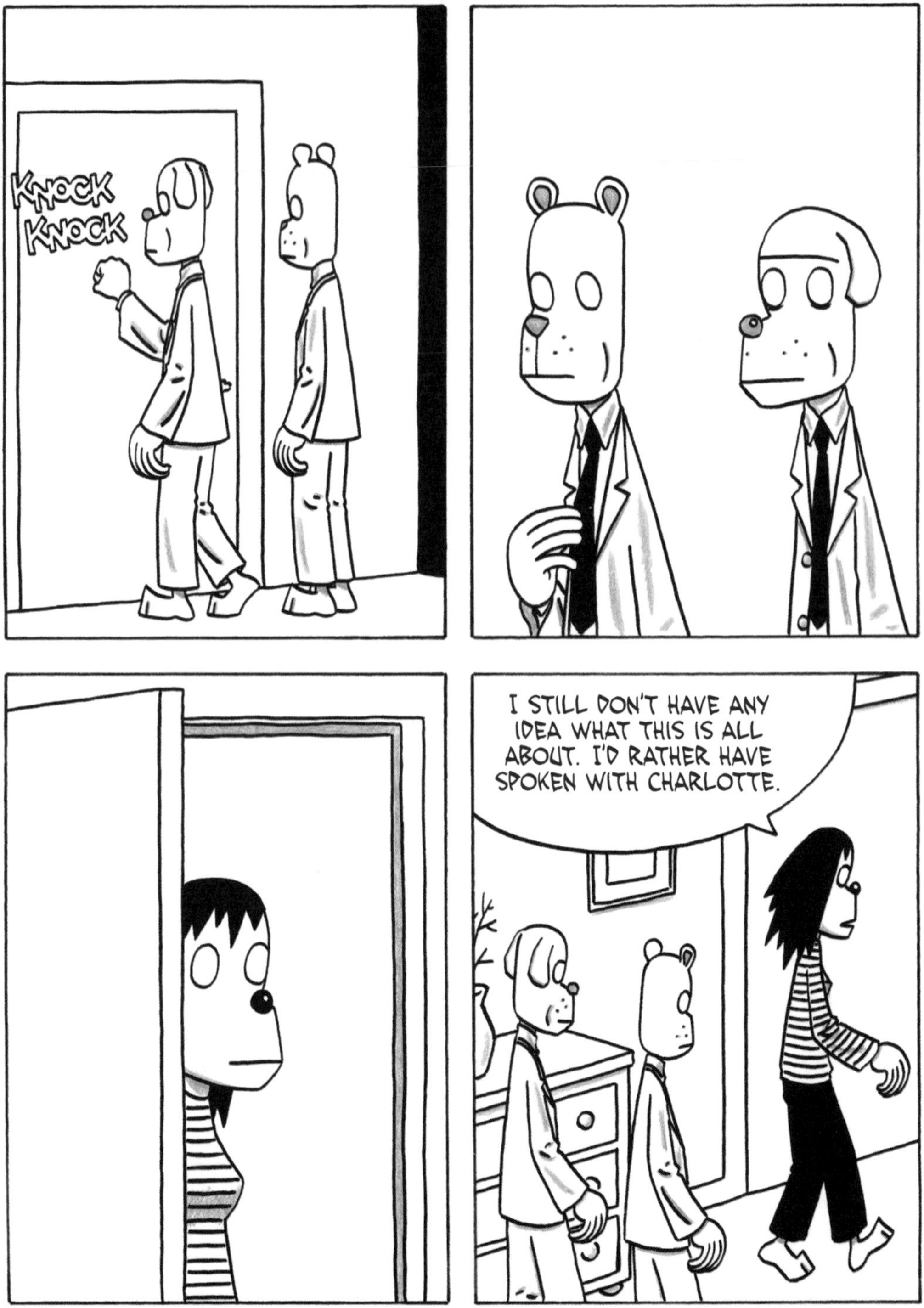
KNOCK KNOCK
I STILL DON'T HAVE ANY IDEA WHAT THIS IS ALL ABOUT. I'D RATHER HAVE SPOKEN WITH CHARLOTTE.

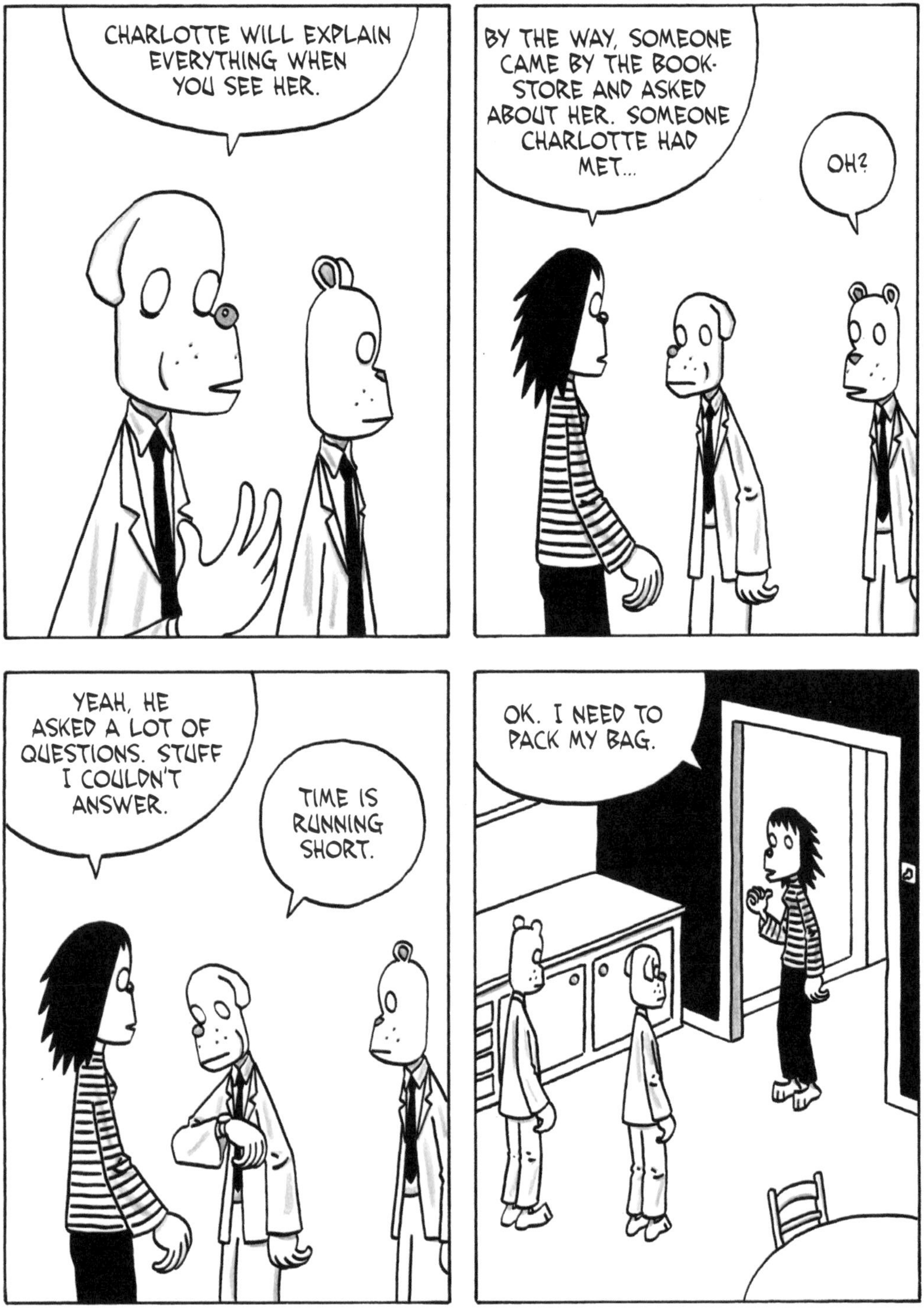
CHARLOTTE WILL EXPLAIN EVERYTHING WHEN YOU SEE HER.
BY THE WAY, SOMEONE CAME BY THE BOOK-STORE AND ASKED ABOUT HER. SOMEONE CHARLOTTE HAD MET...
OH?
YEAH, HE ASKED A LOT OF QUESTIONS. STUFF I COULDN'T ANSWER.
TIME IS RUNNING SHORT.
OK. I NEED TO PACK MY BAG.

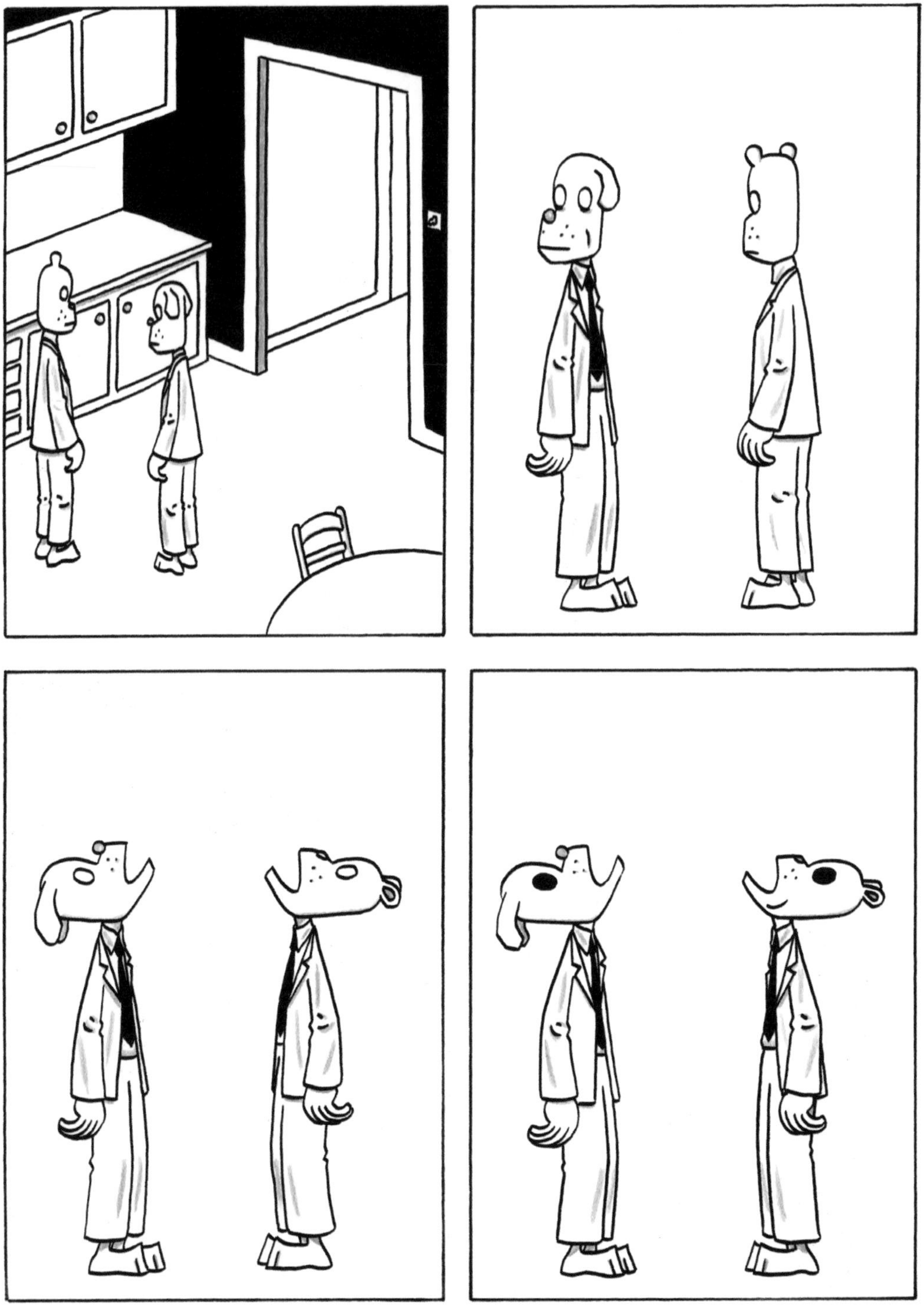

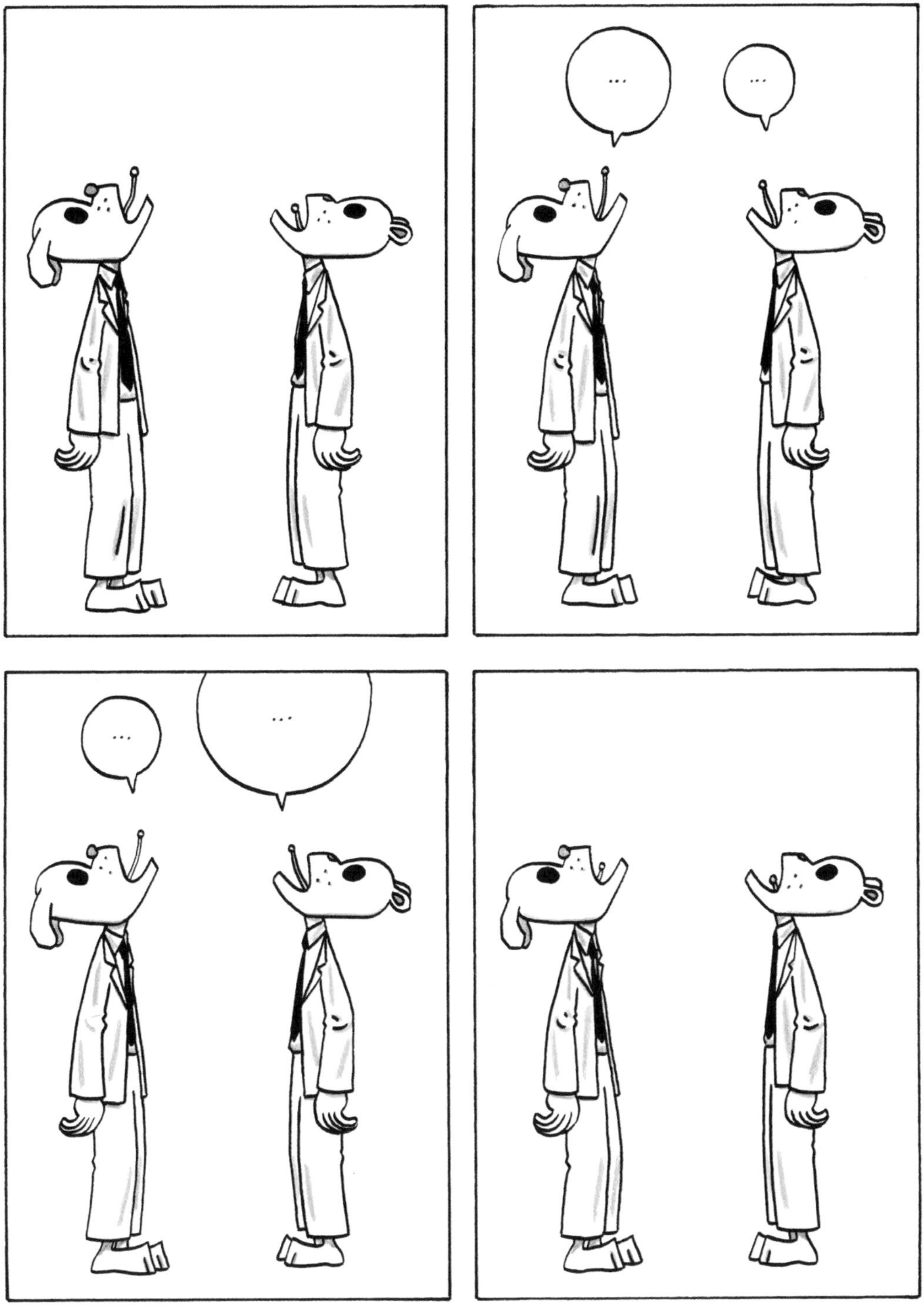
...
...
...
...

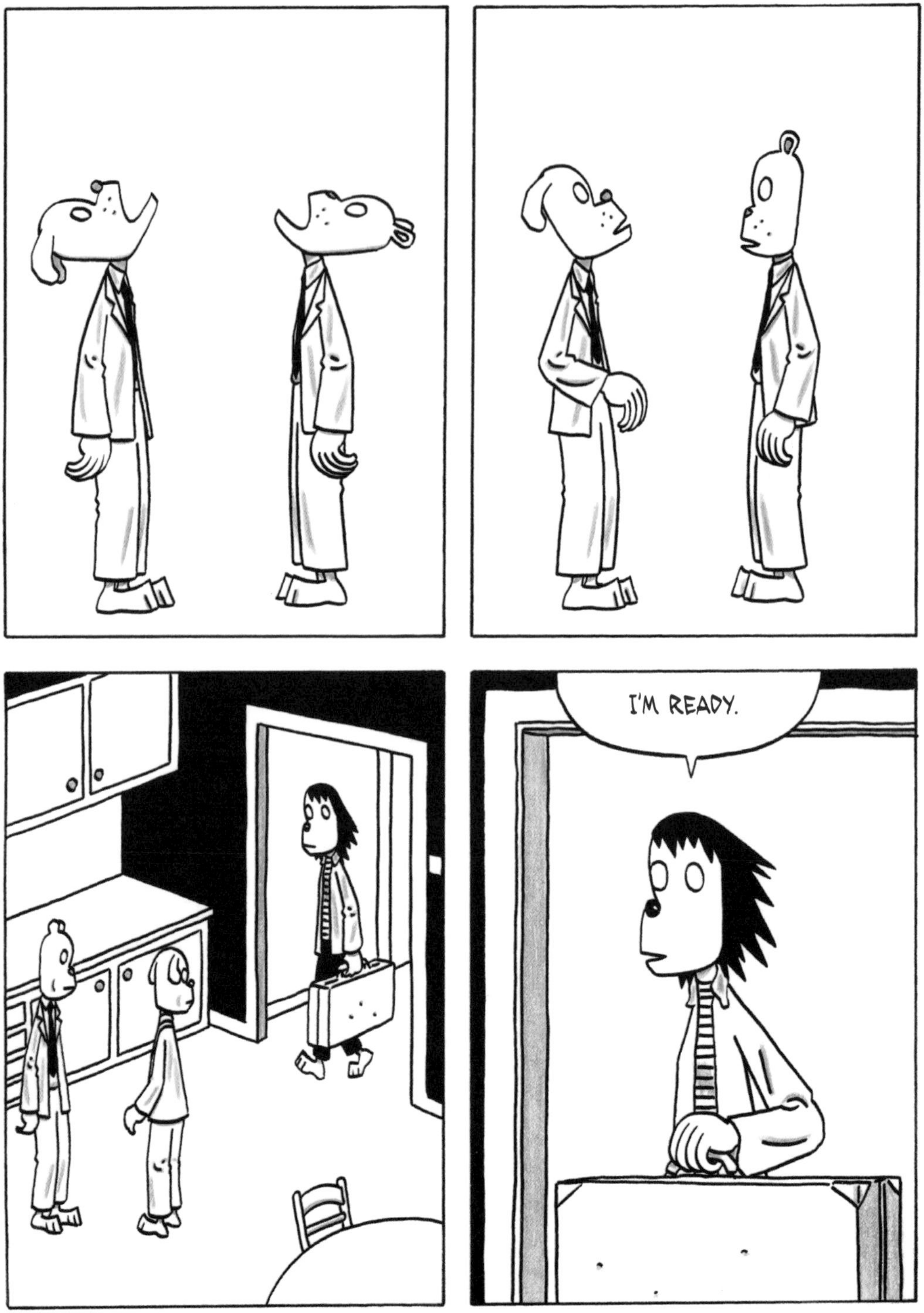
I'M READY.

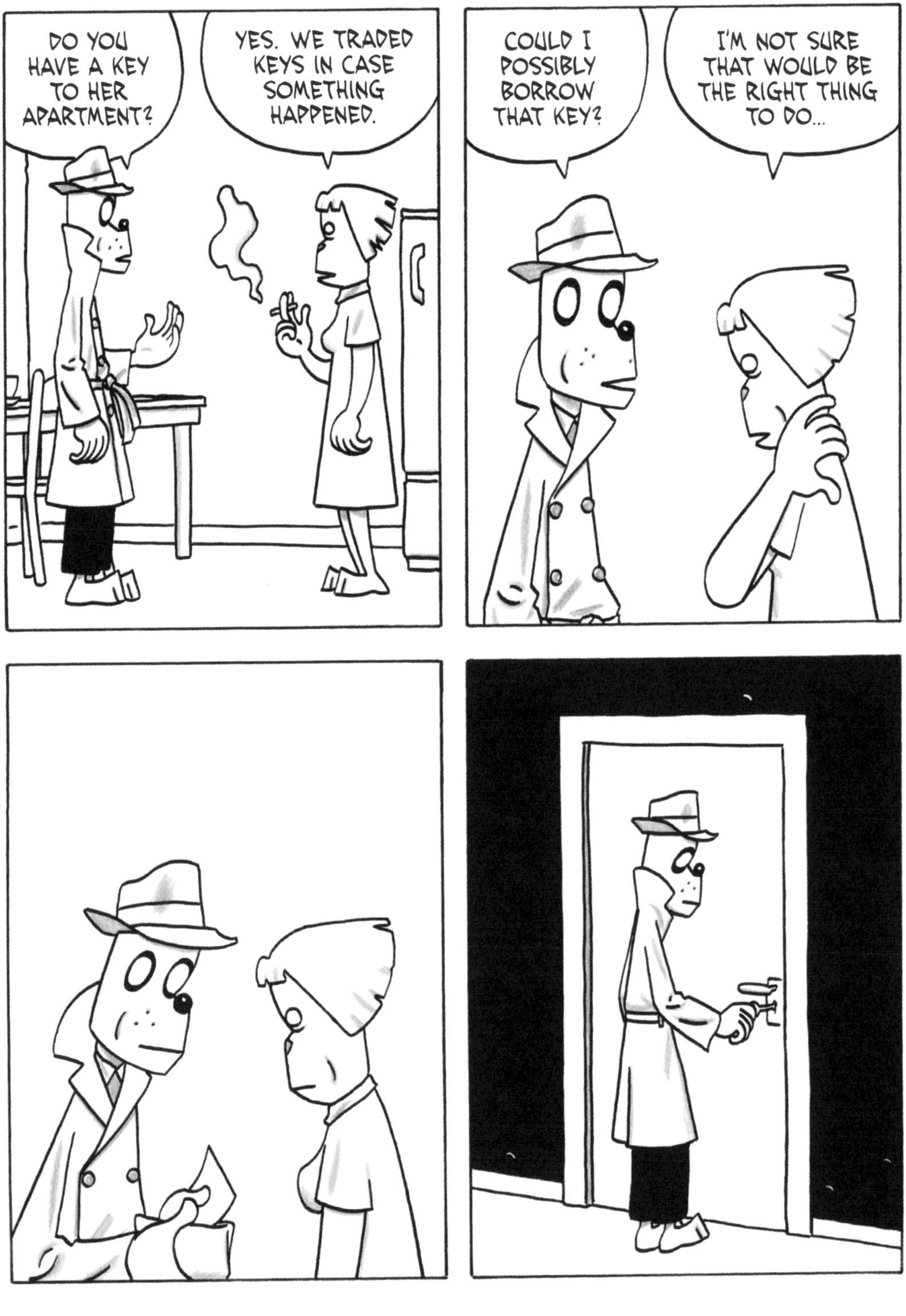
DO YOU HAVE A KEY TO HER APARTMENT?
YES. WE TRADED KEYS IN CASE SOMETHING HAPPENED.
COULD I POSSIBLY BORROW THAT KEY?
I'M NOT SURE THAT WOULD BE THE RIGHT THING TO DO...

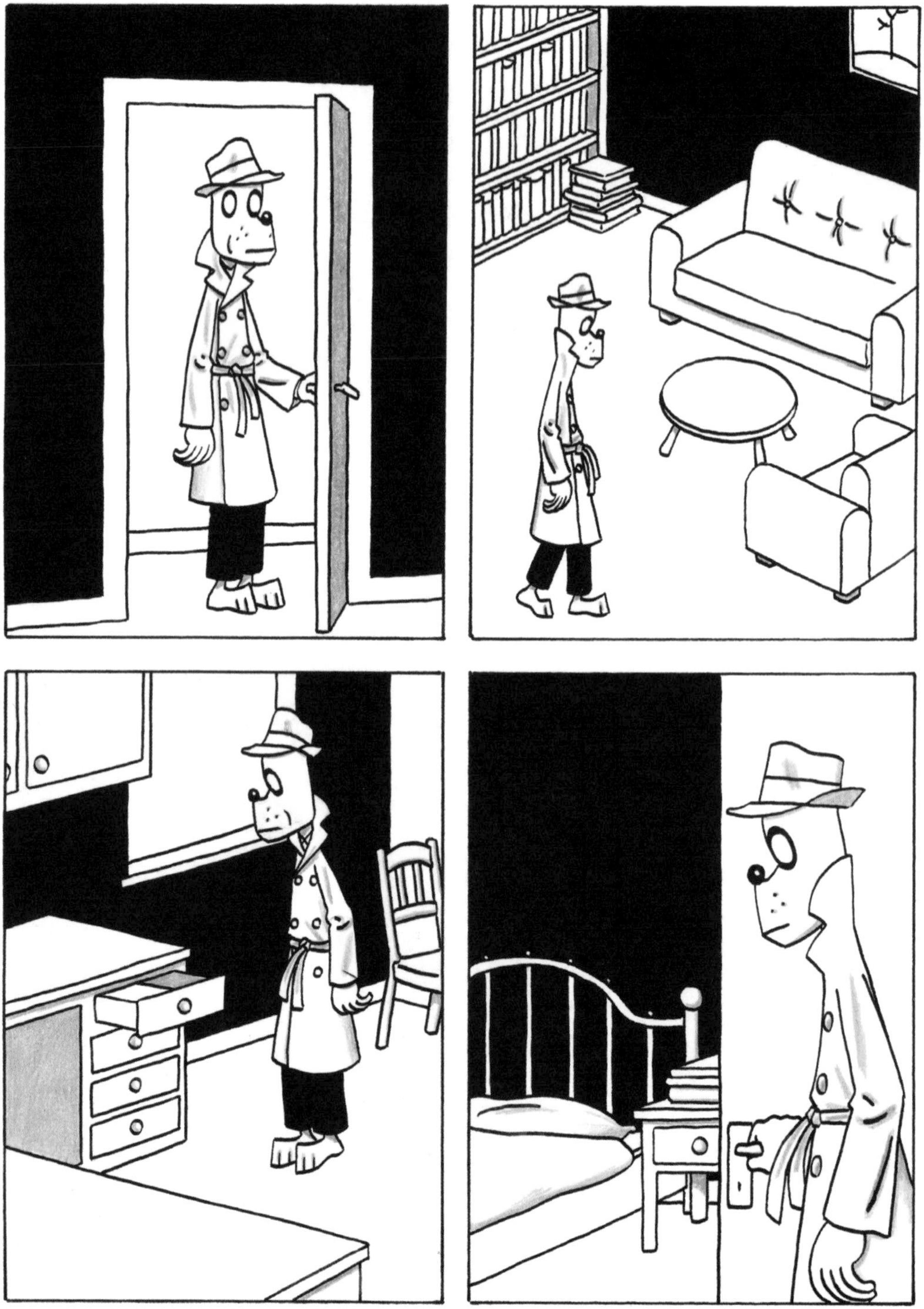

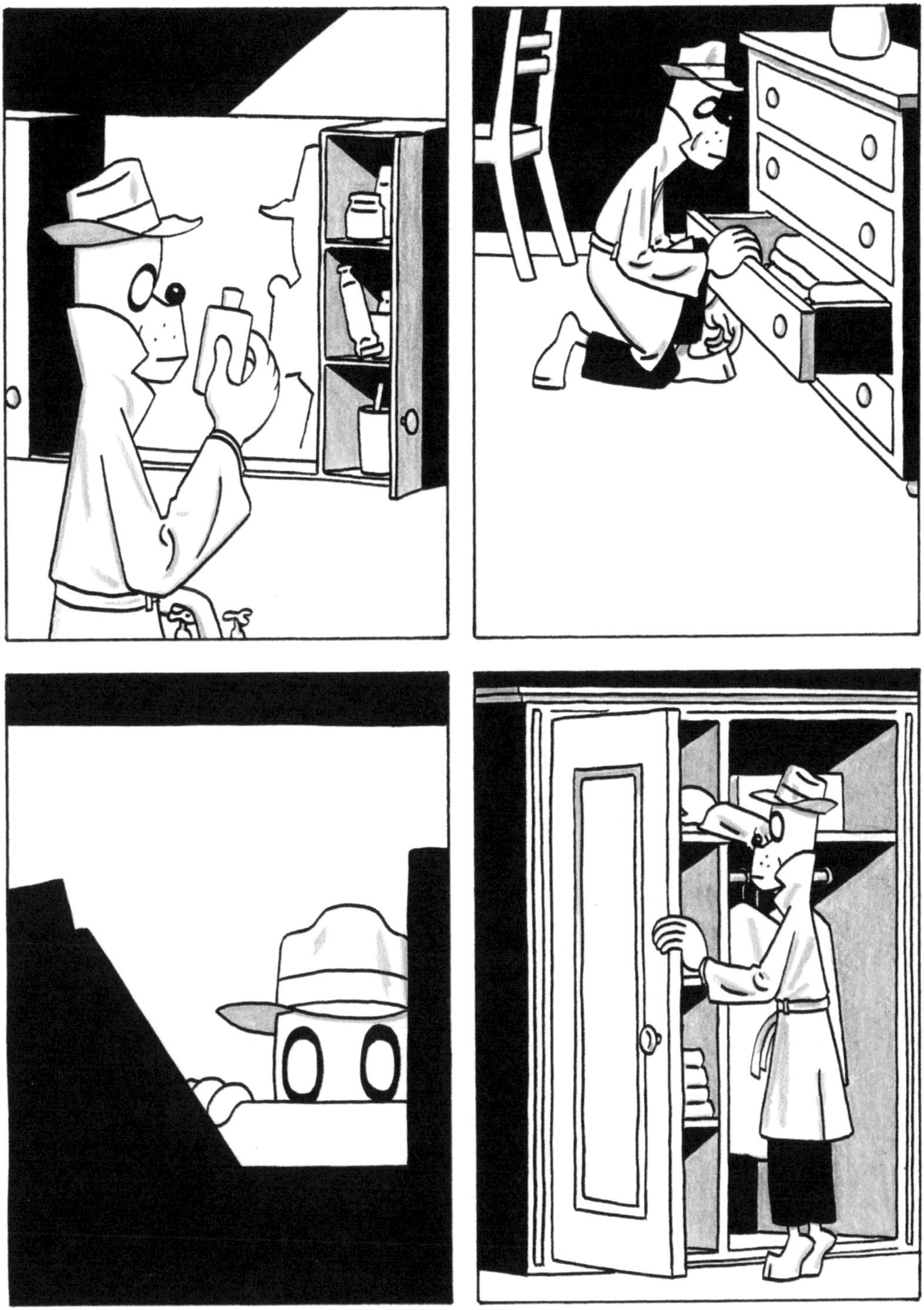

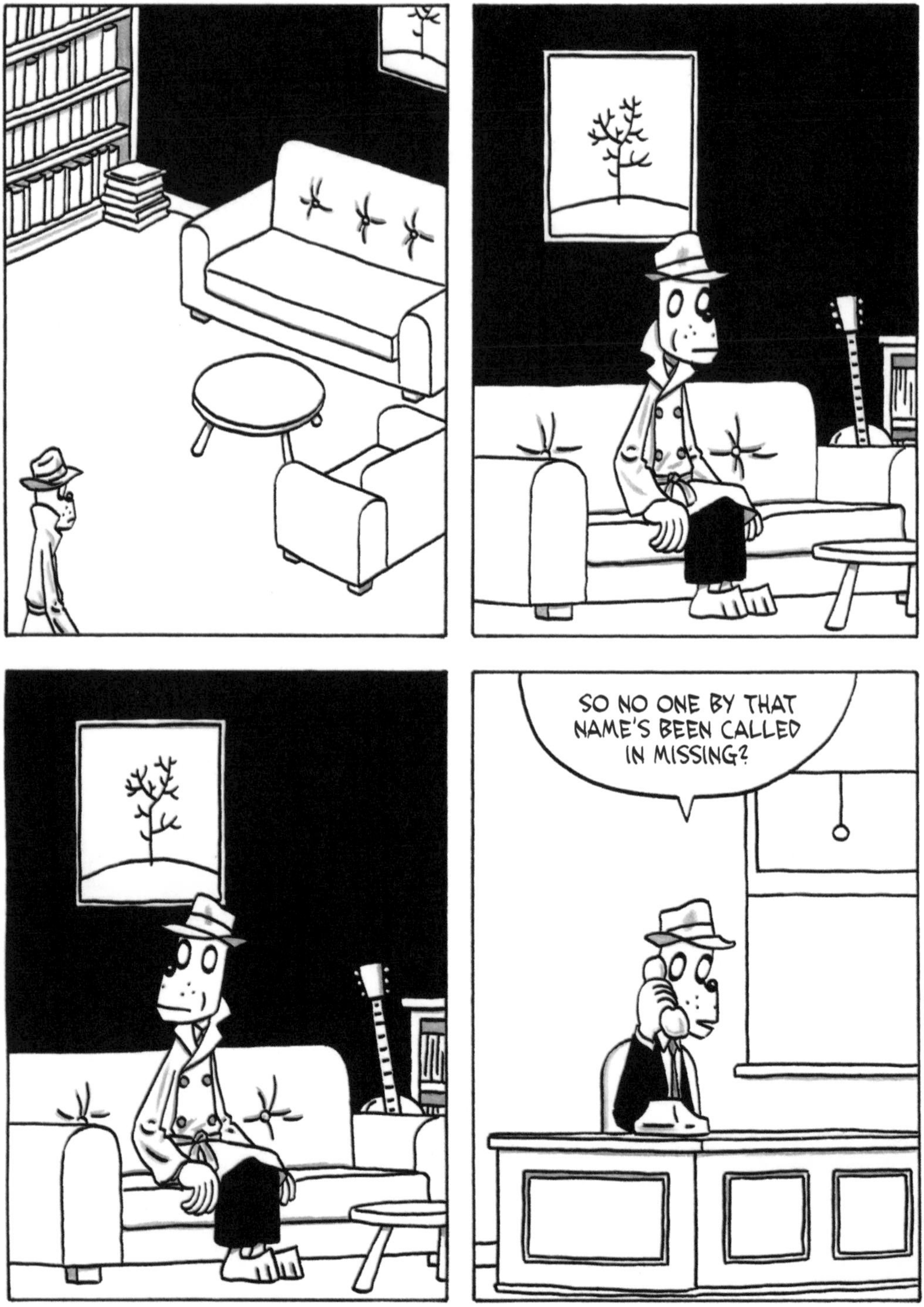
SO NO ONE BY THAT
NAME'S BEEN CALLED
IN MISSING?

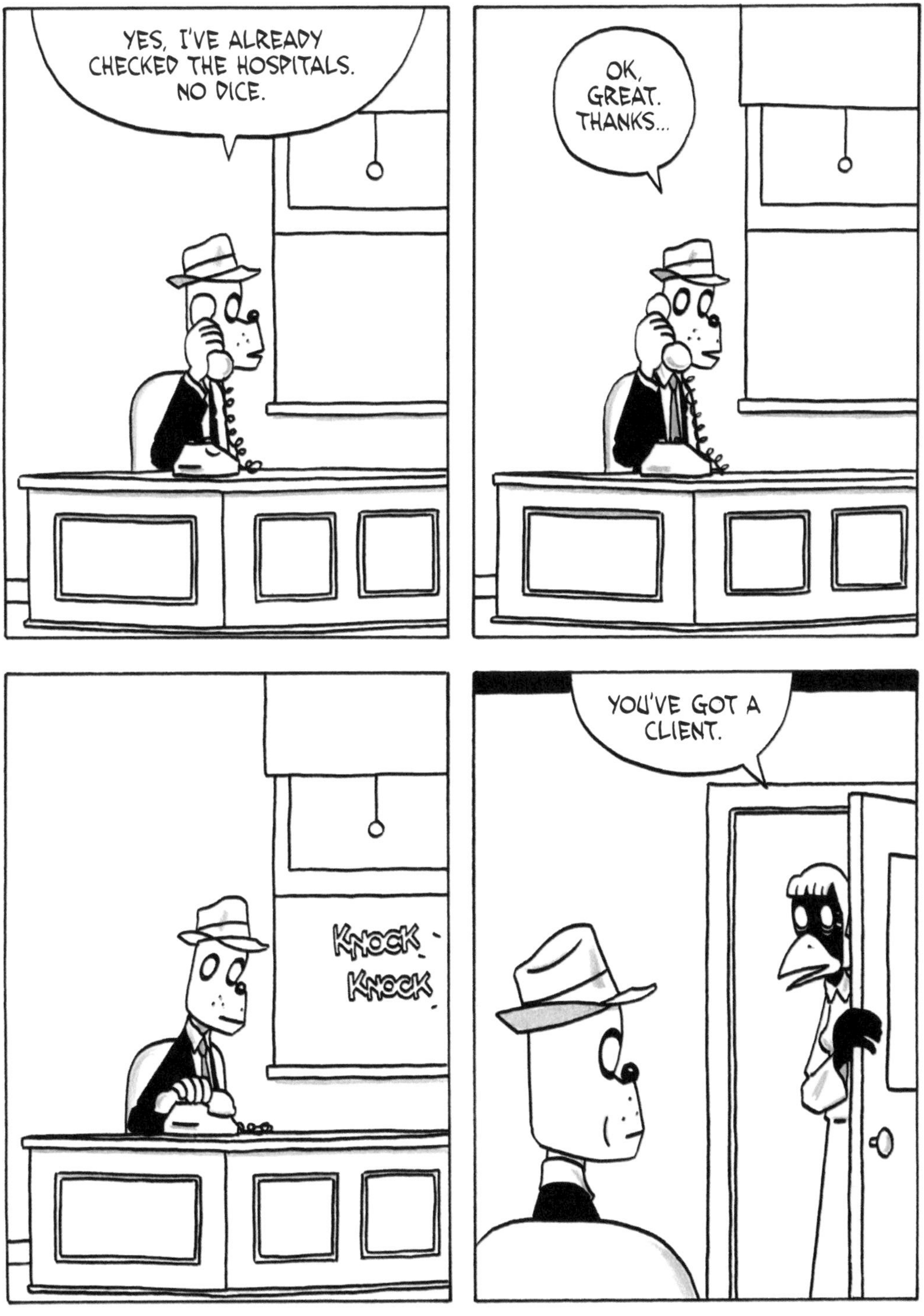
YES, I'VE ALREADY CHECKED THE HOSPITALS. NO DICE.
OK, GREAT. THANKS...
KNOCK KNOCK
YOU'VE GOT A CLIENT.

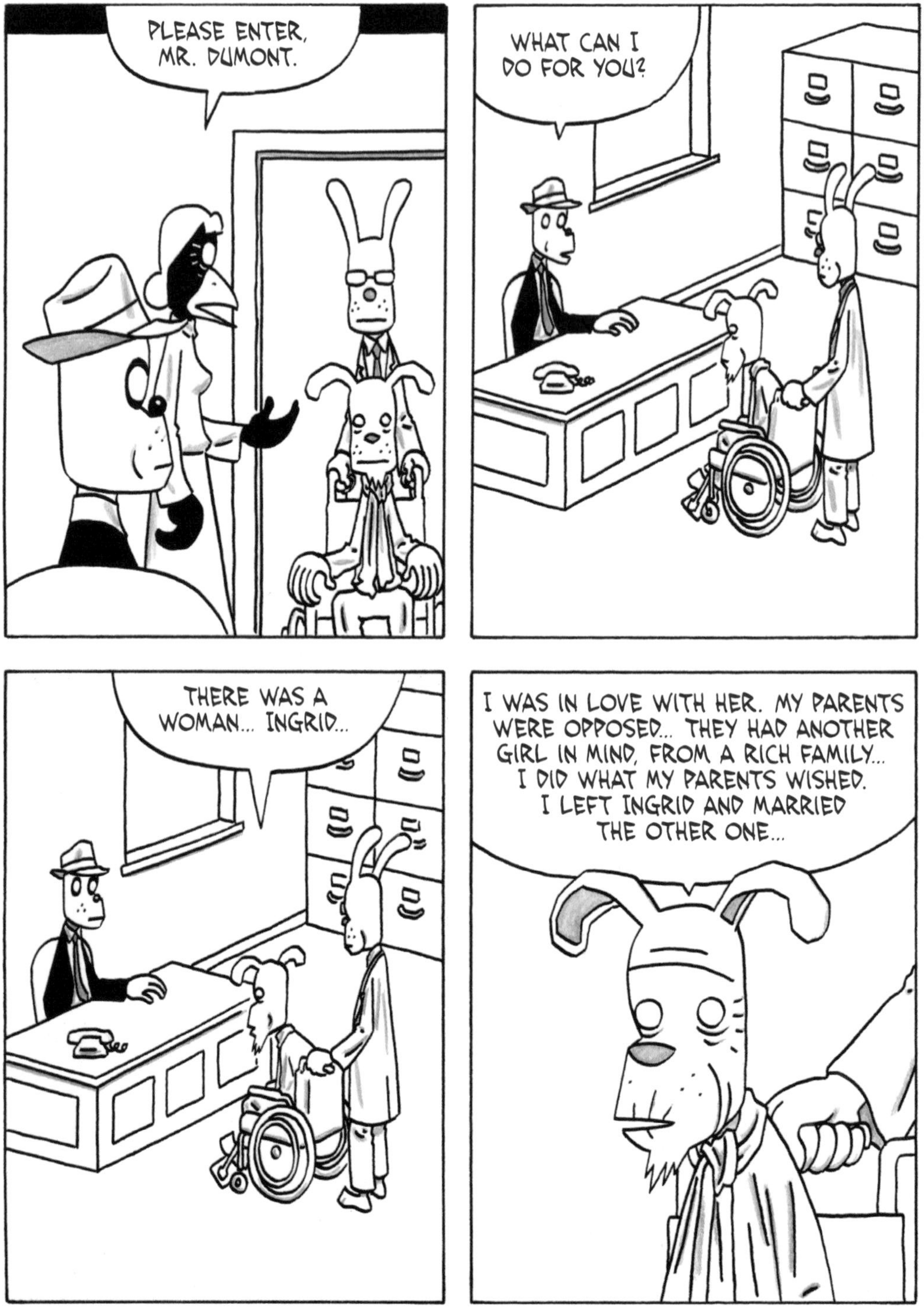
PLEASE ENTER, MR. DUMONT.
WHAT CAN I DO FOR YOU?
THERE WAS A WOMAN... INGRID...
I WAS IN LOVE WITH HER. MY PARENTS WERE OPPOSED... THEY HAD ANOTHER GIRL IN MIND, FROM A RICH FAMILY... I DID WHAT MY PARENTS WISHED. I LEFT INGRID AND MARRIED THE OTHER ONE...

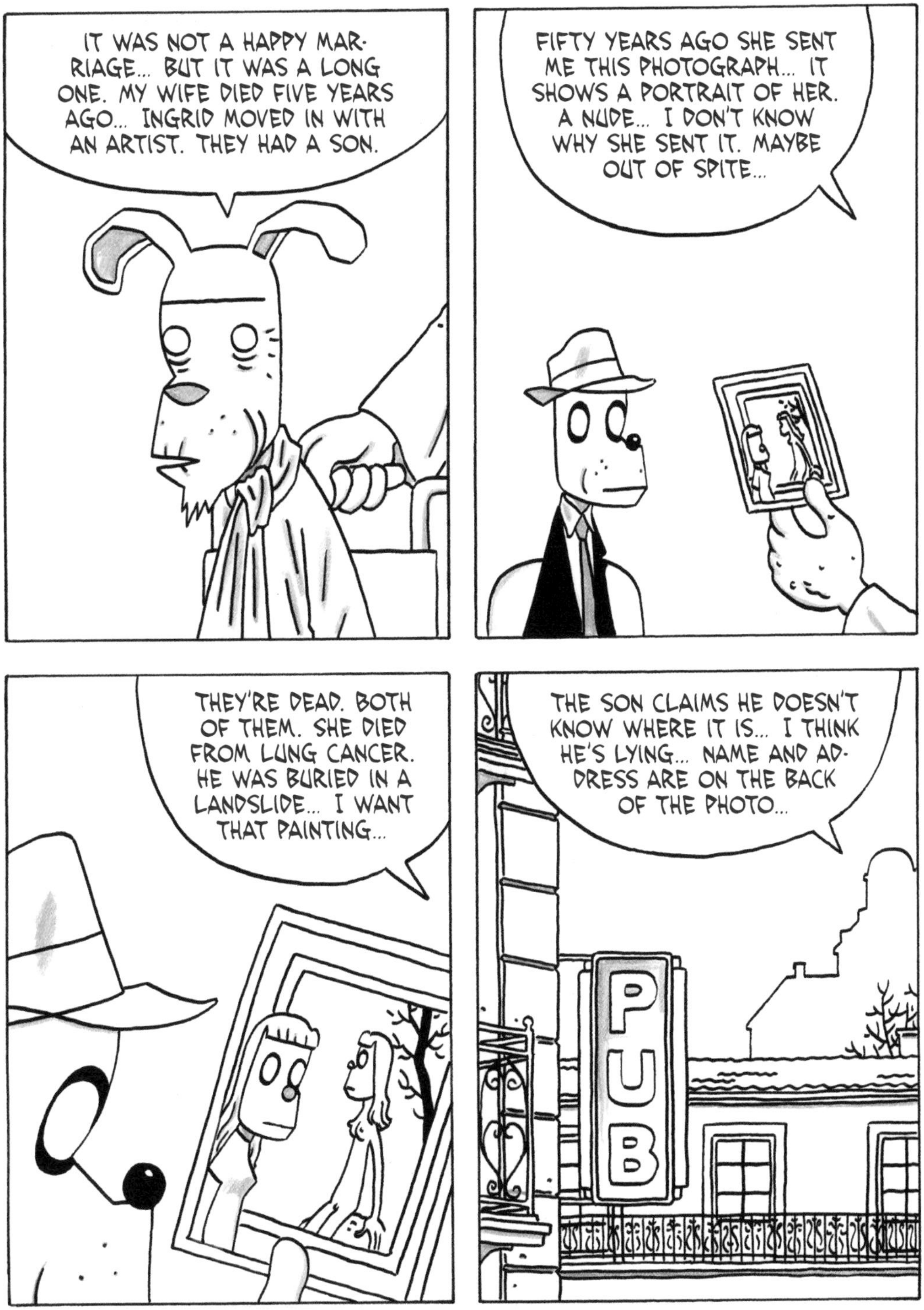
IT WAS NOT A HAPPY MAR-RIAGE... BUT IT WAS A LONG ONE. MY WIFE DIED FIVE YEARS AGO... INGRID MOVED IN WITH AN ARTIST. THEY HAD A SON.
FIFTY YEARS AGO SHE SENT ME THIS PHOTOGRAPH... IT SHOWS A PORTRAIT OF HER. A NUDE... I DON'T KNOW WHY SHE SENT IT. MAYBE OUT OF SPITE...
THEY'RE DEAD. BOTH OF THEM. SHE DIED FROM LUNG CANCER. HE WAS BURIED IN A LANDSLIDE... I WANT THAT PAINTING...
THE SON CLAIMS HE DOESN'T KNOW WHERE IT IS... I THINK HE'S LYING... NAME AND AD-DRESS ARE ON THE BACK OF THE PHOTO...
PUB

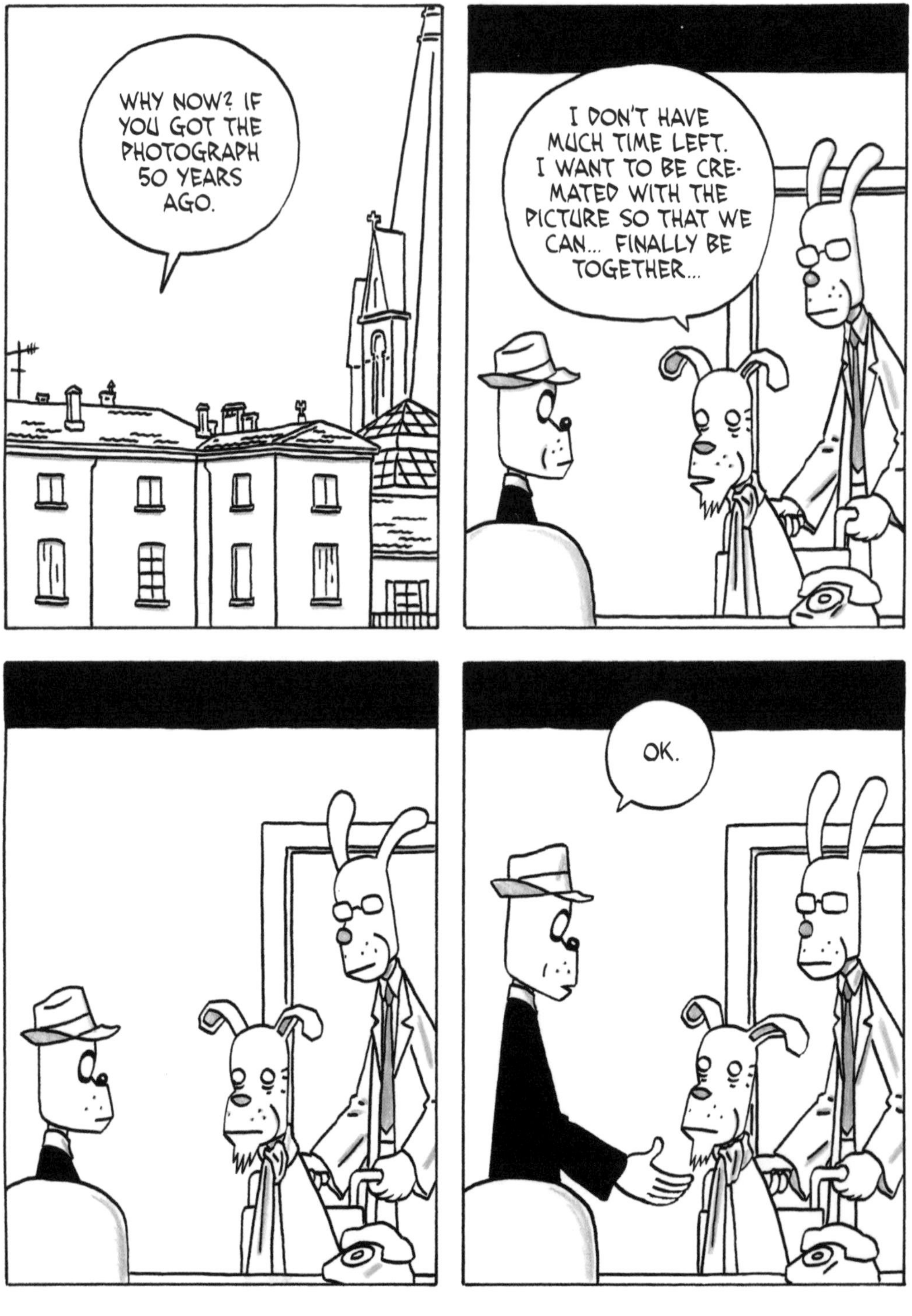
WHY NOW? IF YOU GOT THE PHOTOGRAPH 50 YEARS AGO.
I DON'T HAVE MUCH TIME LEFT. I WANT TO BE CRE-MATED WITH THE PICTURE SO THAT WE CAN... FINALLY BE TOGETHER...
OK.

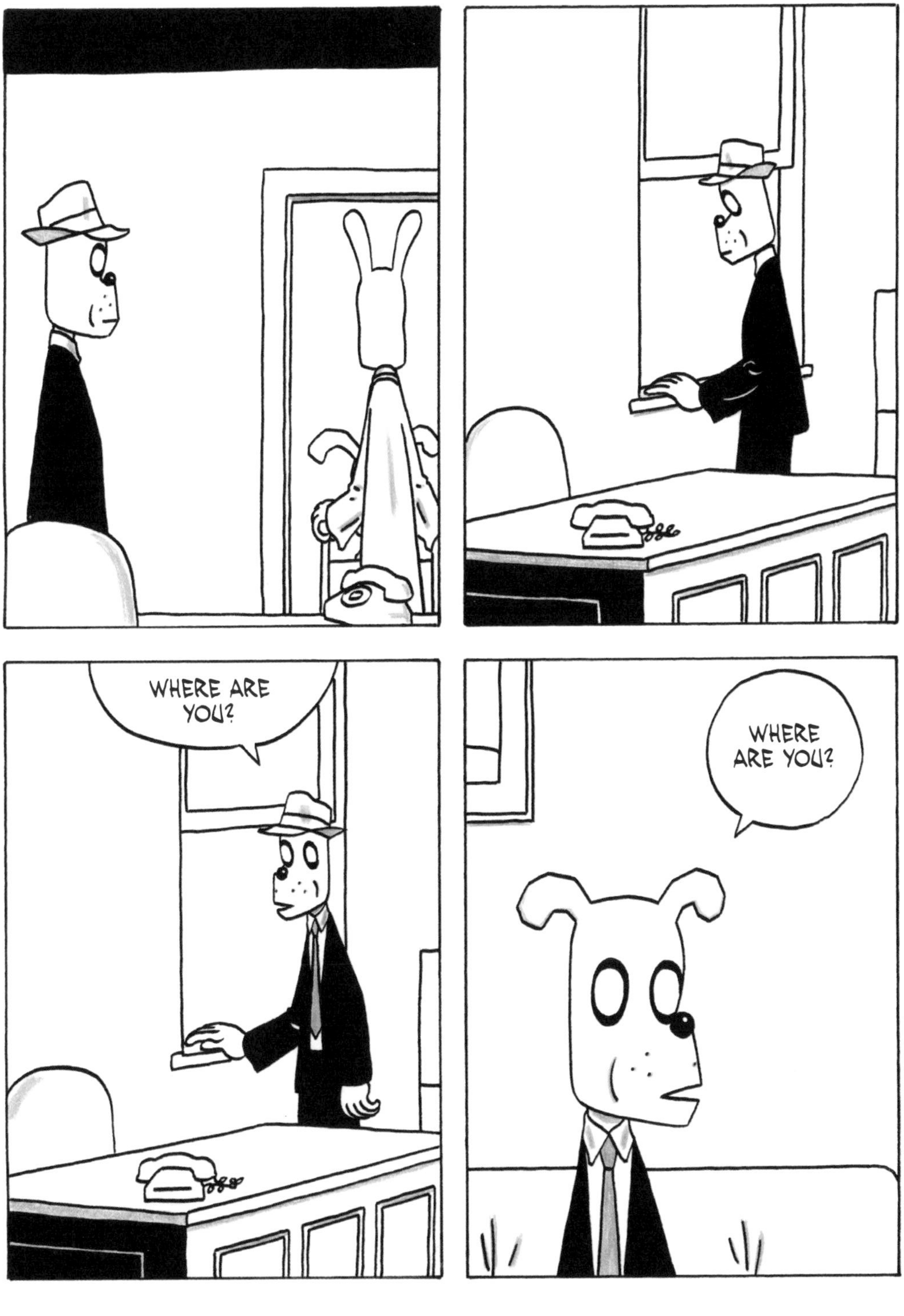
WHERE ARE YOU?
WHERE ARE YOU?

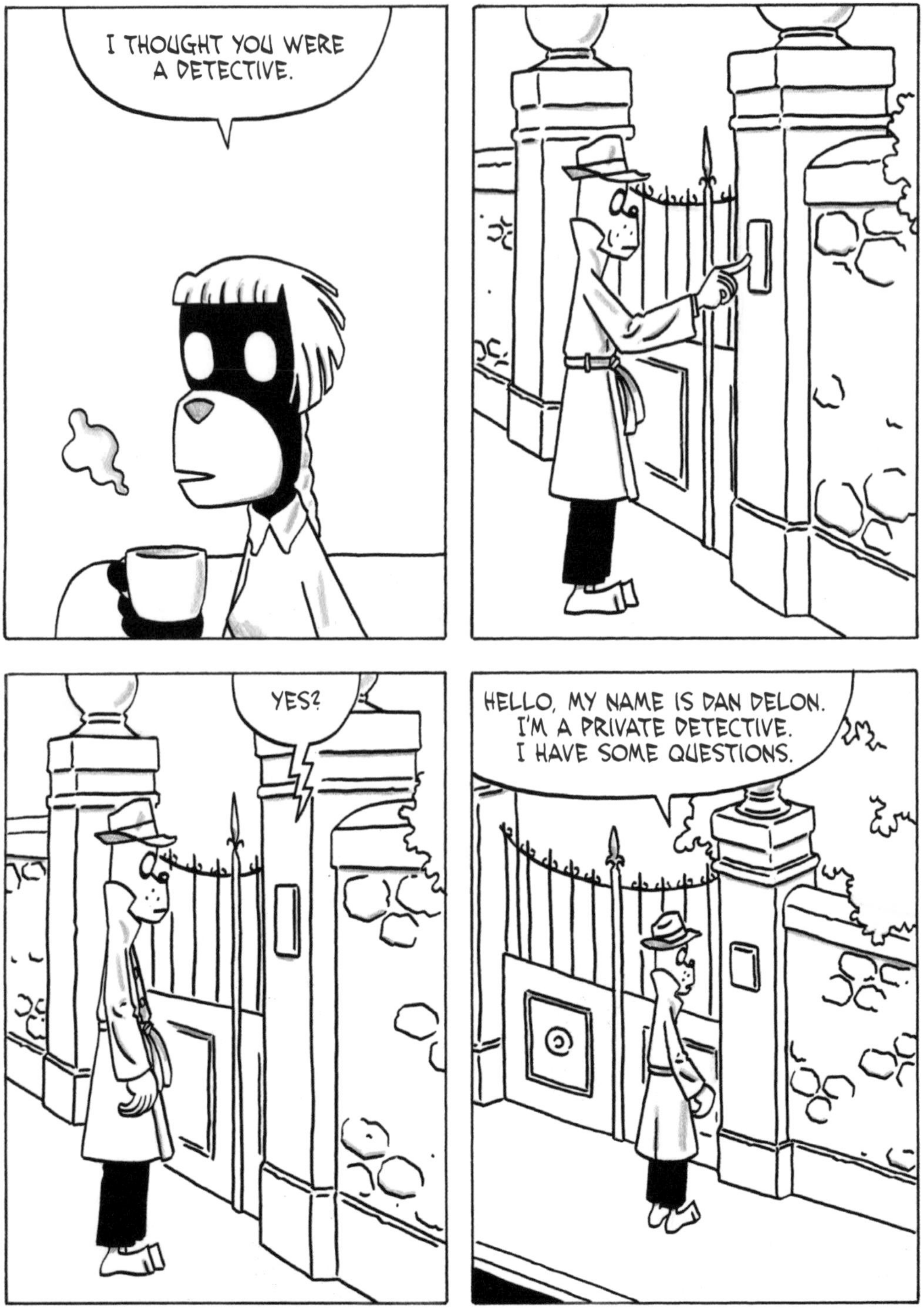
I THOUGHT YOU WERE A DETECTIVE.
YES?
HELLO, MY NAME IS DAN DELON. I'M A PRIVATE DETECTIVE. I HAVE SOME QUESTIONS.

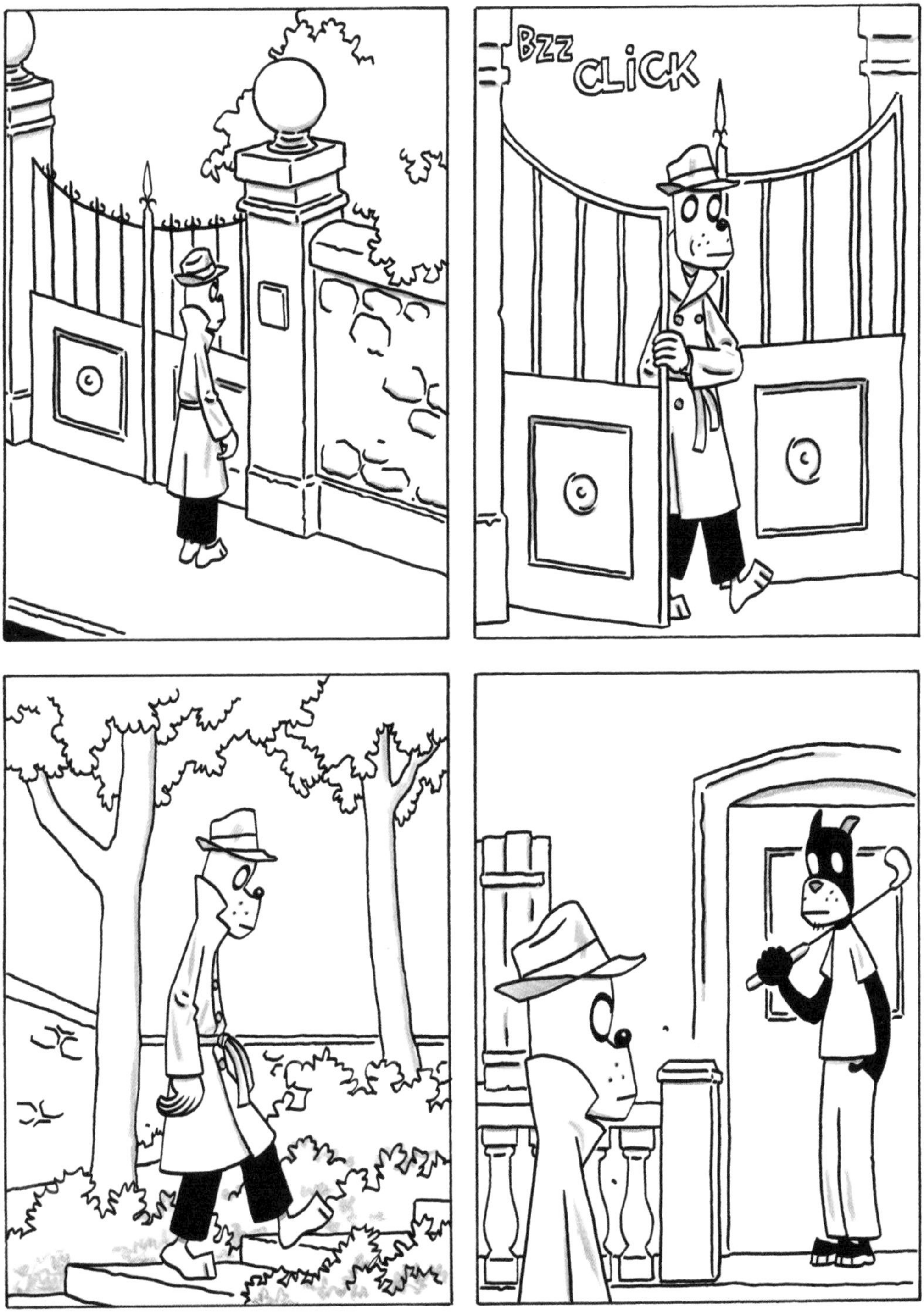
BZZ
CLICK

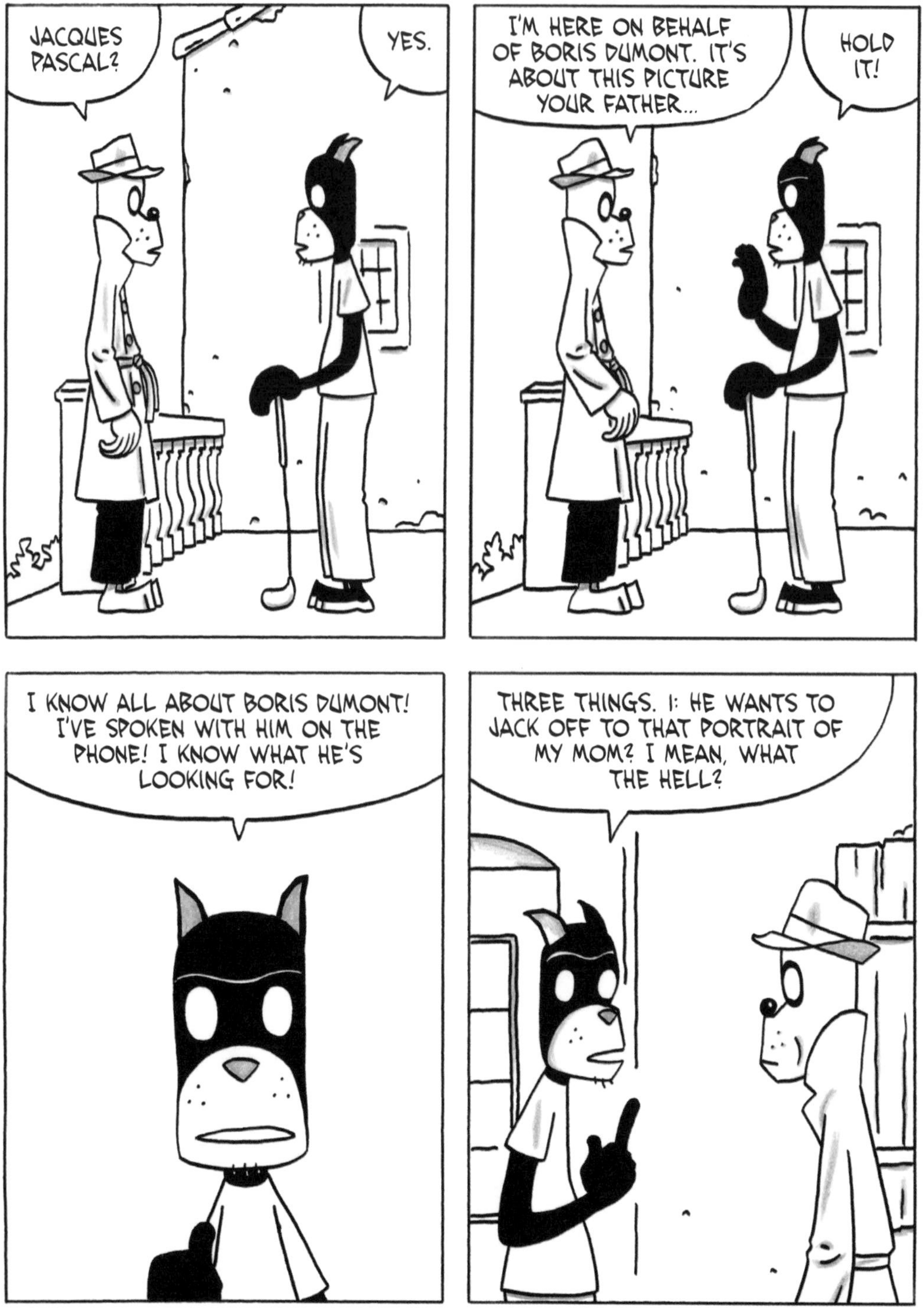
JACQUES PASCAL?
YES.
I'M HERE ON BEHALF OF BORIS DUMONT. IT'S ABOUT THIS PICTURE YOUR FATHER...
HOLD IT!
I KNOW ALL ABOUT BORIS DUMONT! I'VE SPOKEN WITH HIM ON THE PHONE! I KNOW WHAT HE'S LOOKING FOR!
THREE THINGS. 1: HE WANTS TO JACK OFF TO THAT PORTRAIT OF MY MOM? I MEAN, WHAT THE HELL?

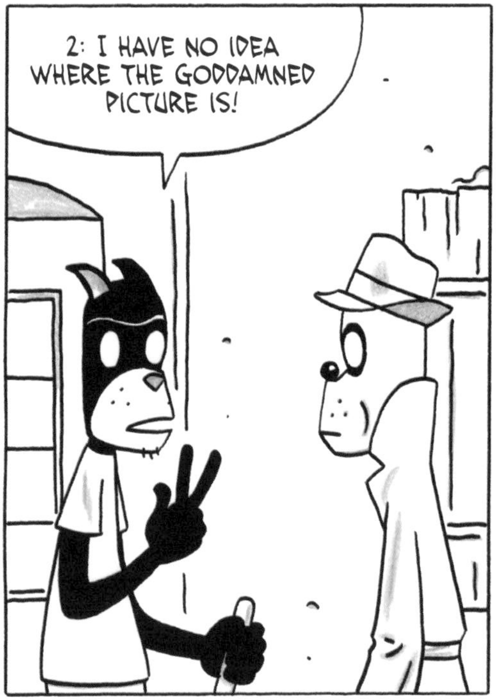
2: I HAVE NO IDEA WHERE THE GODDAMNED PICTURE IS!

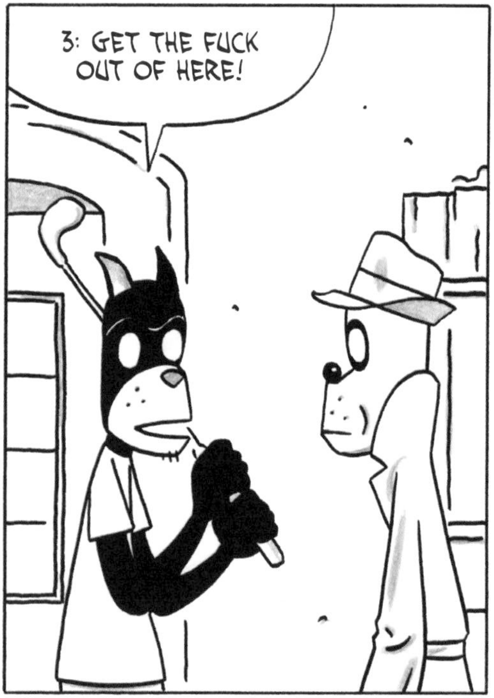
3: GET THE FUCK OUT OF HERE!

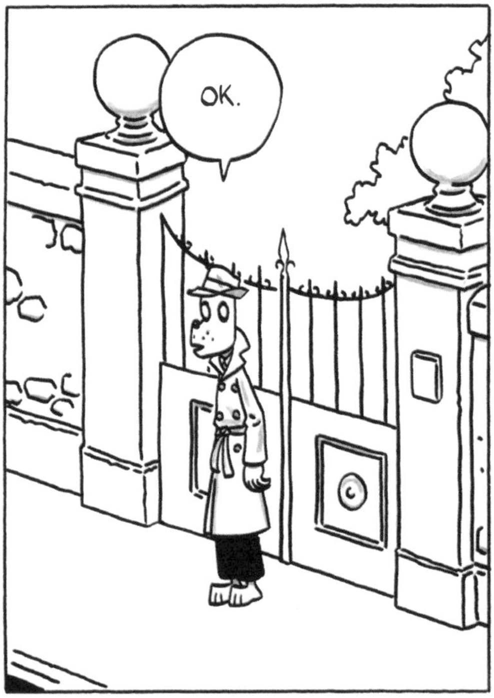
OK.

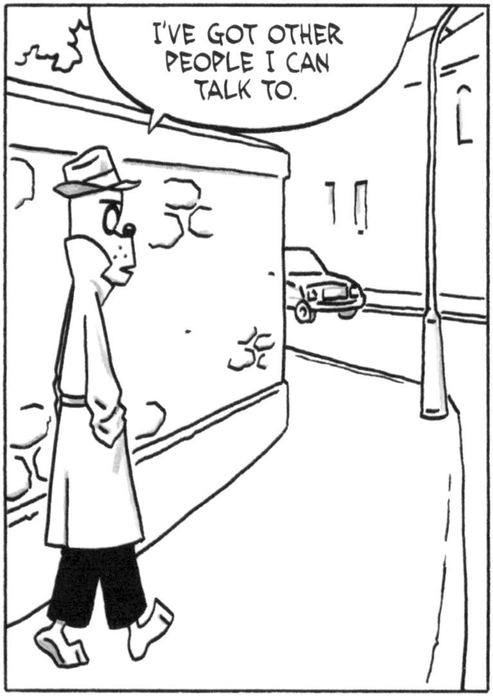
I'VE GOT OTHER PEOPLE I CAN TALK TO.

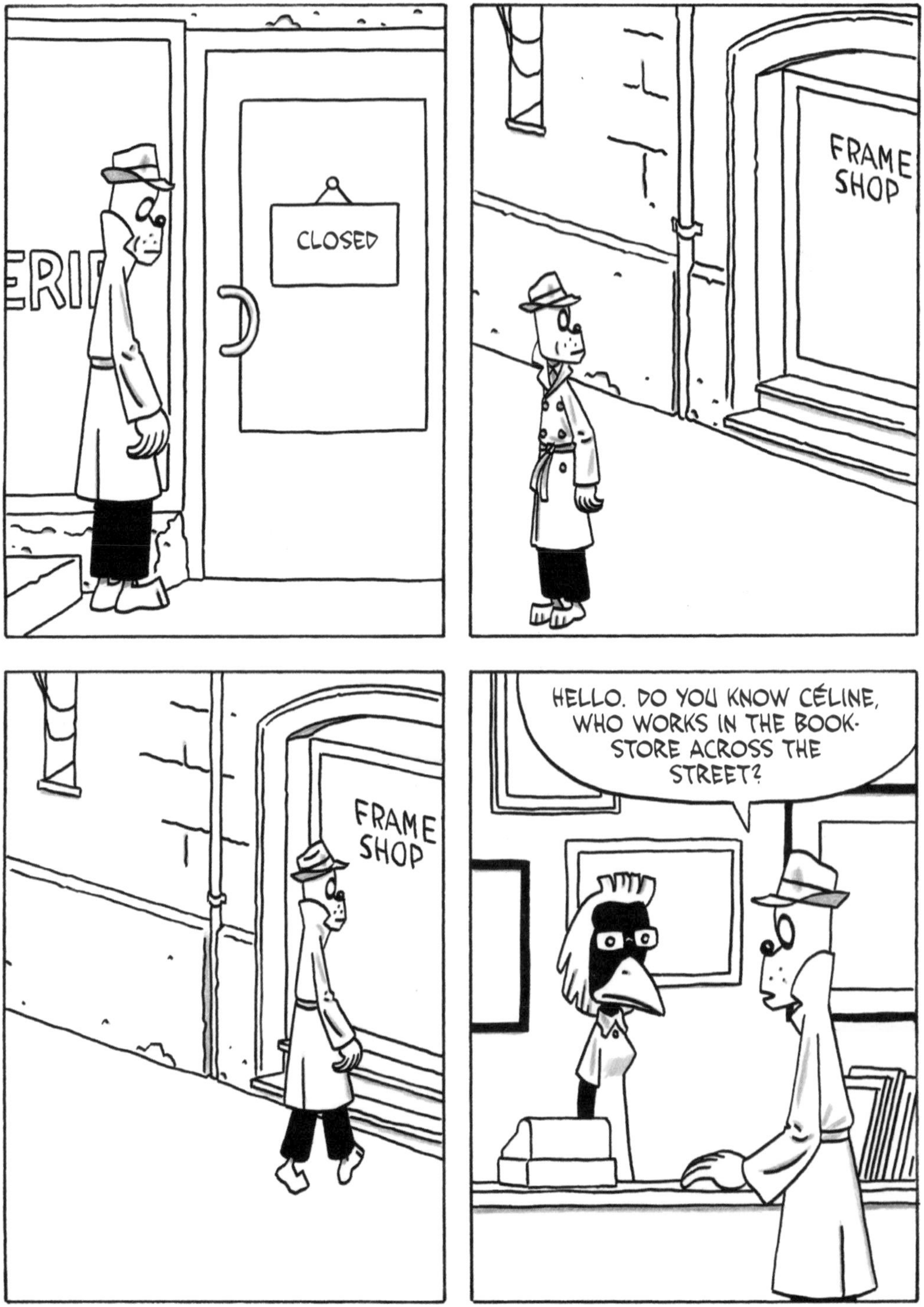
CLOSED
FRAME SHOP
FRAME SHOP
HELLO. DO YOU KNOW CÉLINE, WHO WORKS IN THE BOOK-STORE ACROSS THE STREET?

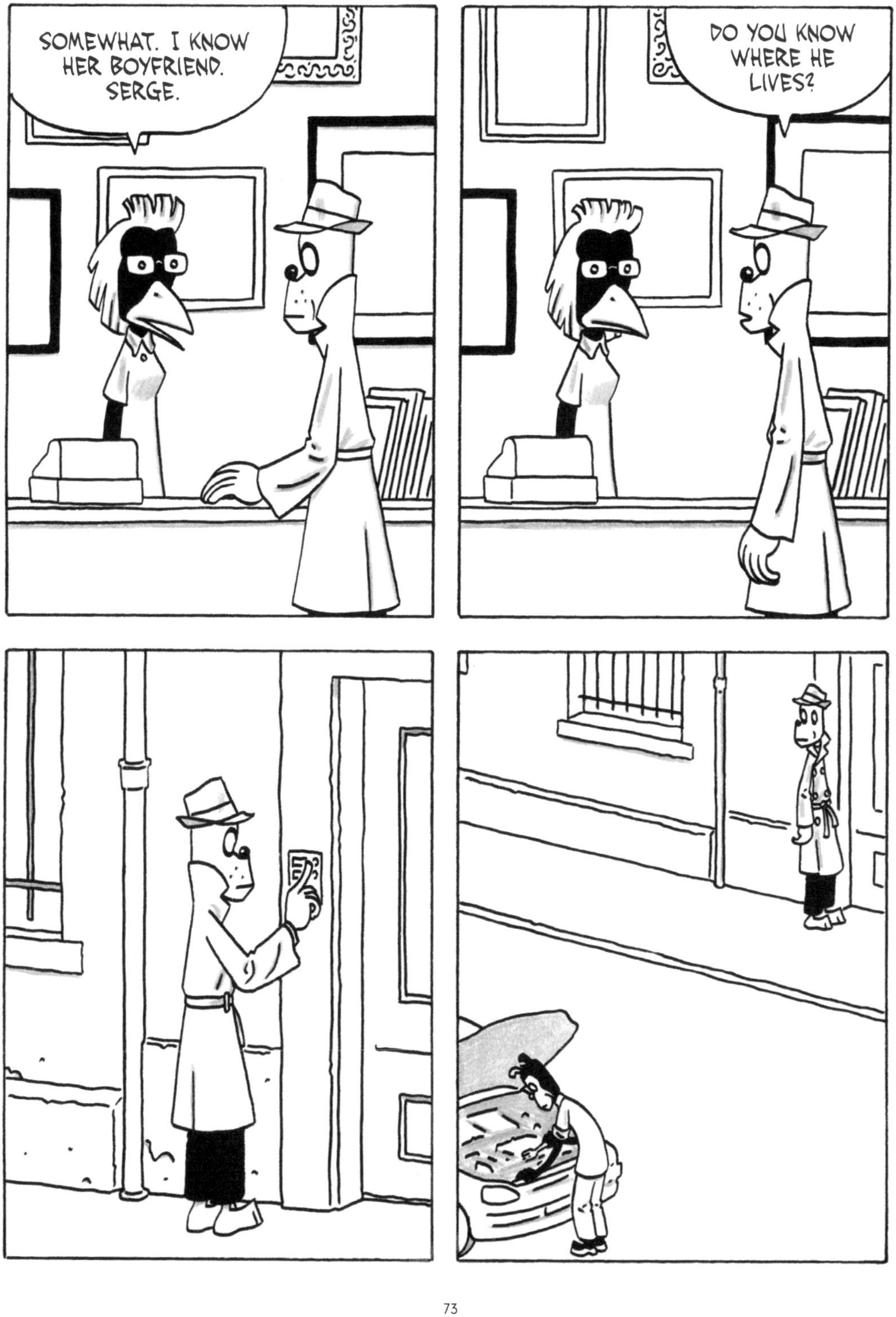
SOMEWHAT. I KNOW HER BOYFRIEND. SERGE.
DO YOU KNOW WHERE HE LIVES?

SERGE NOEL?

YEP, THAT'S ME. YOU KNOW ANYTHING ABOUT CARS?

THEY'VE GOT FOUR WHEELS.

HA!

MY NAME IS DAN DELON. I'M A PRIVATE DETECTIVE.

I'D LIKE TO HAVE A WORD WITH CÉLINE.

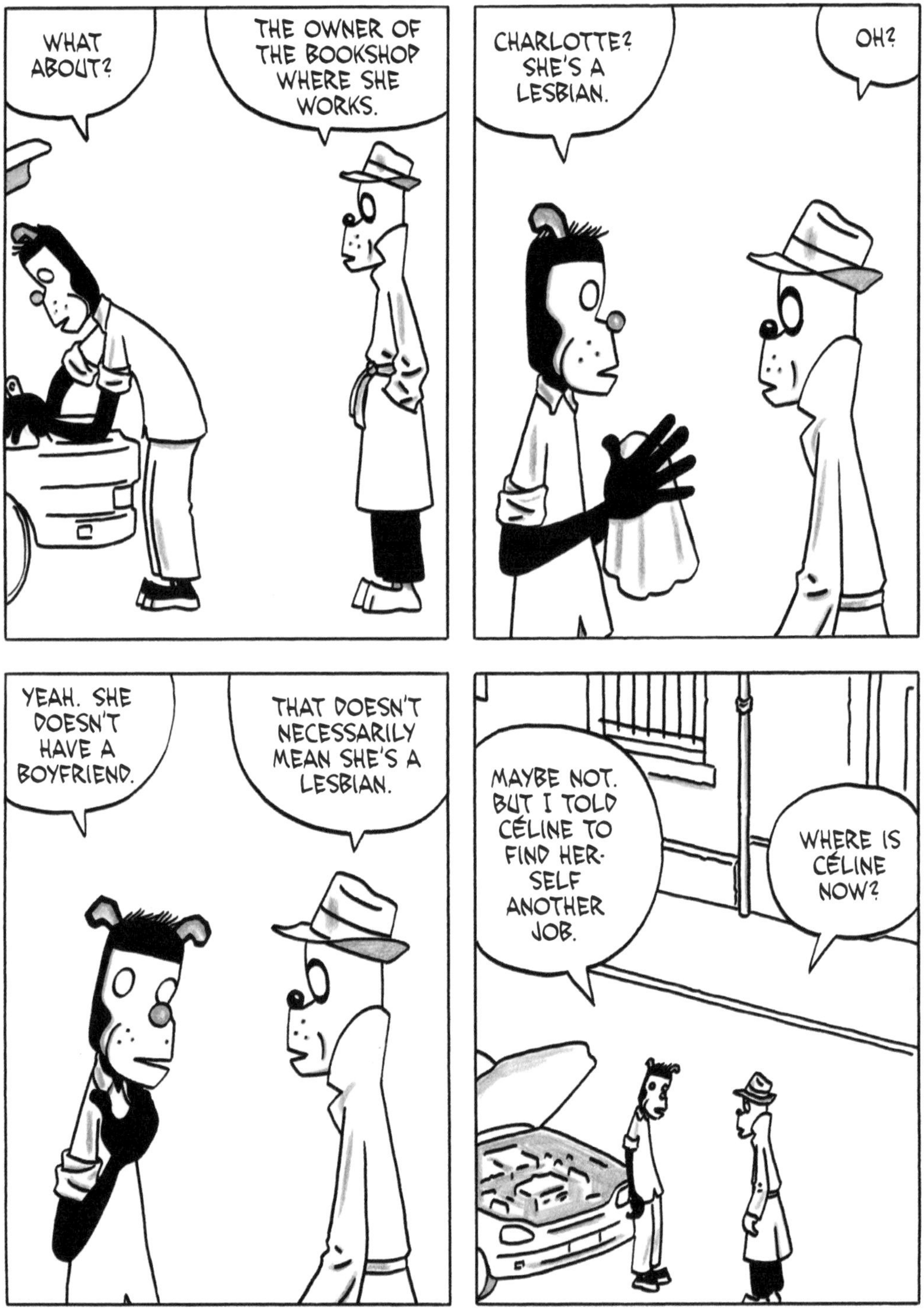
WHAT ABOUT?
THE OWNER OF THE BOOKSHOP WHERE SHE WORKS.
CHARLOTTE? SHE'S A LESBIAN.
OH?
YEAH. SHE DOESN'T HAVE A BOYFRIEND.
THAT DOESN'T NECESSARILY MEAN SHE'S A LESBIAN.
MAYBE NOT. BUT I TOLD CÉLINE TO FIND HER-SELF ANOTHER JOB.
WHERE IS CÉLINE NOW?

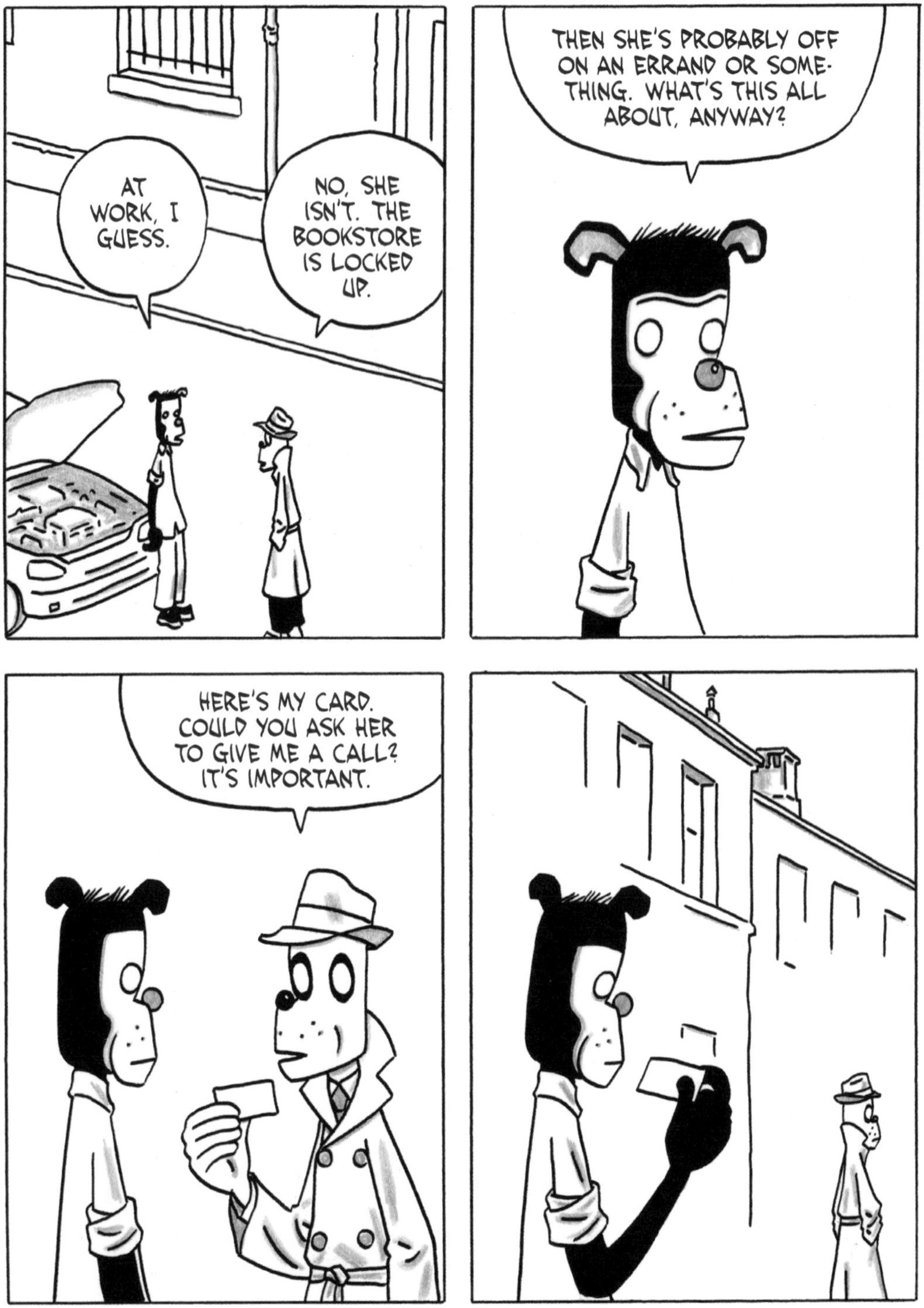
AT WORK, I GUESS.
NO, SHE ISN'T. THE BOOKSTORE IS LOCKED UP.
THEN SHE'S PROBABLY OFF ON AN ERRAND OR SOME-THING. WHAT'S THIS ALL ABOUT, ANYWAY?
HERE'S MY CARD. COULD YOU ASK HER TO GIVE ME A CALL? IT'S IMPORTANT.

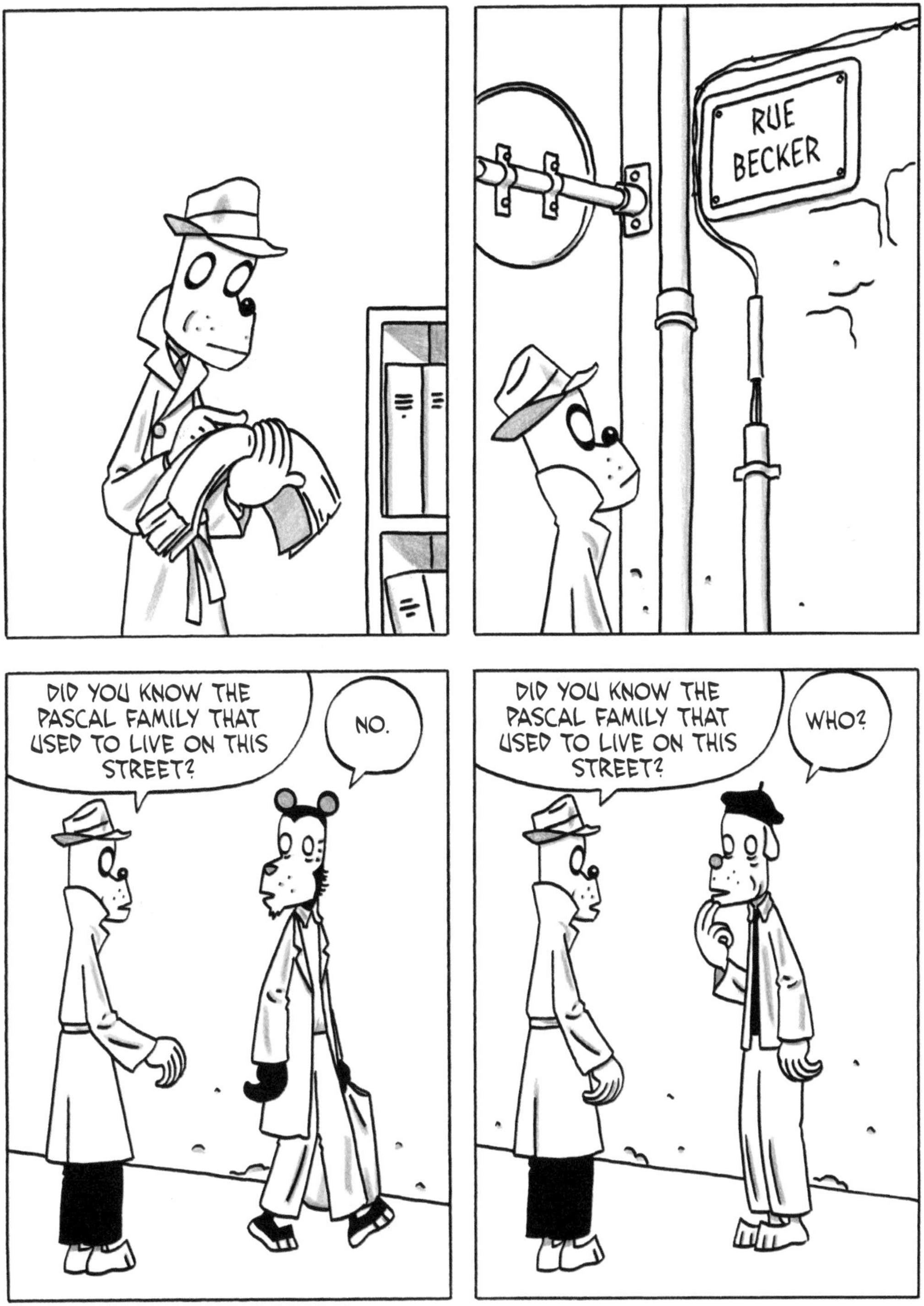
RUE BECKER
DID YOU KNOW THE PASCAL FAMILY THAT USED TO LIVE ON THIS STREET?
NO.
DID YOU KNOW THE PASCAL FAMILY THAT USED TO LIVE ON THIS STREET?
WHO?

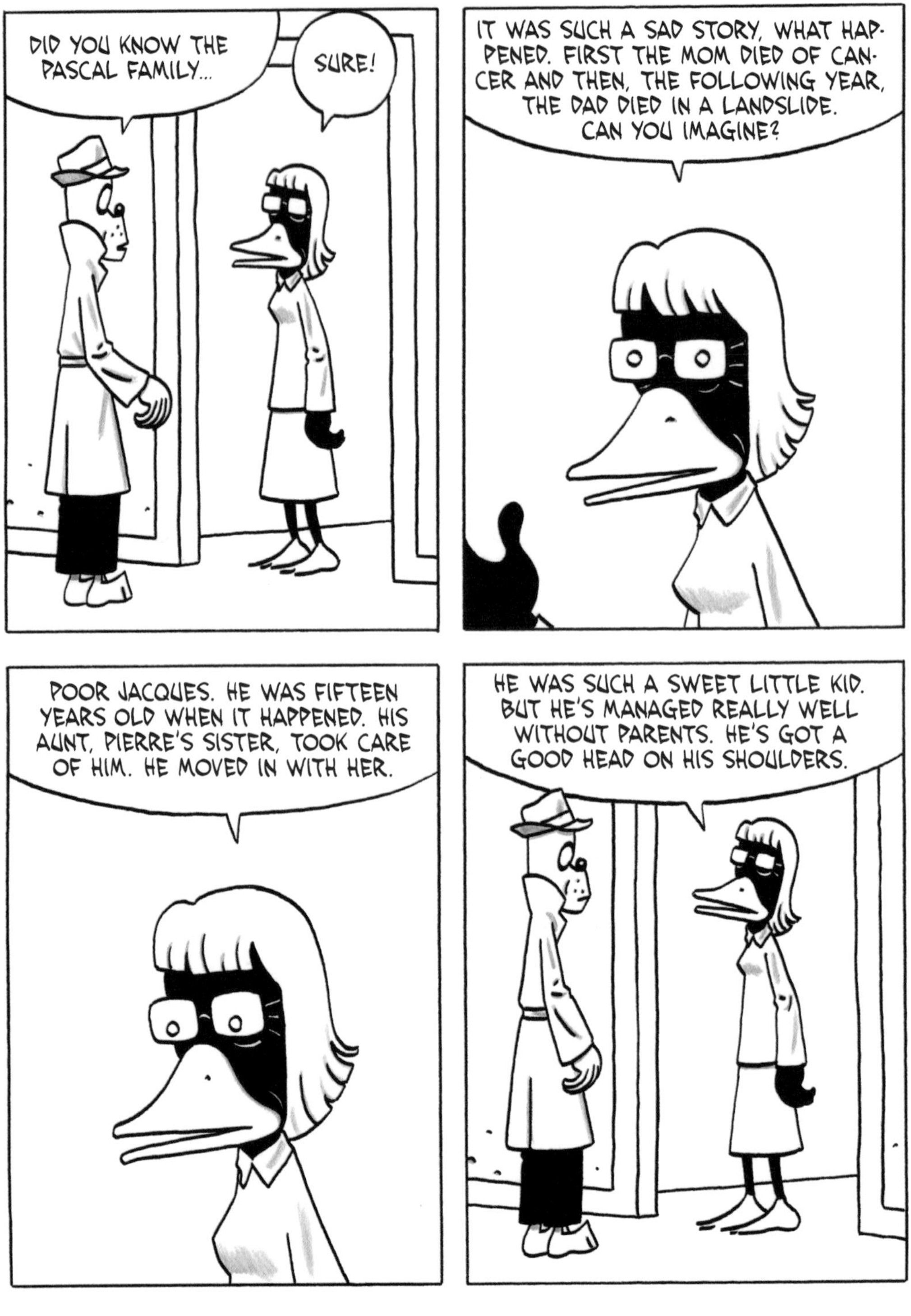
DID YOU KNOW THE PASCAL FAMILY...
SURE!
IT WAS SUCH A SAD STORY, WHAT HAPPENED. FIRST THE MOM DIED OF CANCER AND THEN, THE FOLLOWING YEAR, THE DAD DIED IN A LANDSLIDE. CAN YOU IMAGINE?
POOR JACQUES. HE WAS FIFTEEN YEARS OLD WHEN IT HAPPENED. HIS AUNT, PIERRE'S SISTER, TOOK CARE OF HIM. HE MOVED IN WITH HER.
HE WAS SUCH A SWEET LITTLE KID. BUT HE'S MANAGED REALLY WELL WITHOUT PARENTS. HE'S GOT A GOOD HEAD ON HIS SHOULDERS.

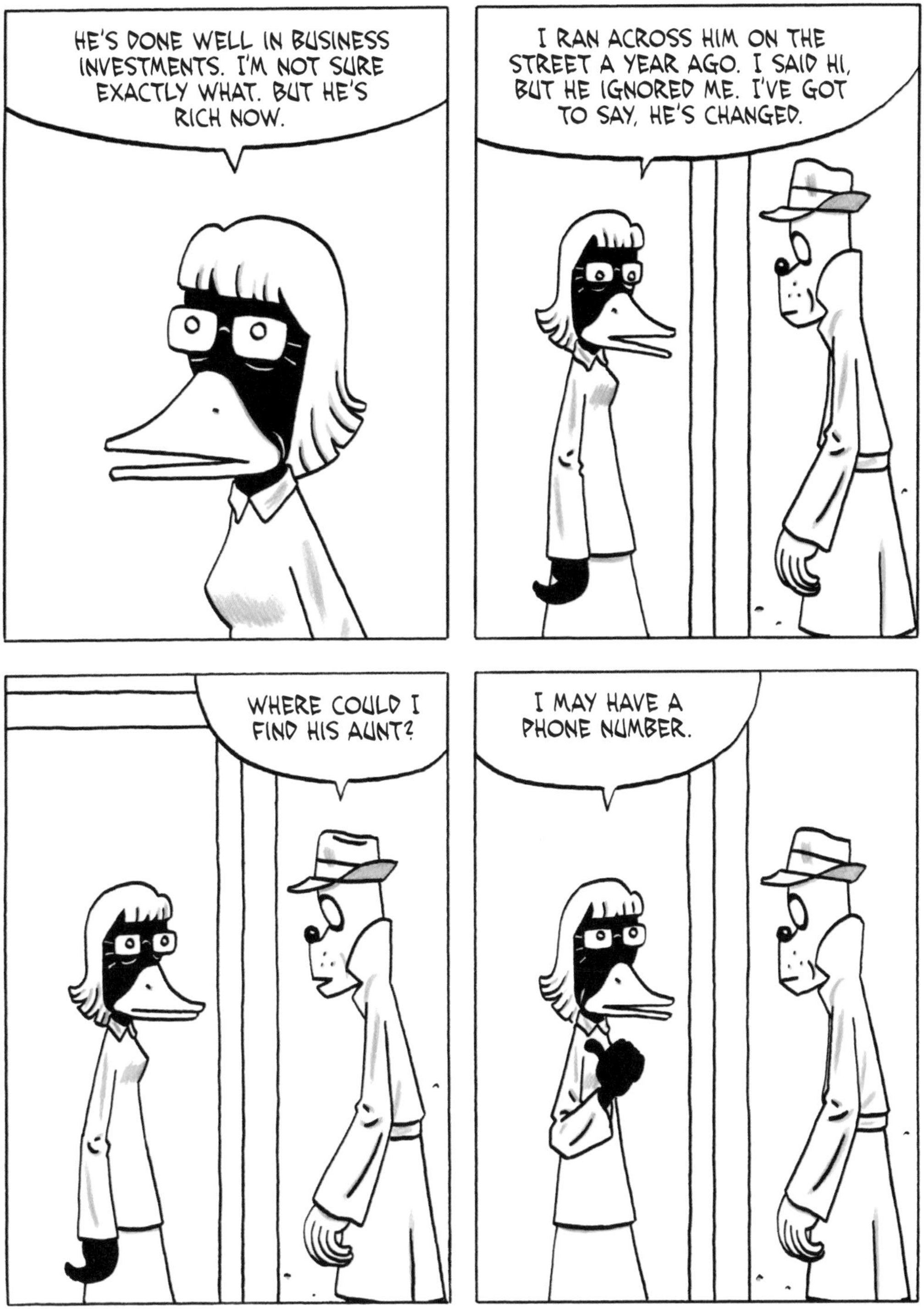

HE'S DONE WELL IN BUSINESS INVESTMENTS. I'M NOT SURE EXACTLY WHAT. BUT HE'S RICH NOW.
I RAN ACROSS HIM ON THE STREET A YEAR AGO. I SAID HI, BUT HE IGNORED ME. I'VE GOT TO SAY, HE'S CHANGED.
WHERE COULD I FIND HIS AUNT?
I MAY HAVE A PHONE NUMBER.

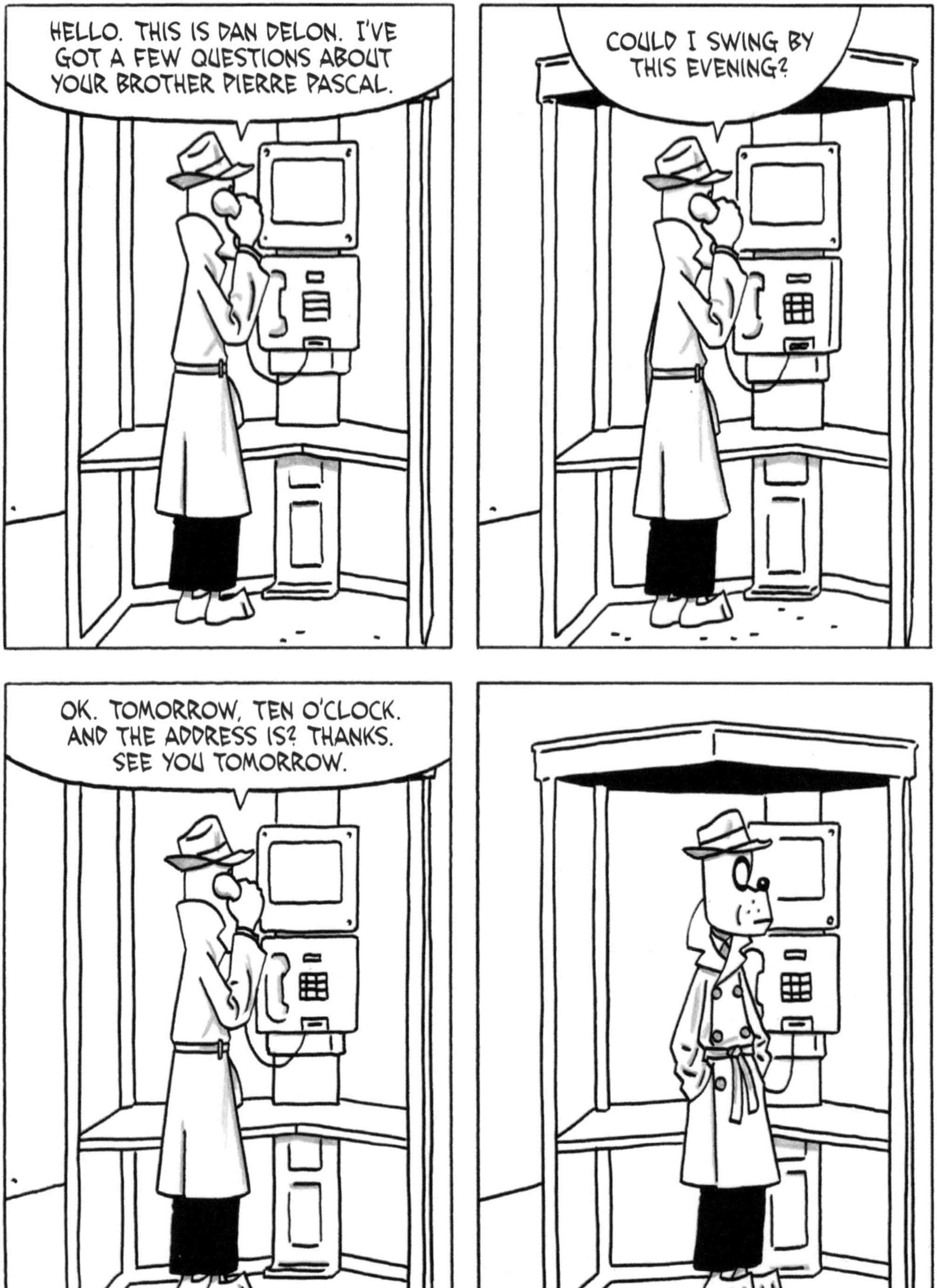
HELLO. THIS IS DAN DELON. I'VE GOT A FEW QUESTIONS ABOUT YOUR BROTHER PIERRE PASCAL.
COULD I SWING BY THIS EVENING?
OK. TOMORROW, TEN O'CLOCK. AND THE ADDRESS IS? THANKS. SEE YOU TOMORROW.

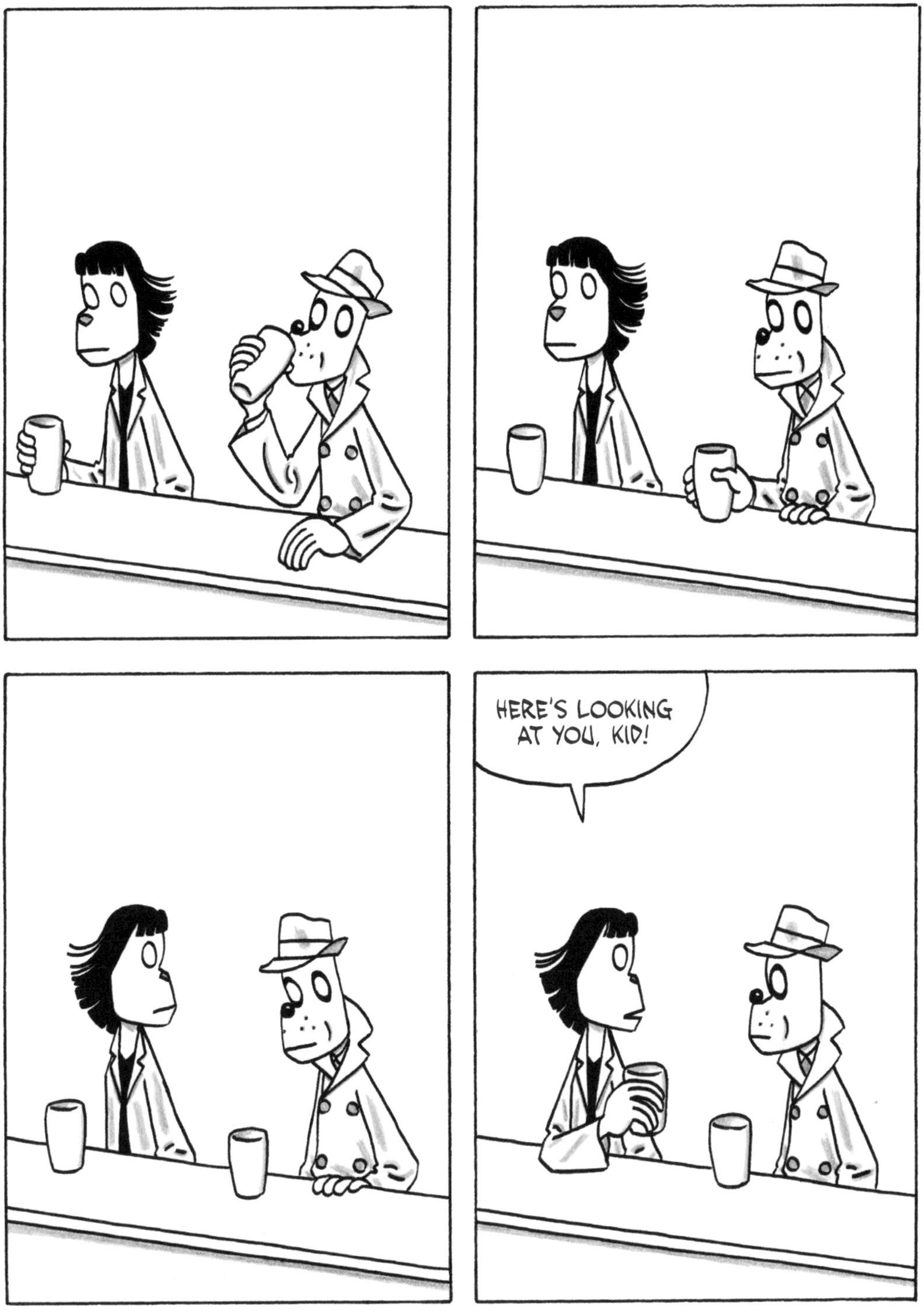
HERE'S LOOKING AT YOU, KID!

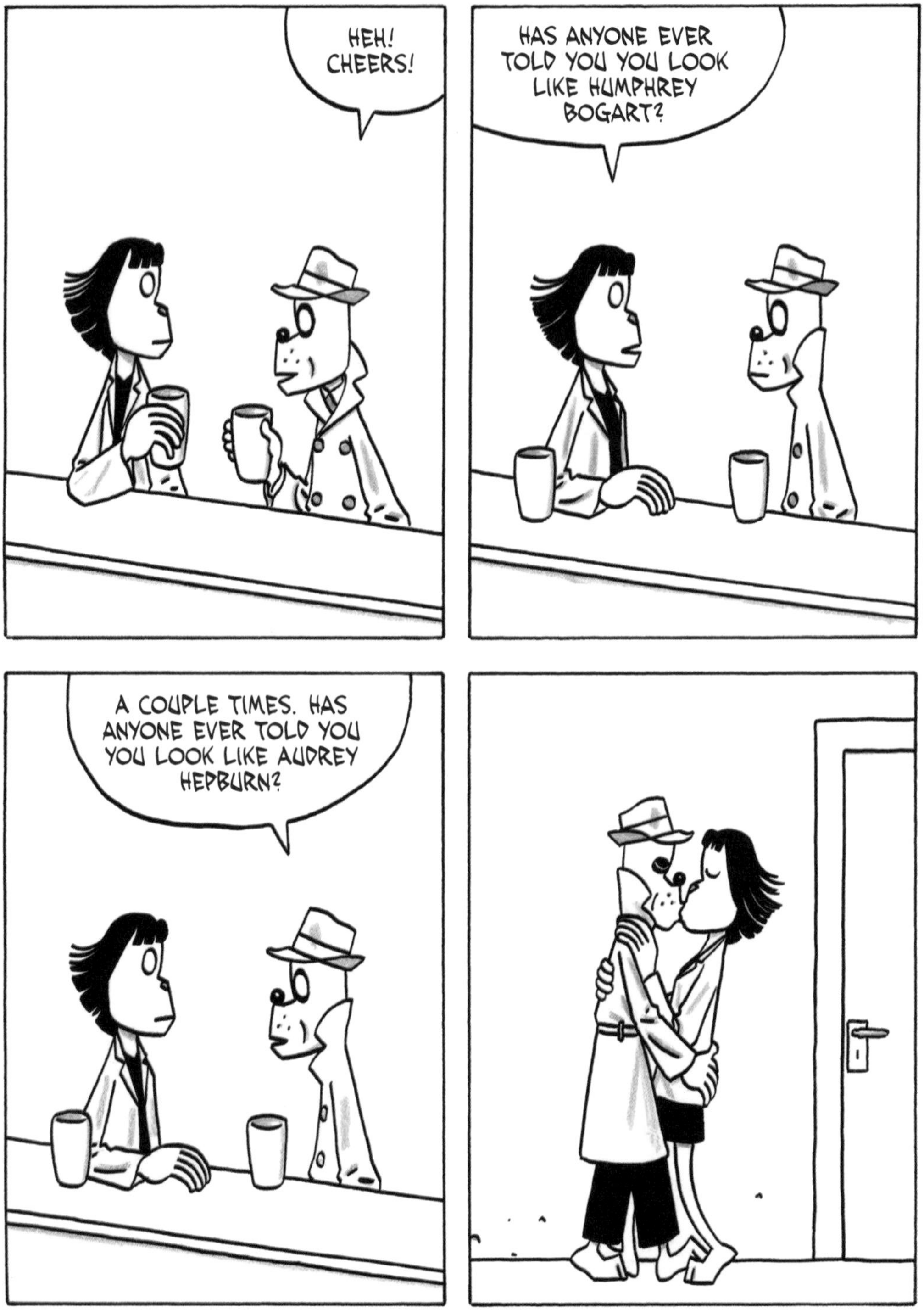
HEH! CHEERS!
HAS ANYONE EVER TOLD YOU YOU LOOK LIKE HUMPHREY BOGART?
A COUPLE TIMES. HAS ANYONE EVER TOLD YOU YOU LOOK LIKE AUDREY HEPBURN?

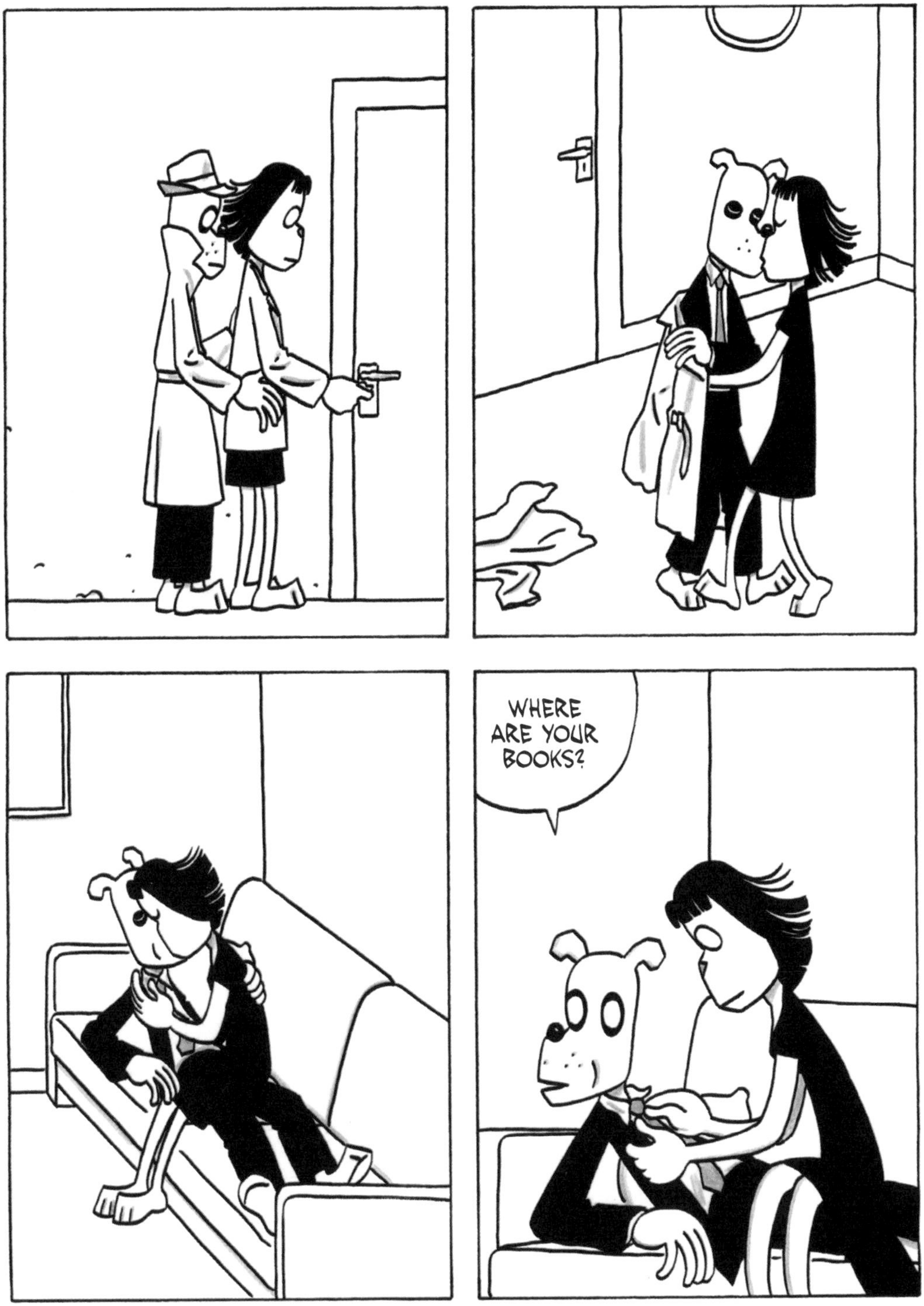
WHERE ARE YOUR BOOKS?

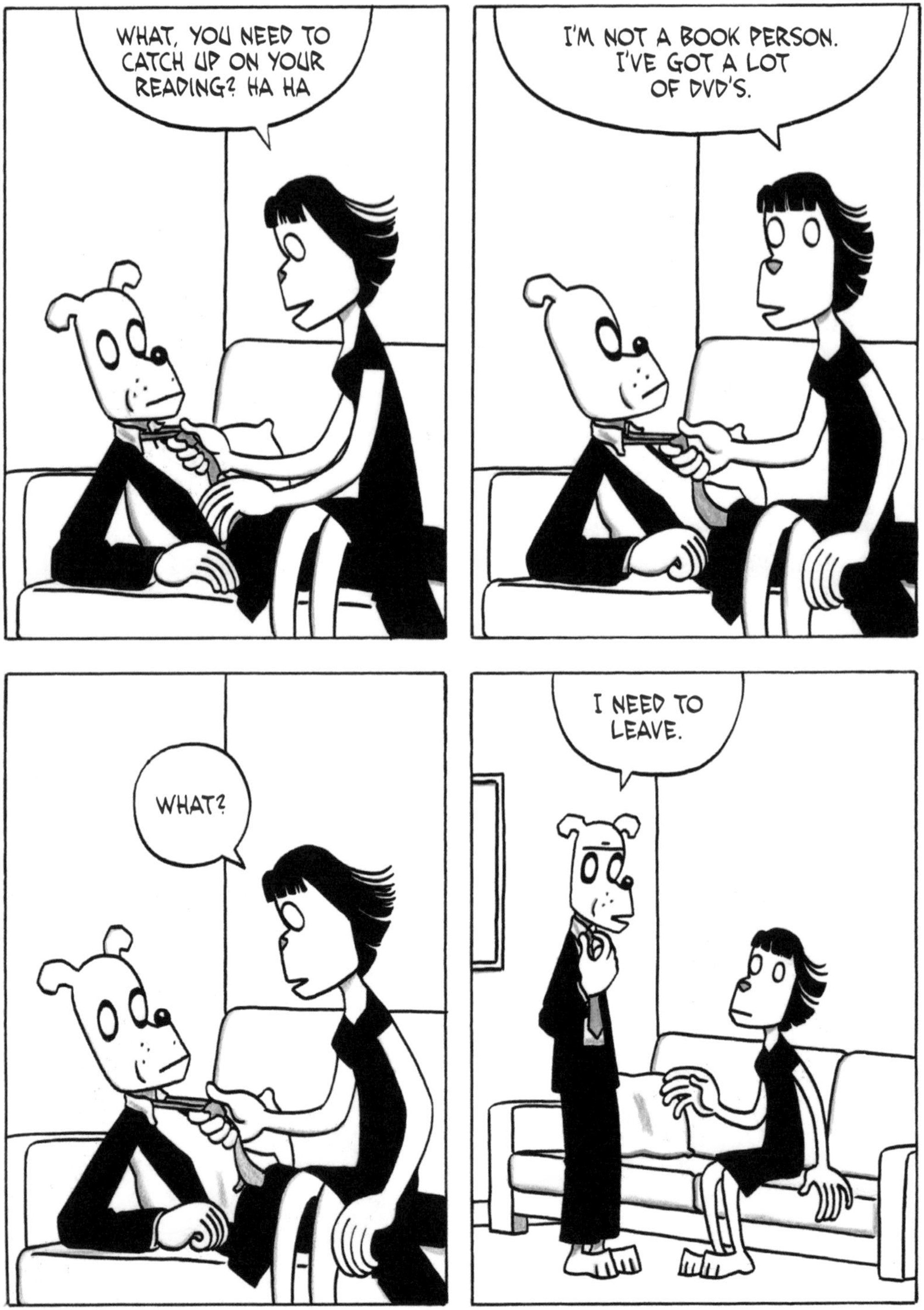
WHAT, YOU NEED TO CATCH UP ON YOUR READING? HA HA
I'M NOT A BOOK PERSON. I'VE GOT A LOT OF DVD'S.
WHAT?
I NEED TO LEAVE.

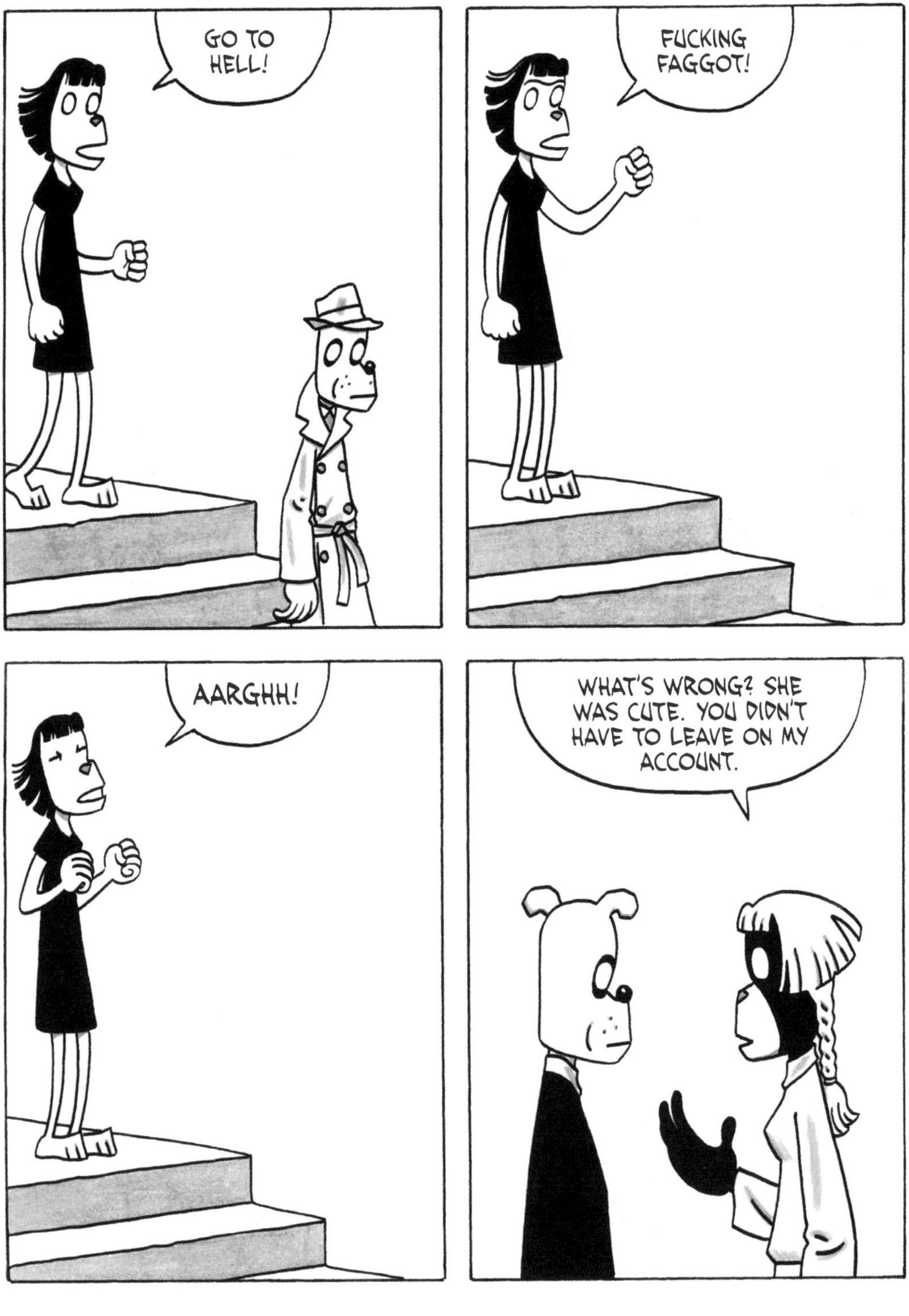
GO TO HELL!
FUCKING FAGGOT!
AARGHH!
WHAT'S WRONG? SHE WAS CUTE. YOU DIDN'T HAVE TO LEAVE ON MY ACCOUNT.

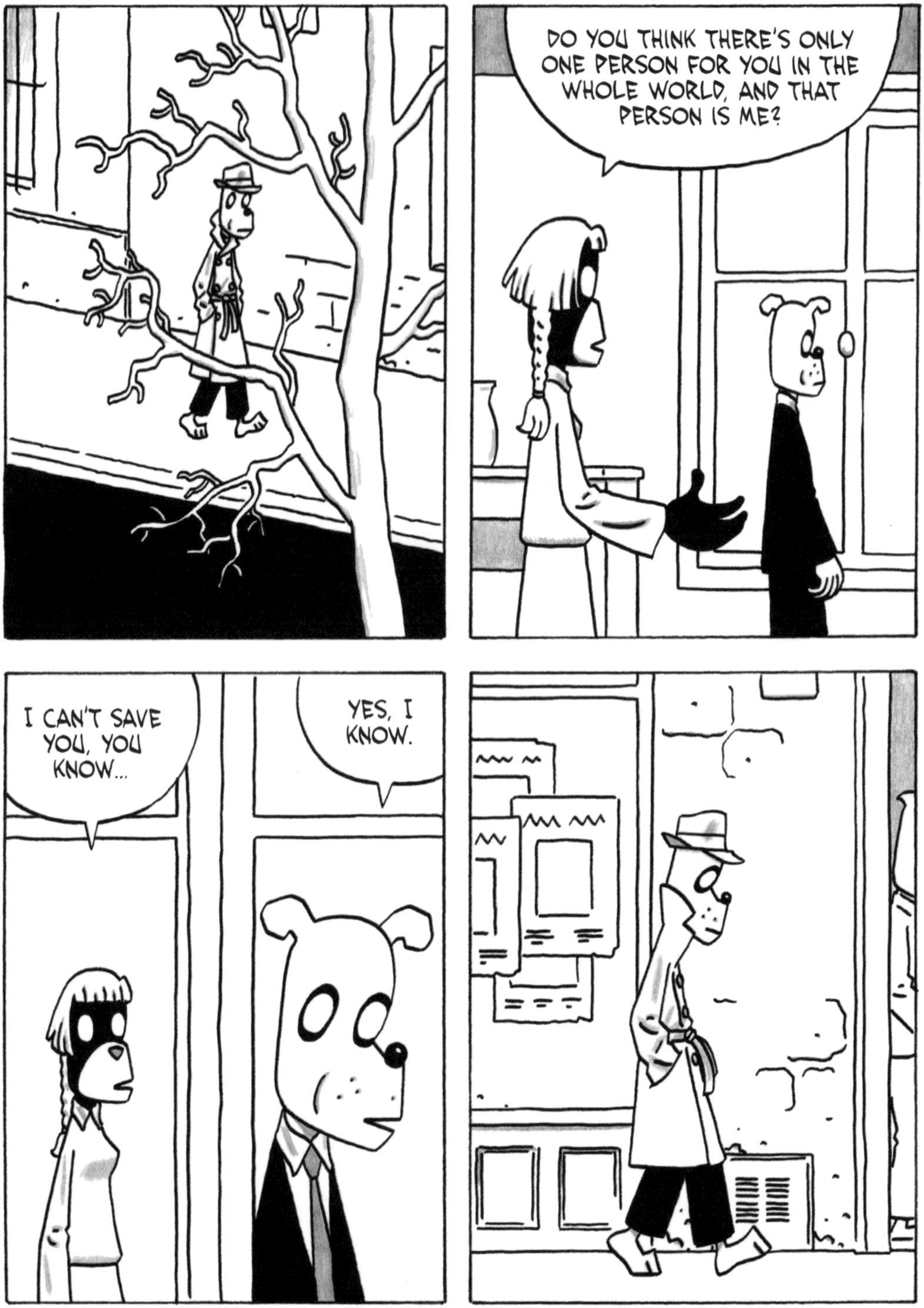
DO YOU THINK THERE'S ONLY ONE PERSON FOR YOU IN THE WHOLE WORLD, AND THAT PERSON IS ME?
I CAN'T SAVE YOU, YOU KNOW...
YES, I KNOW.

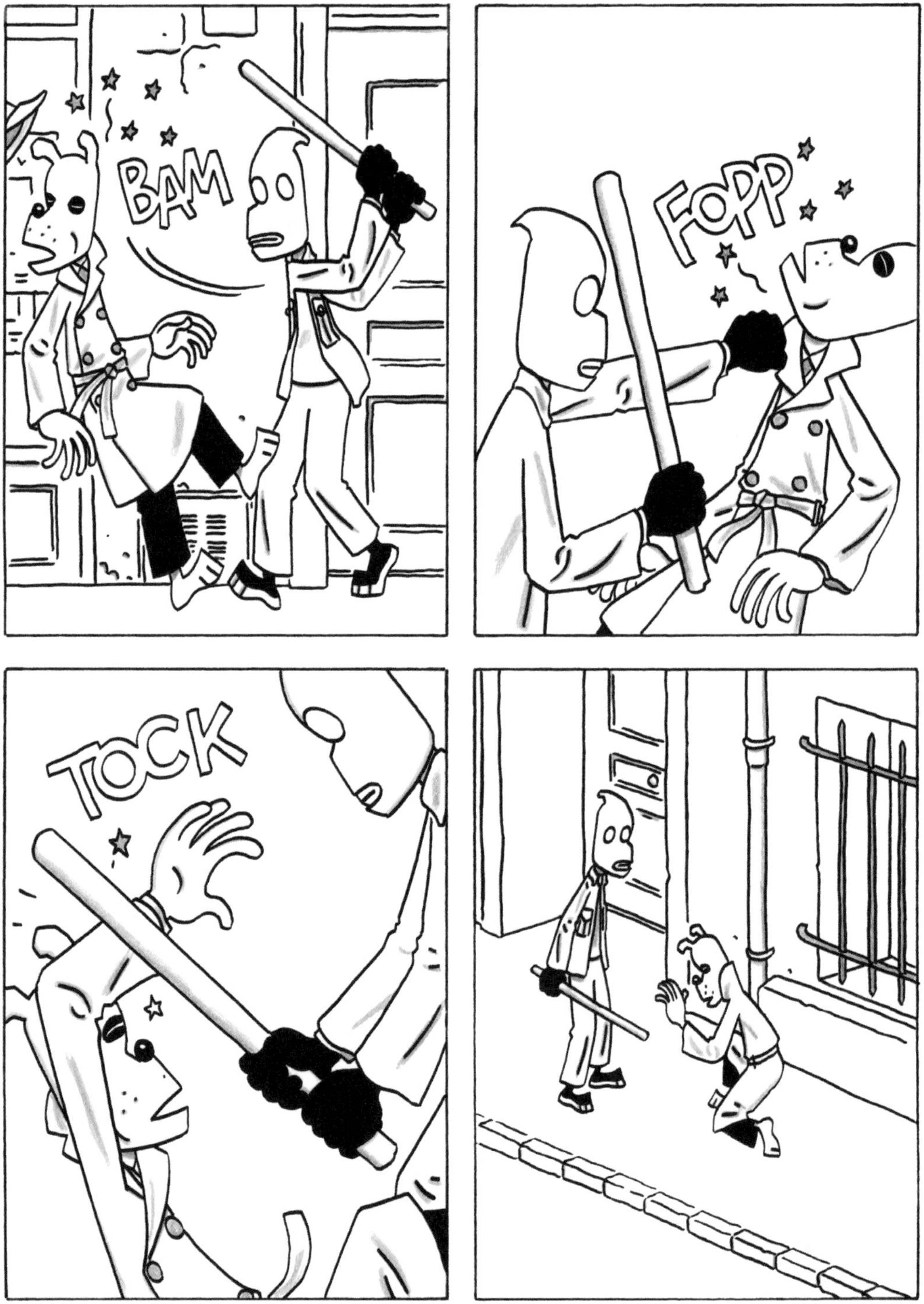
BAM
FOPP
TOCK

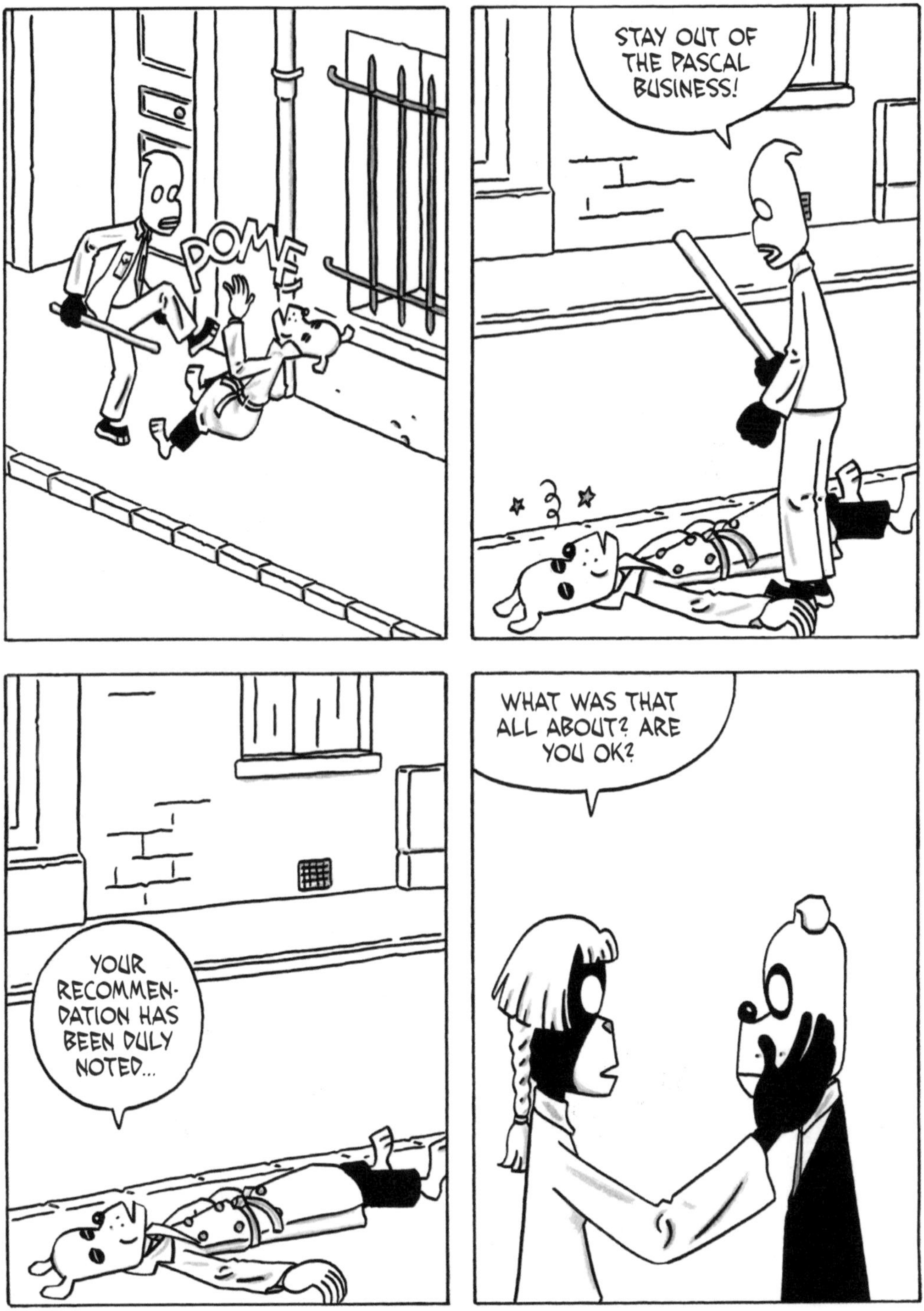
POMF
STAY OUT OF THE PASCAL BUSINESS!
YOUR RECOMMEN-DATION HAS BEEN DULY NOTED...
WHAT WAS THAT ALL ABOUT? ARE YOU OK?

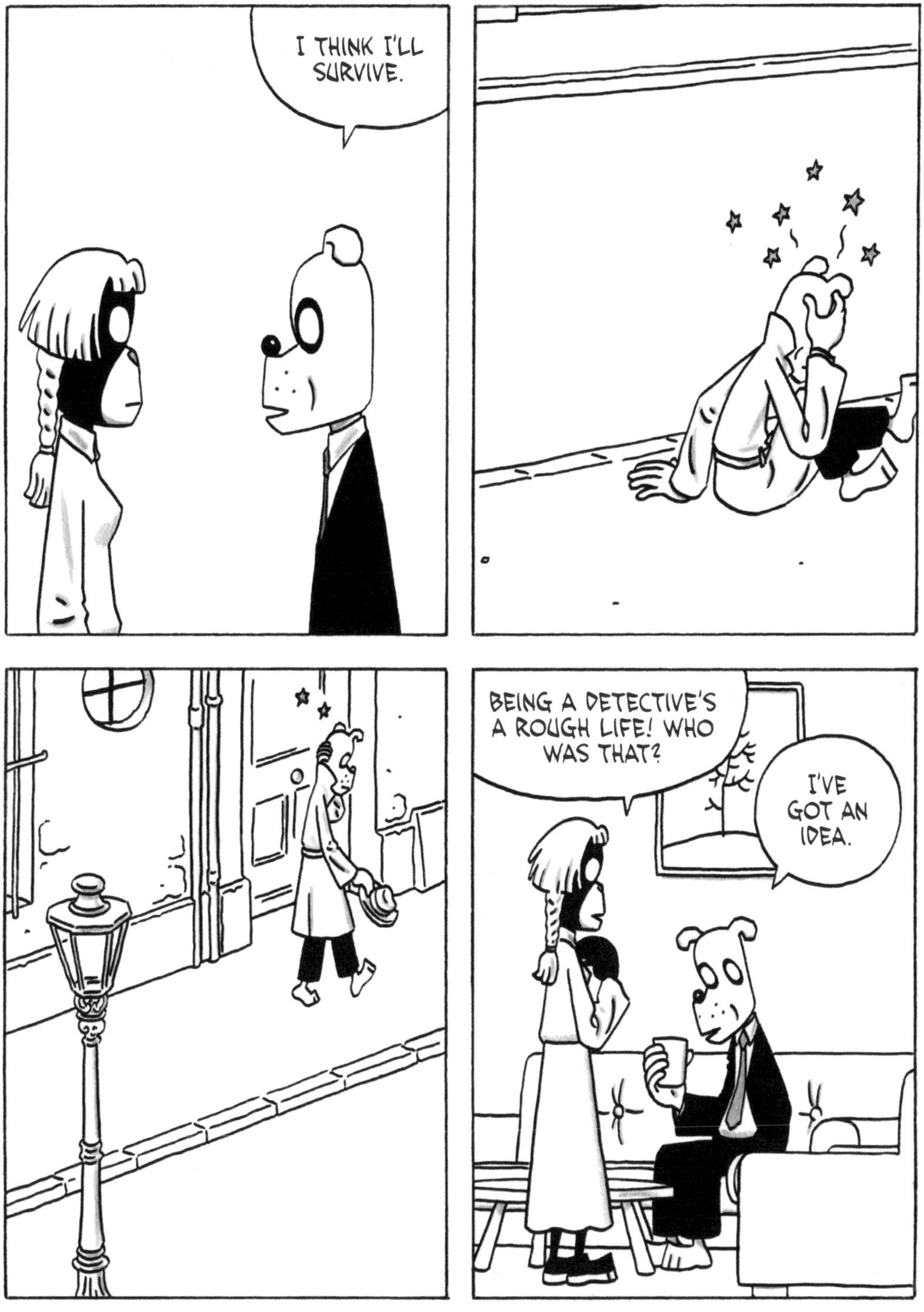
I THINK I'LL SURVIVE.
BEING A DETECTIVE'S A ROUGH LIFE! WHO WAS THAT?
I'VE GOT AN IDEA.

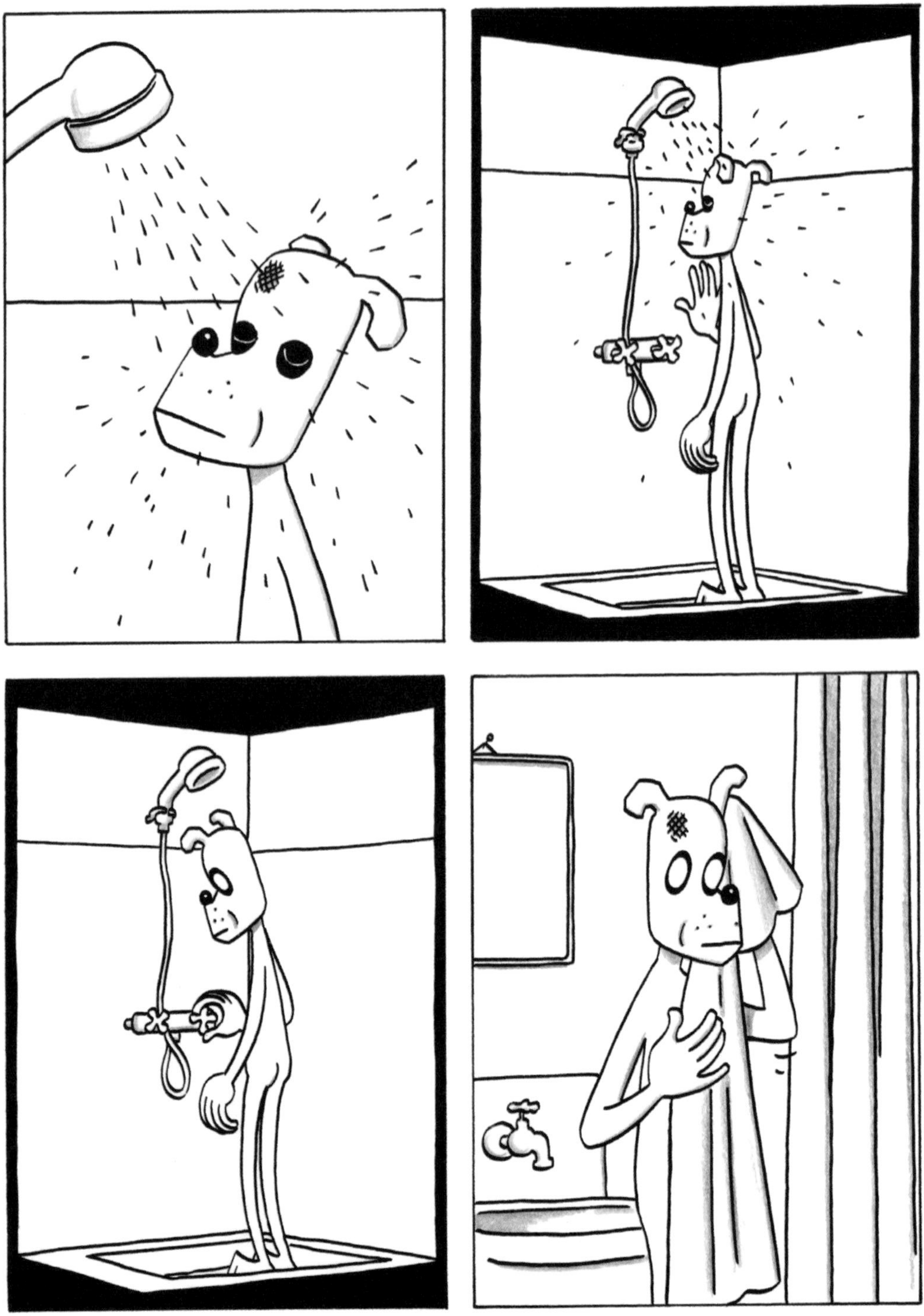

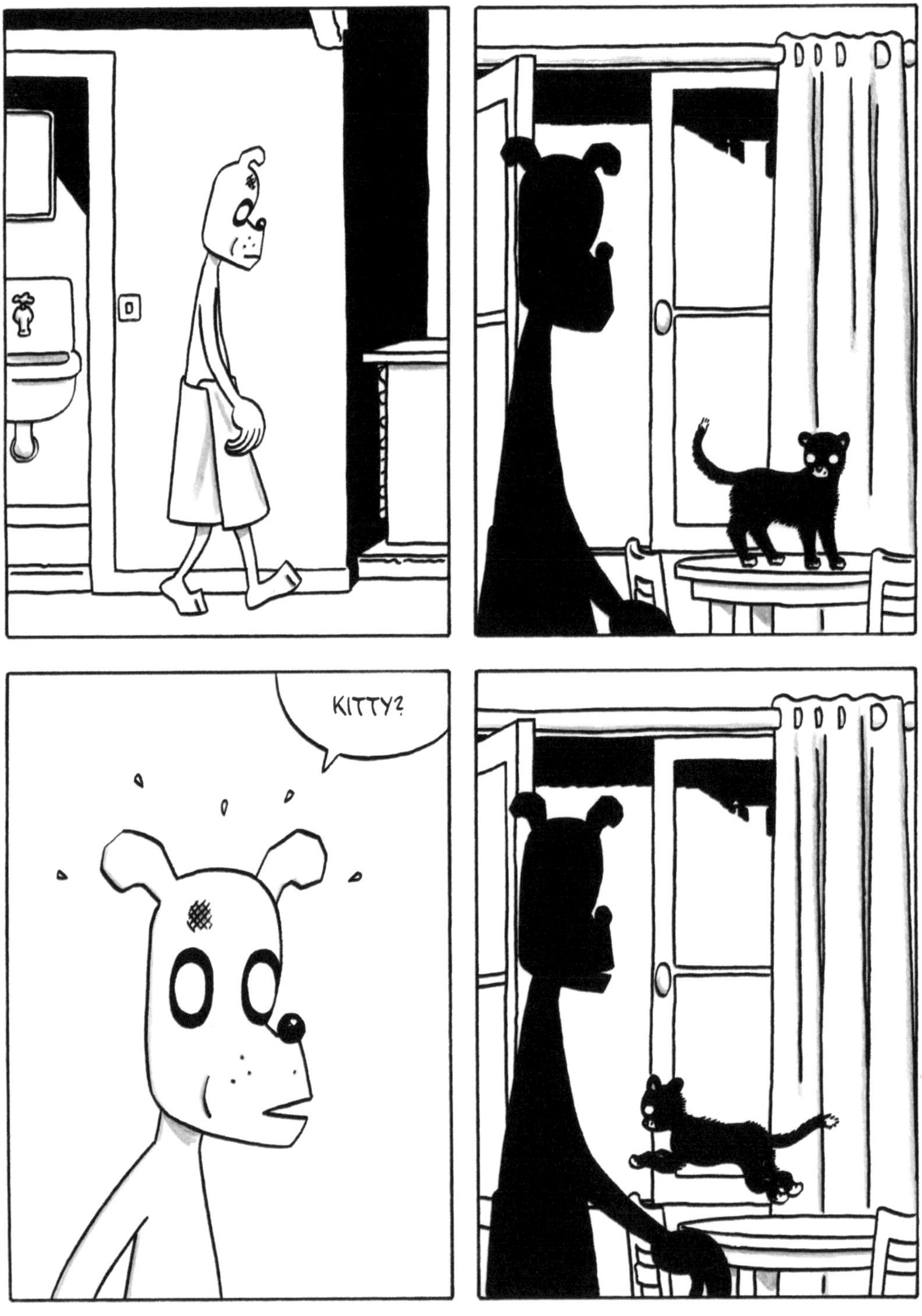
KITTY?

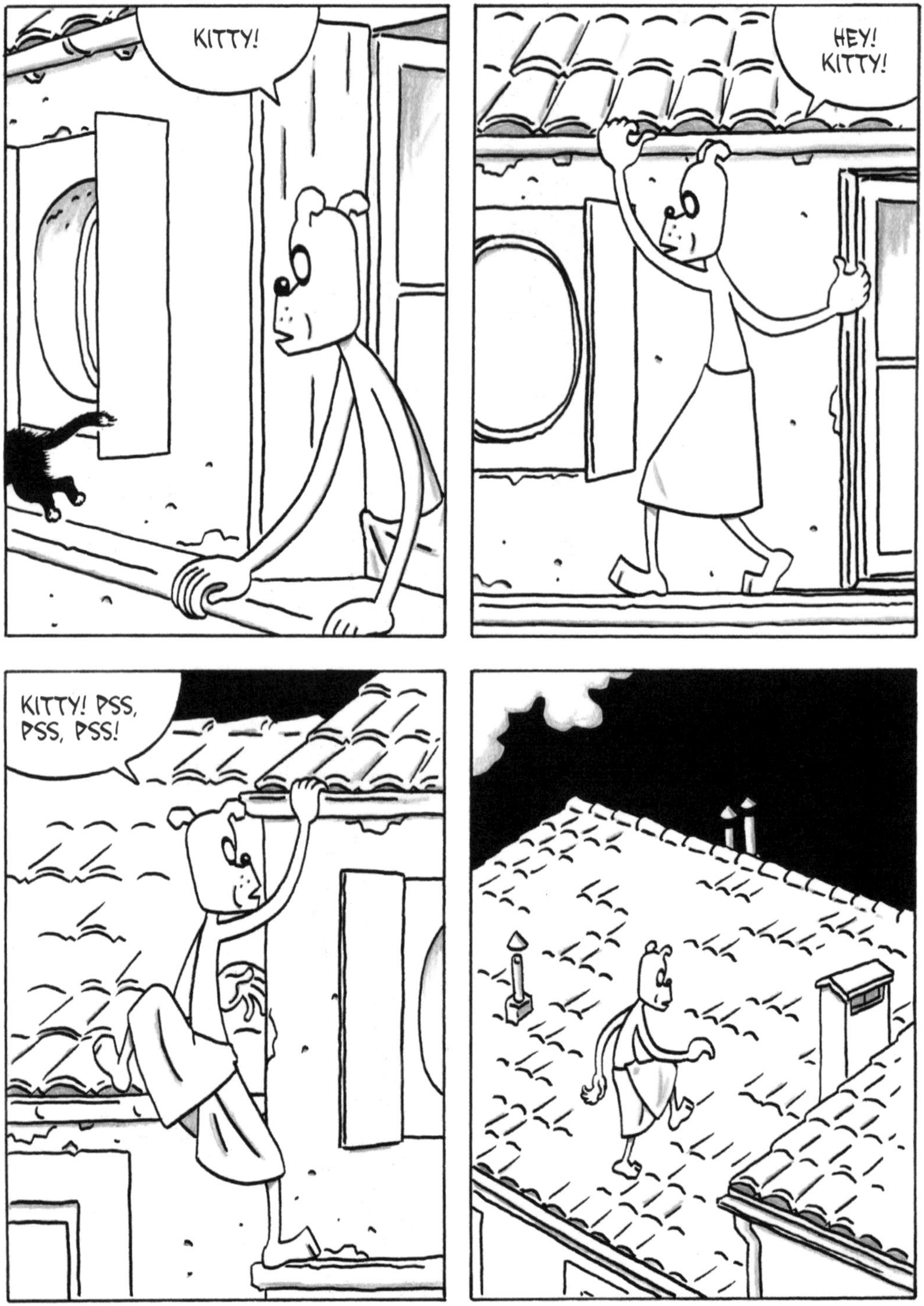
KITTY!
HEY! KITTY!
KITTY! PSS, PSS, PSS!

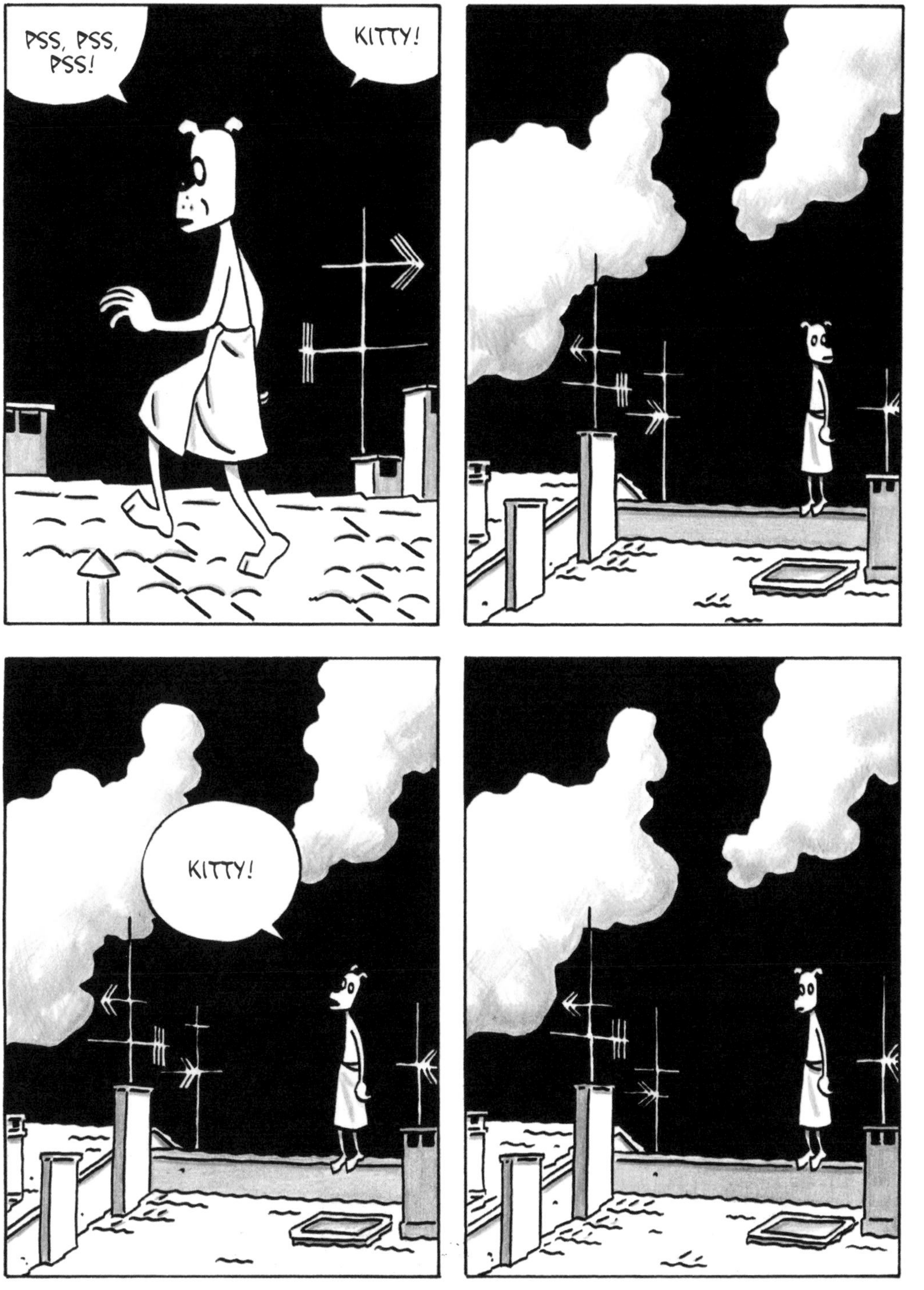
PSS, PSS, PSS!
KITTY!
KITTY!

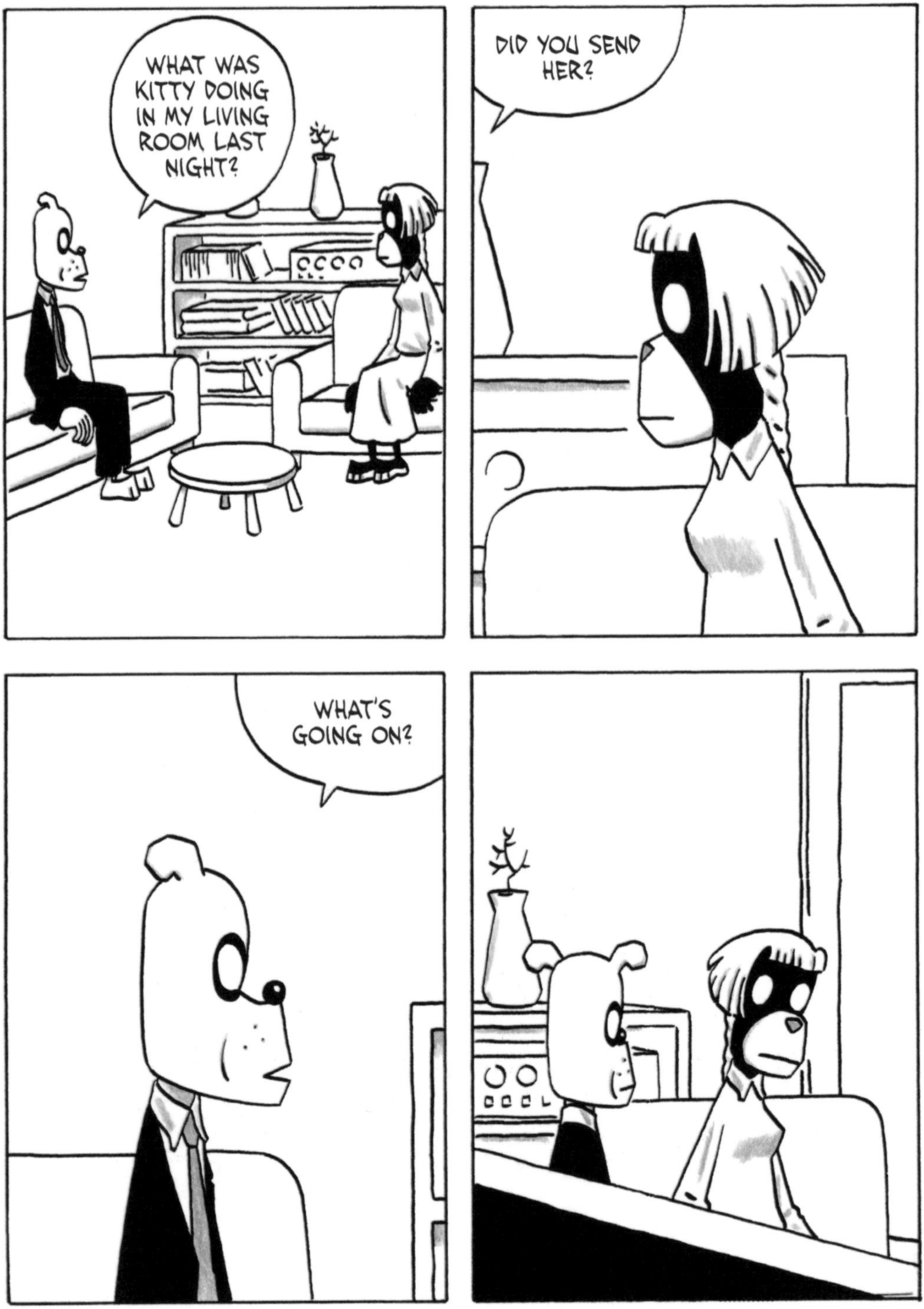
WHAT WAS KITTY DOING IN MY LIVING ROOM LAST NIGHT?
DID YOU SEND HER?
WHAT'S GOING ON?

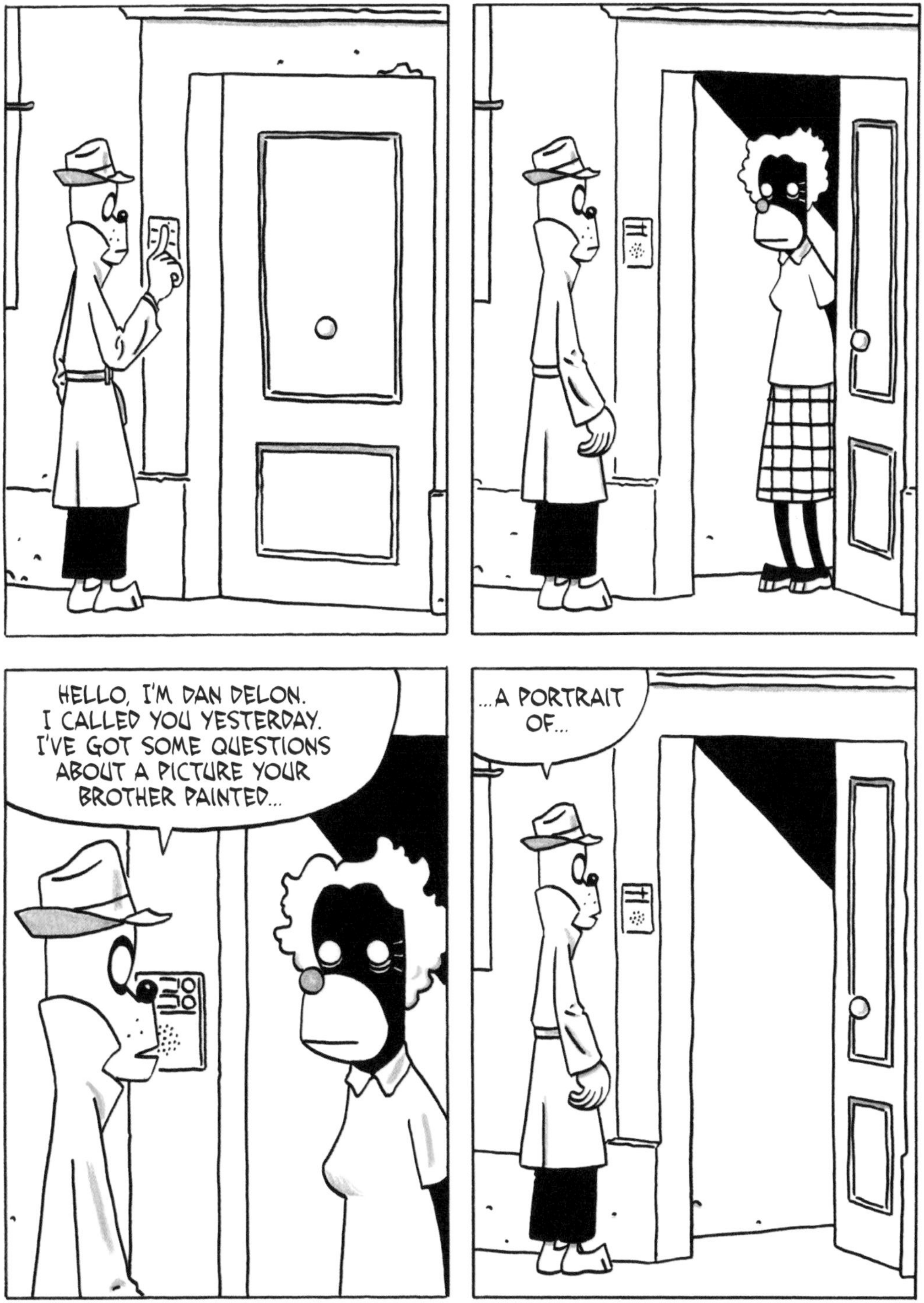
HELLO, I'M DAN DELON. I CALLED YOU YESTERDAY. I'VE GOT SOME QUESTIONS ABOUT A PICTURE YOUR BROTHER PAINTED...
...A PORTRAIT OF...

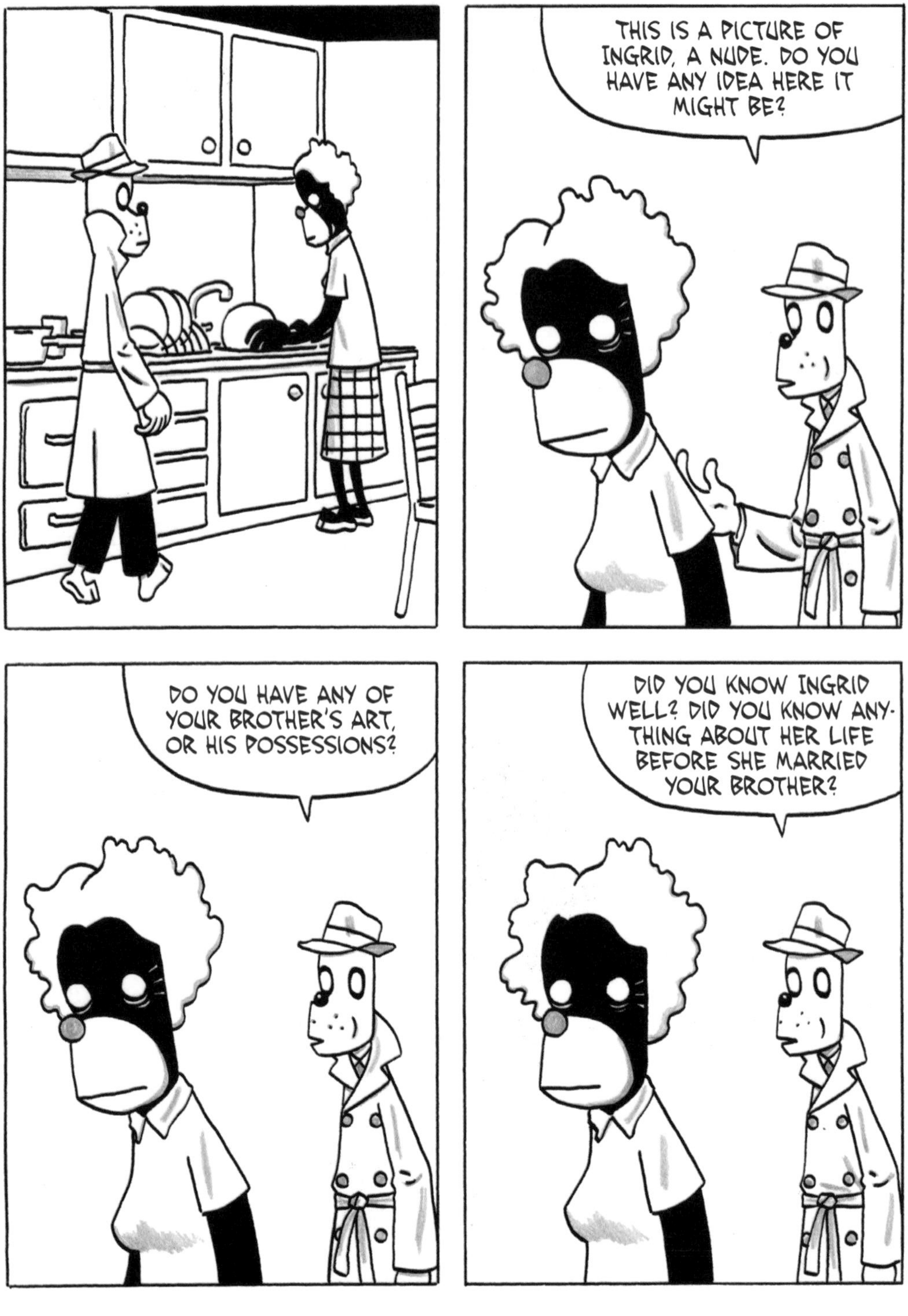
THIS IS A PICTURE OF INGRID, A NUDE. DO YOU HAVE ANY IDEA HERE IT MIGHT BE?
DO YOU HAVE ANY OF YOUR BROTHER'S ART, OR HIS POSSESSIONS?
DID YOU KNOW INGRID WELL? DID YOU KNOW ANY-THING ABOUT HER LIFE BEFORE SHE MARRIED YOUR BROTHER?

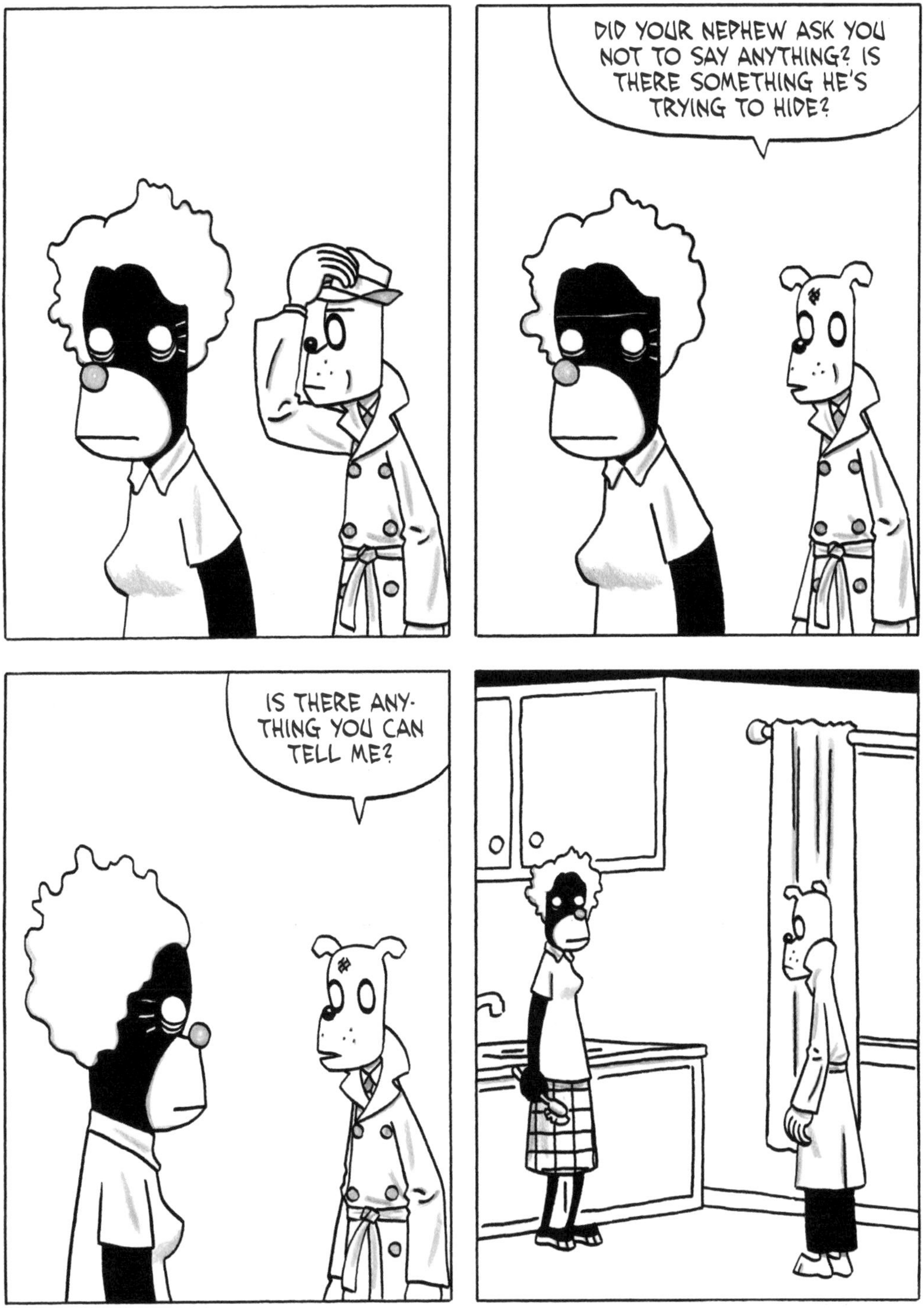
DID YOUR NEPHEW ASK YOU NOT TO SAY ANYTHING? IS THERE SOMETHING HE'S TRYING TO HIDE?
IS THERE ANY-THING YOU CAN TELL ME?

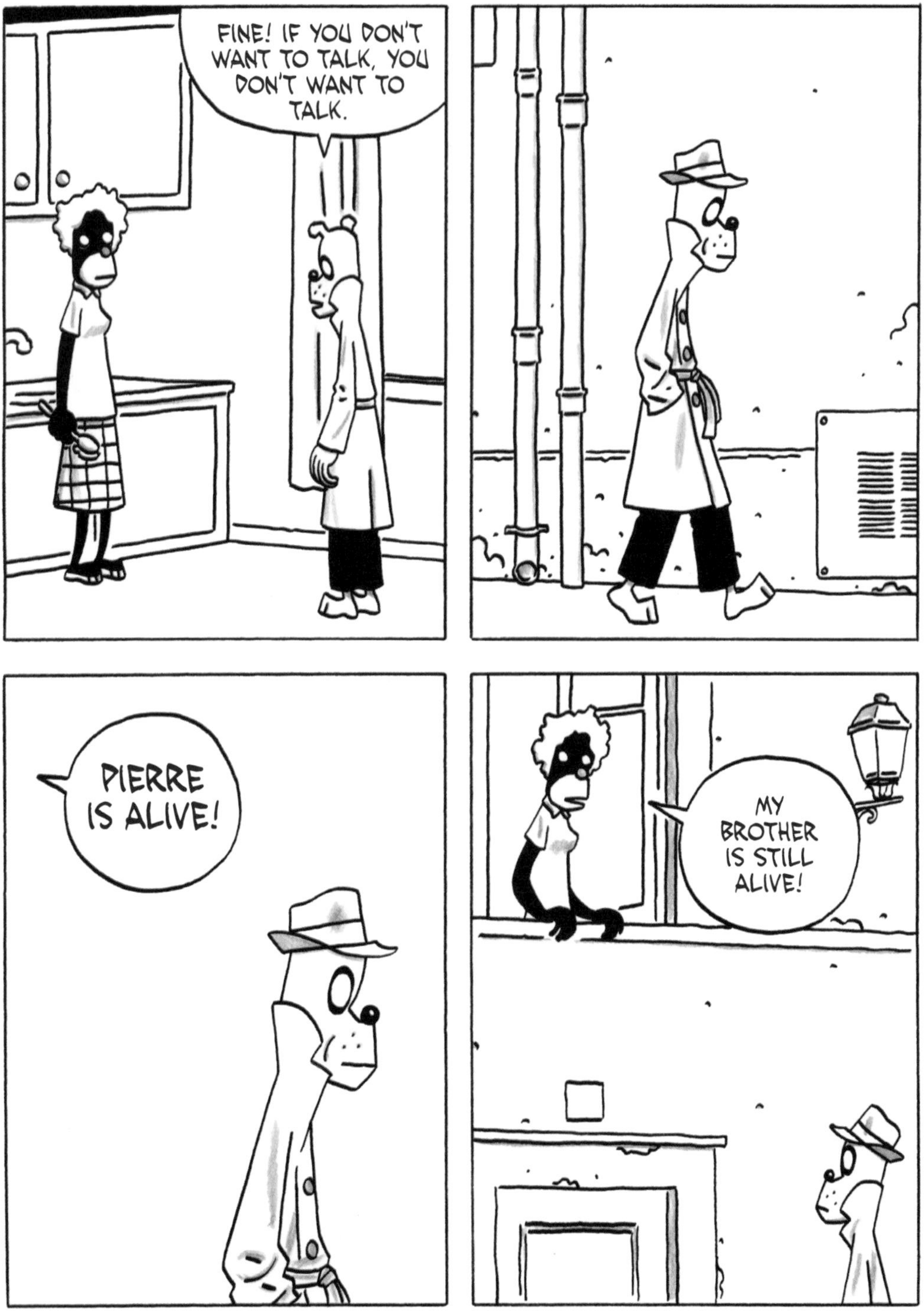
FINE! IF YOU DON'T WANT TO TALK, YOU DON'T WANT TO TALK.
PIERRE IS ALIVE!
MY BROTHER IS STILL ALIVE!

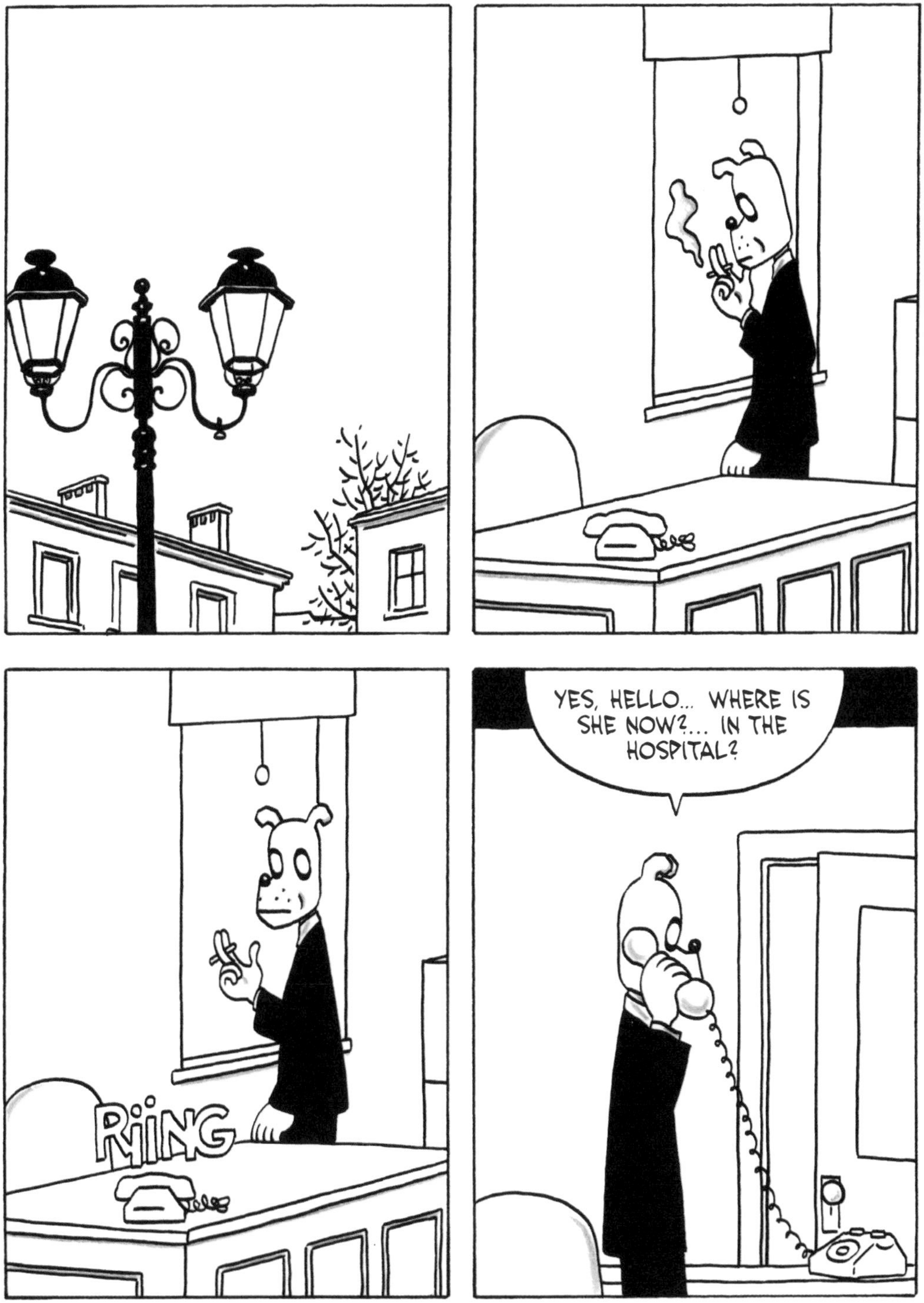
RING
YES, HELLO... WHERE IS SHE NOW?... IN THE HOSPITAL?

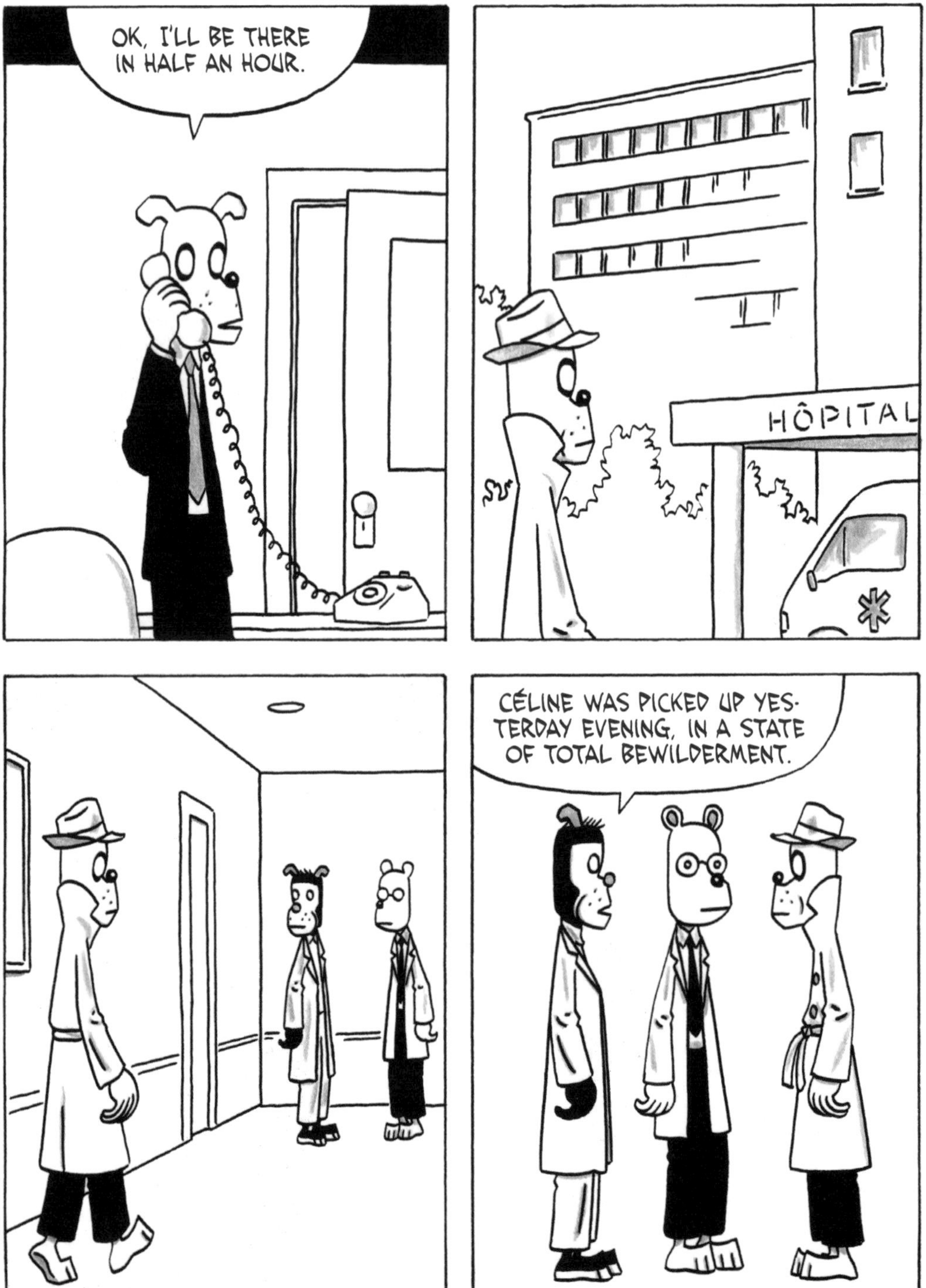
OK, I'LL BE THERE IN HALF AN HOUR.
HÔPITAL
CÉLINE WAS PICKED UP YES-TERDAY EVENING, IN A STATE OF TOTAL BEWILDERMENT.

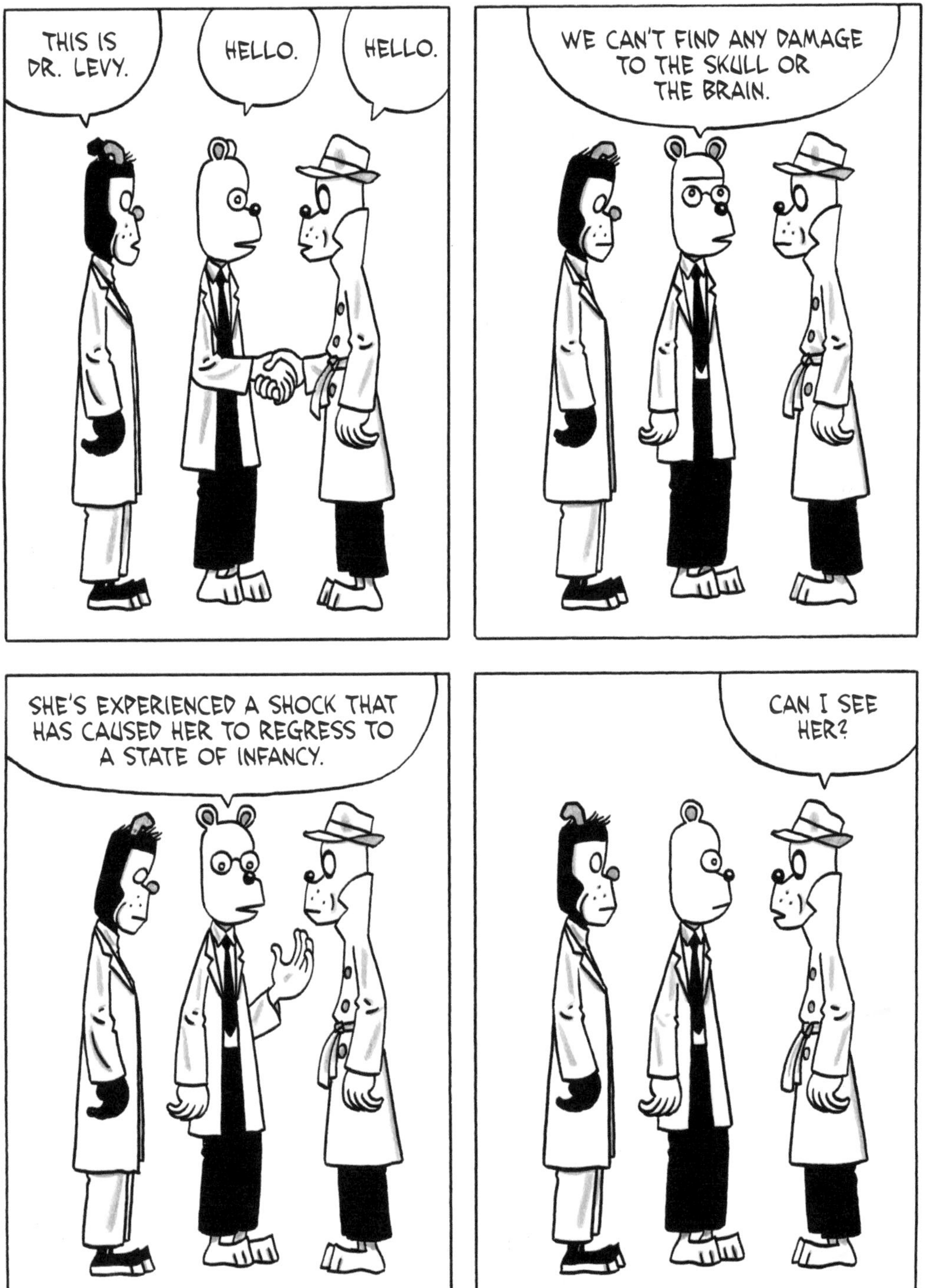
THIS IS DR. LEVY.
HELLO.
HELLO.
WE CAN'T FIND ANY DAMAGE TO THE SKULL OR THE BRAIN.
SHE'S EXPERIENCED A SHOCK THAT HAS CAUSED HER TO REGRESS TO A STATE OF INFANCY.
CAN I SEE HER?

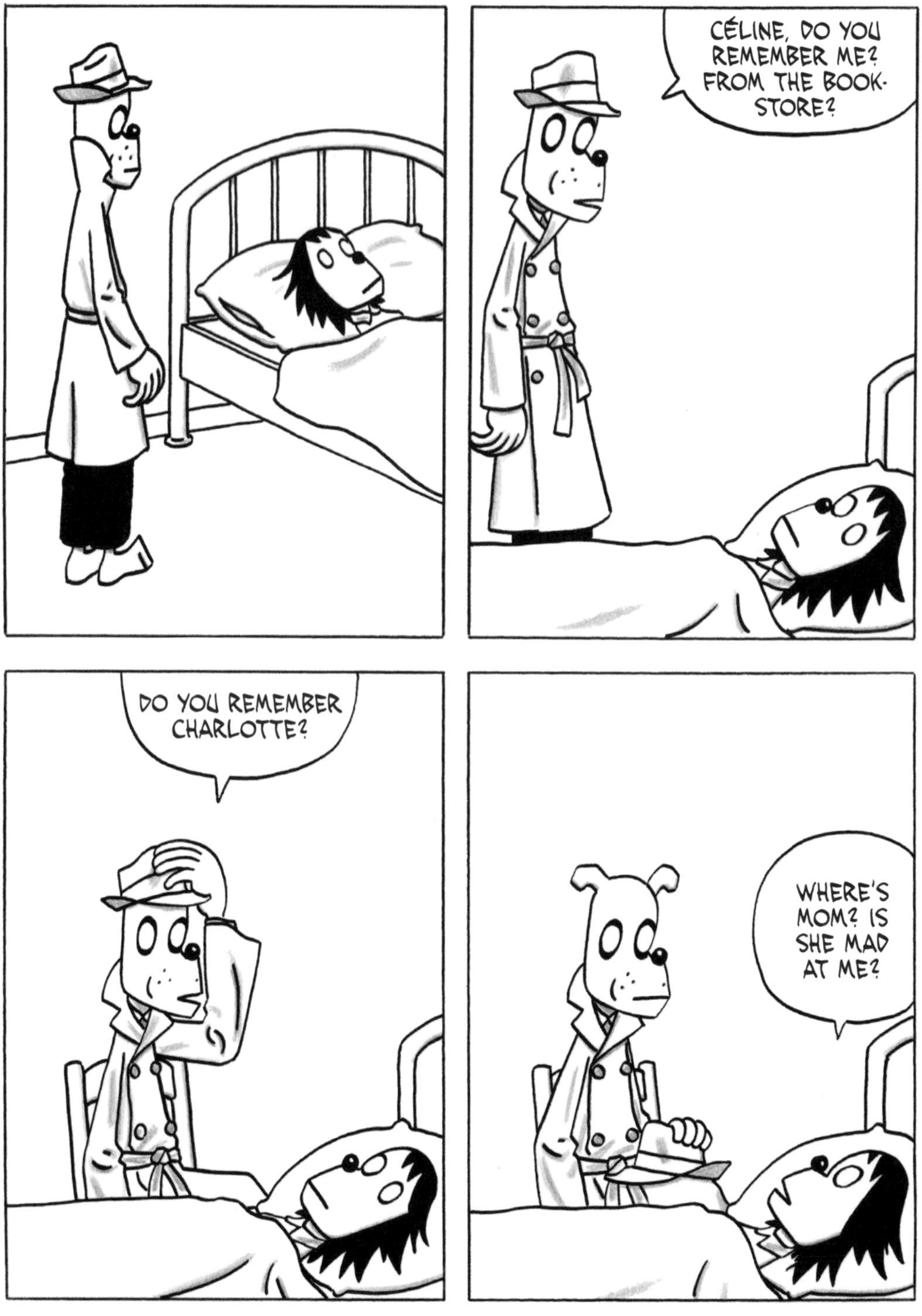
CÉLINE, DO YOU REMEMBER ME? FROM THE BOOK-STORE?
DO YOU REMEMBER CHARLOTTE?
WHERE'S MOM? IS SHE MAD AT ME?

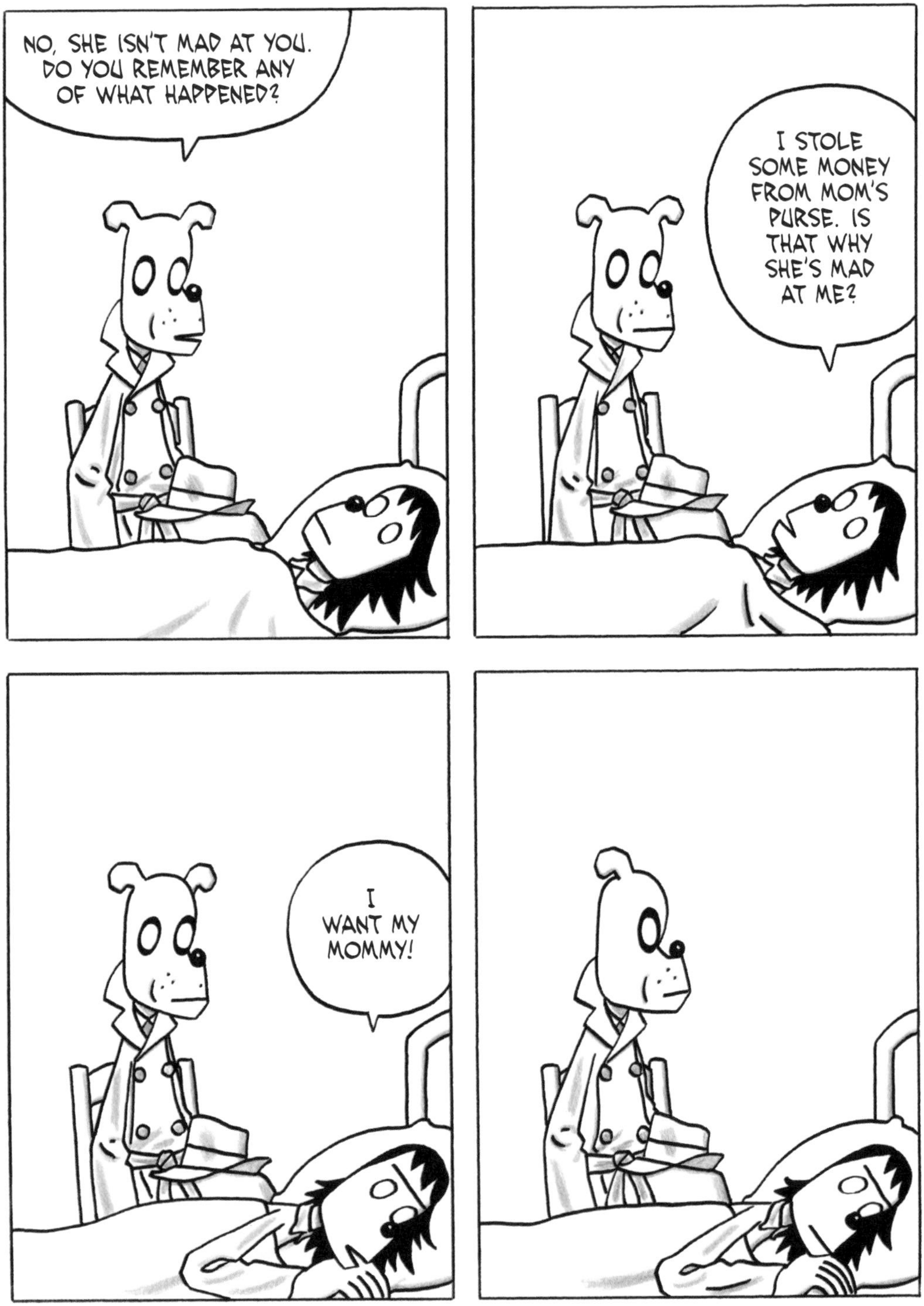
NO, SHE ISN'T MAD AT YOU. DO YOU REMEMBER ANY OF WHAT HAPPENED?
I STOLE SOME MONEY FROM MOM'S PURSE. IS THAT WHY SHE'S MAD AT ME?
I WANT MY MOMMY!

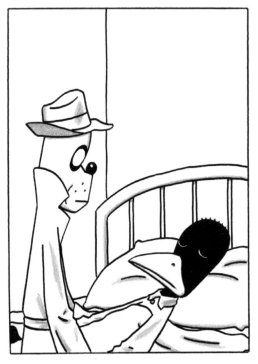
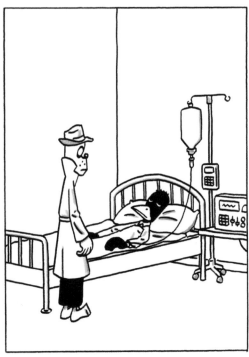

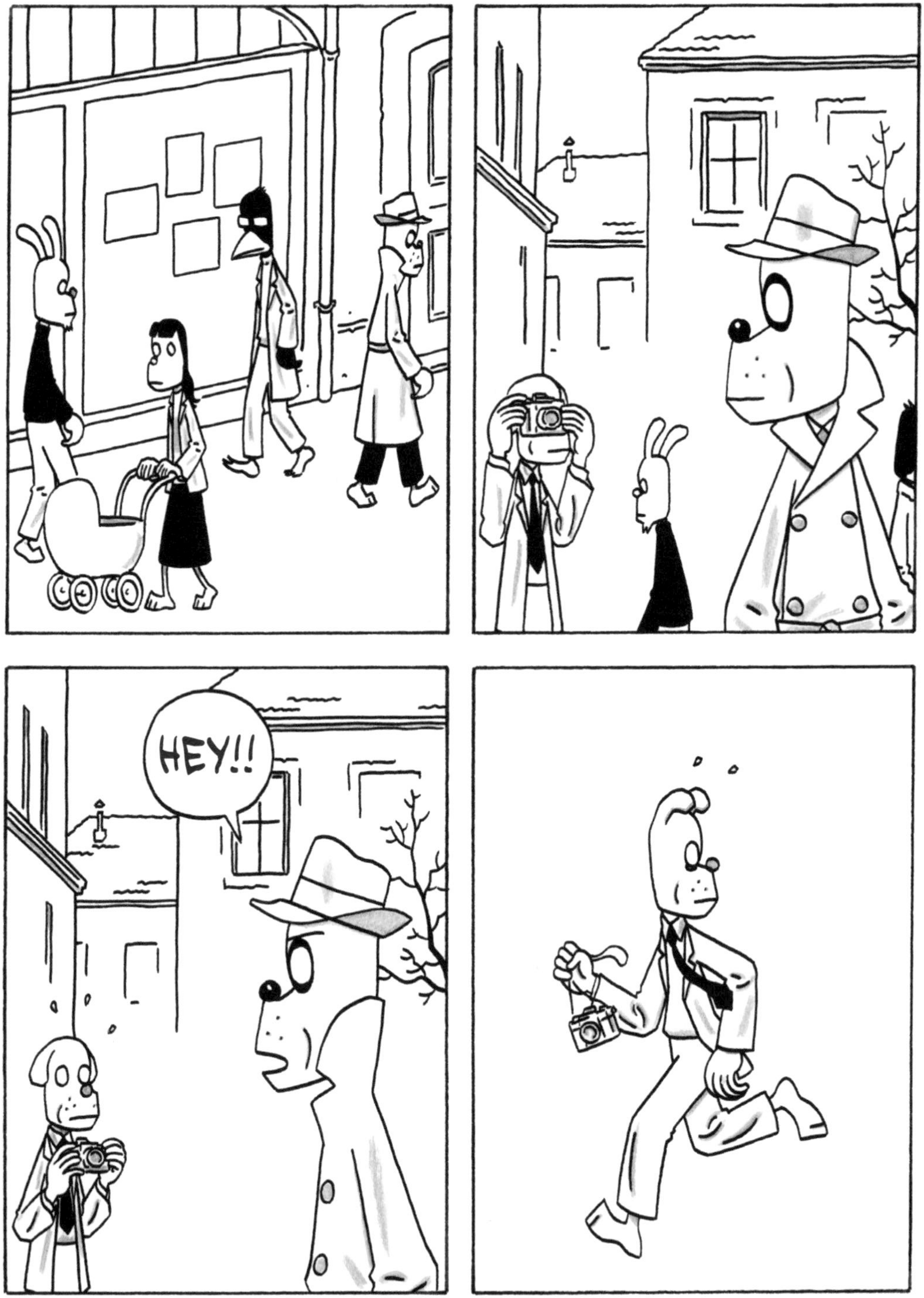
HEY!!

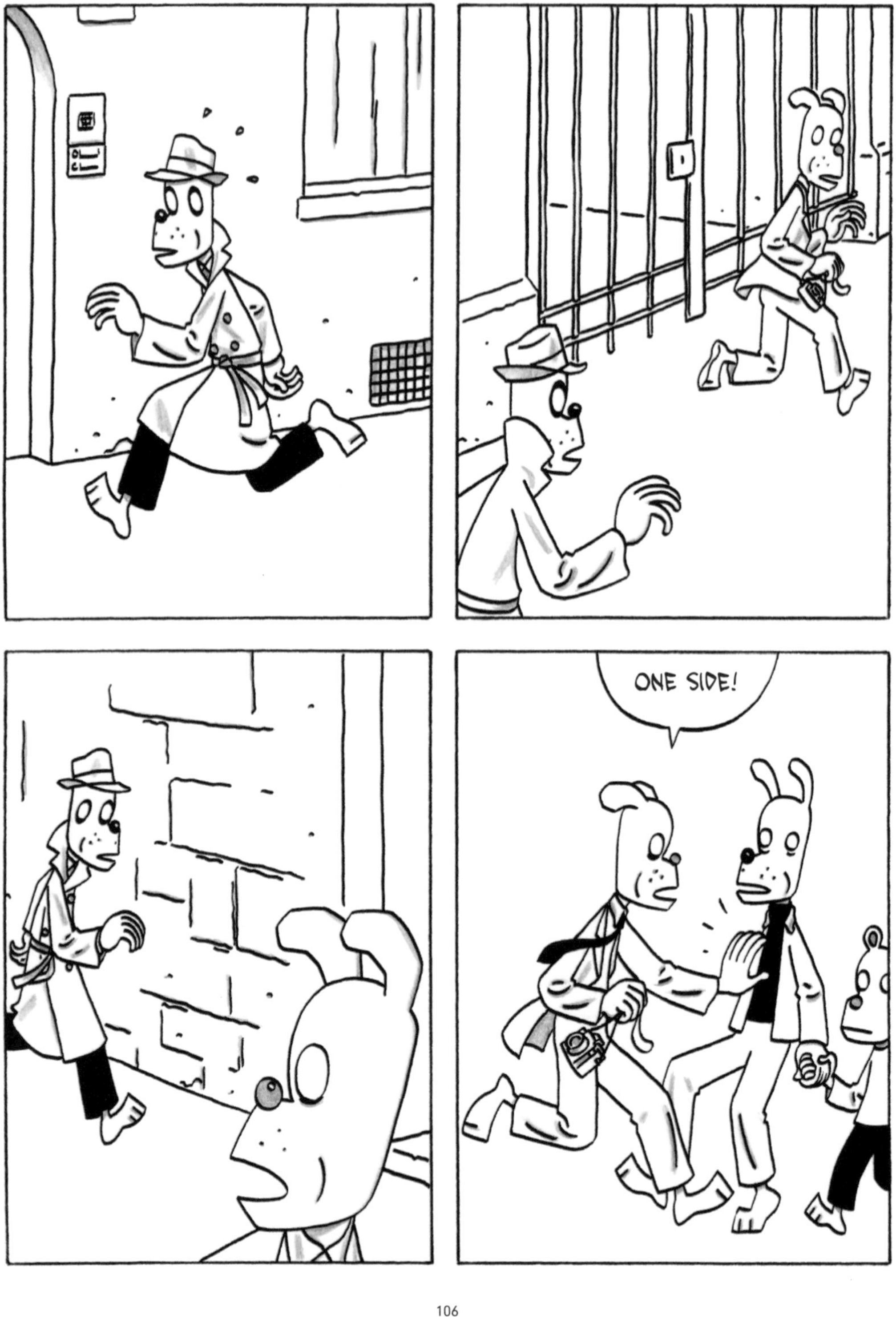
ONE SIDE!

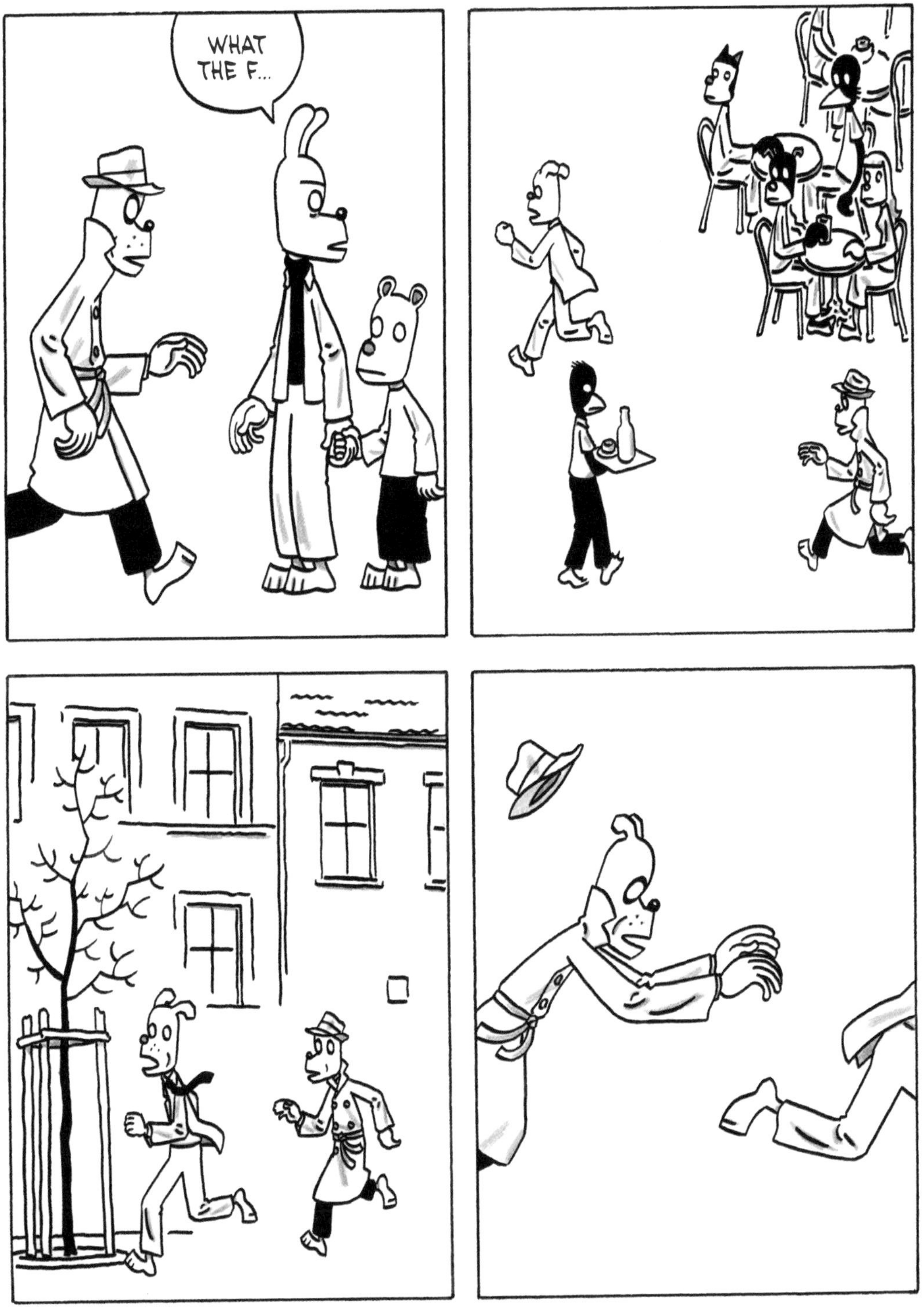
WHAT THE F...

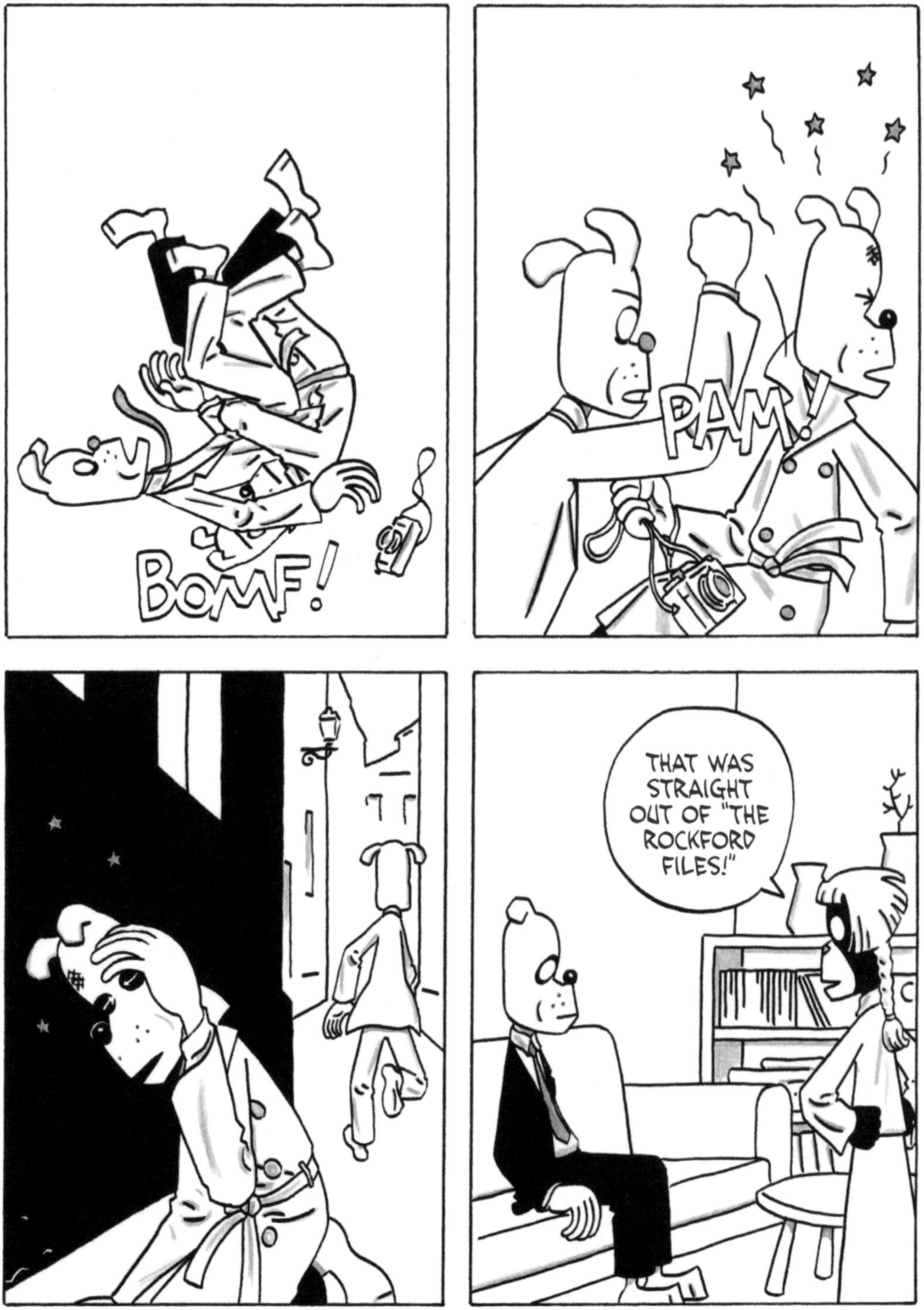
BOMF!
PAM!
THAT WAS STRAIGHT OUT OF "THE ROCKFORD FILES!"

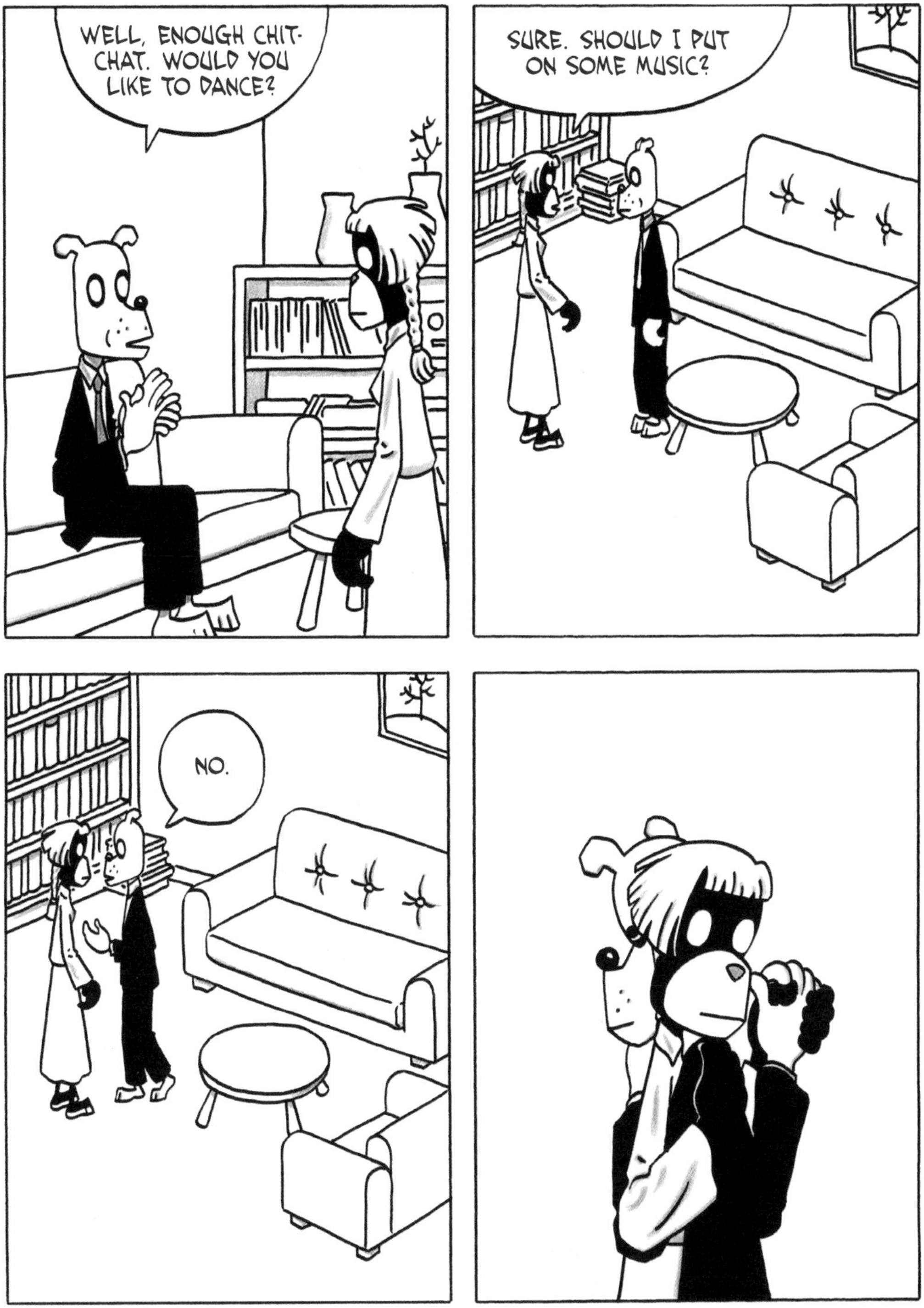
WELL, ENOUGH CHIT-CHAT. WOULD YOU LIKE TO DANCE?
SURE. SHOULD I PUT ON SOME MUSIC?
NO.

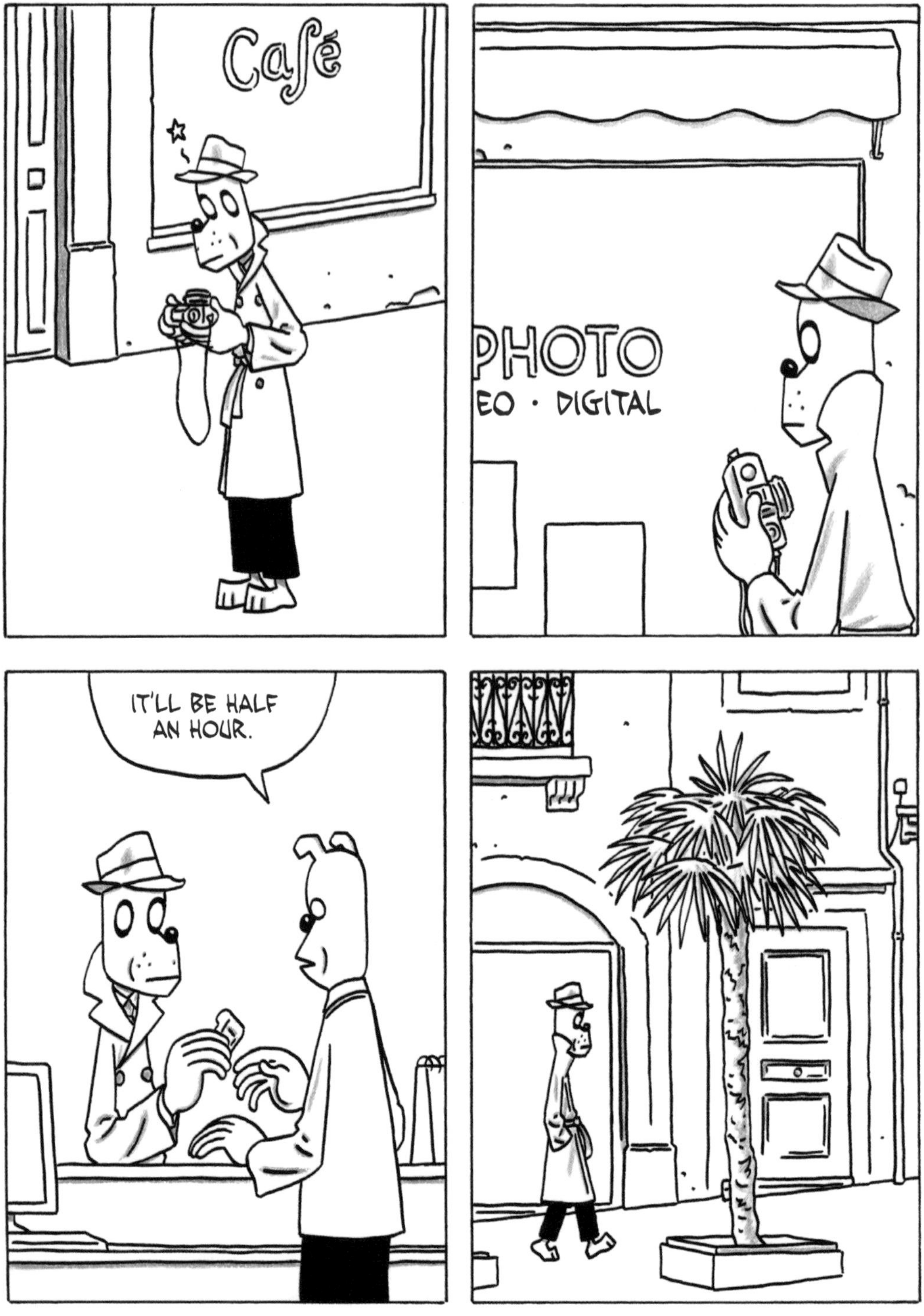
Café
PHOTO
EO · DIGITAL
IT'LL BE HALF AN HOUR.

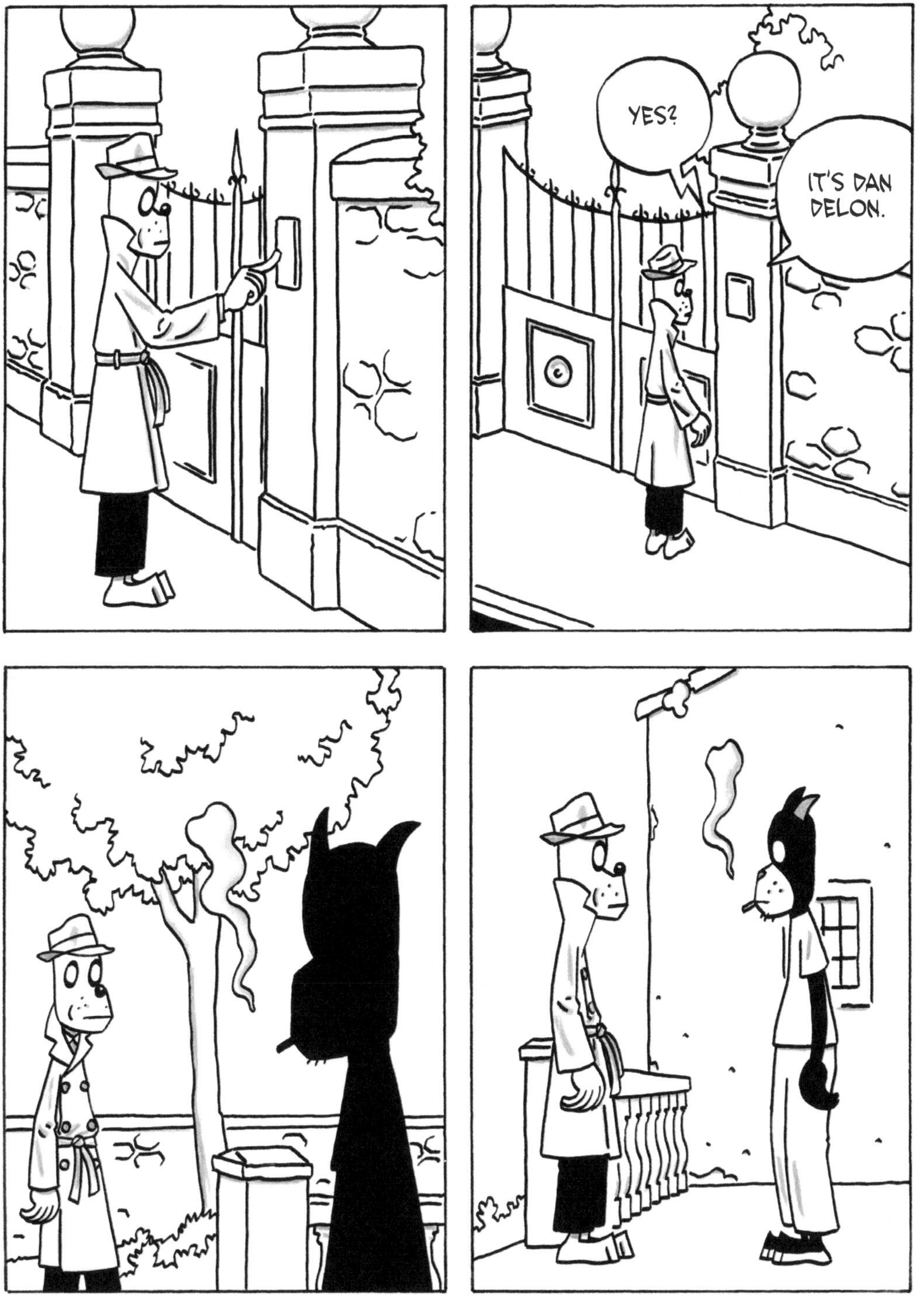
YES?
IT'S DAN DELON.

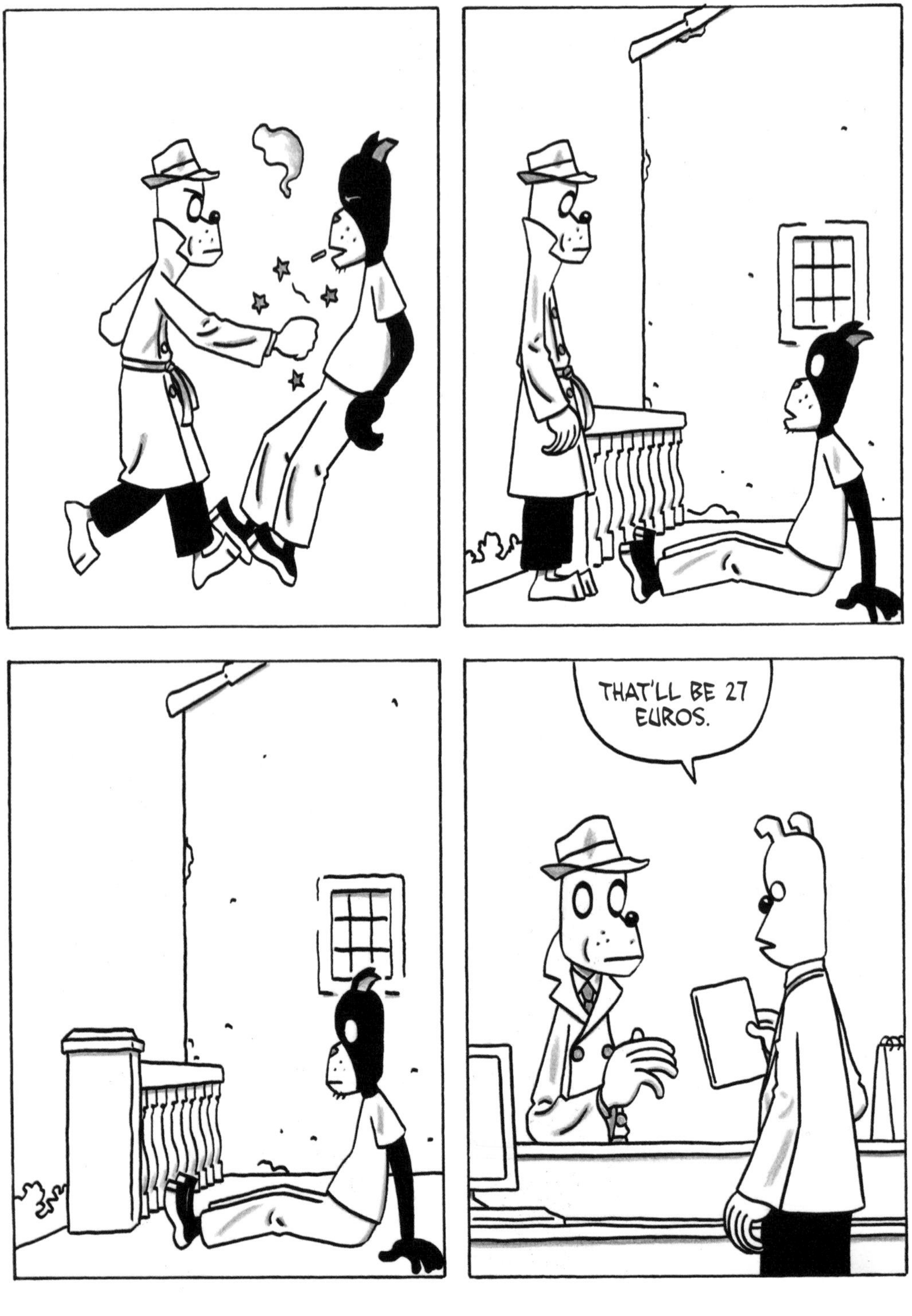
THAT'LL BE 27 EUROS.

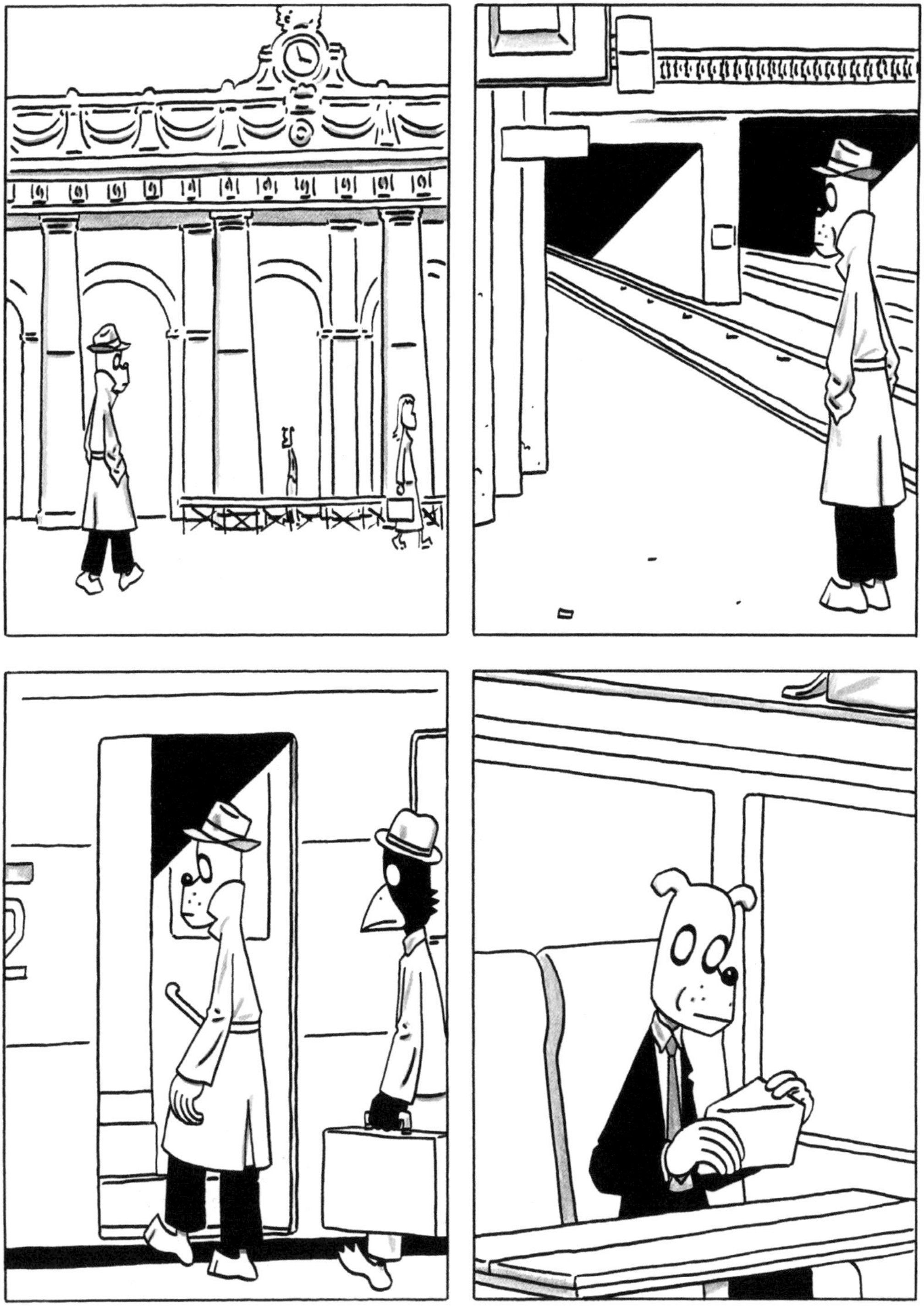

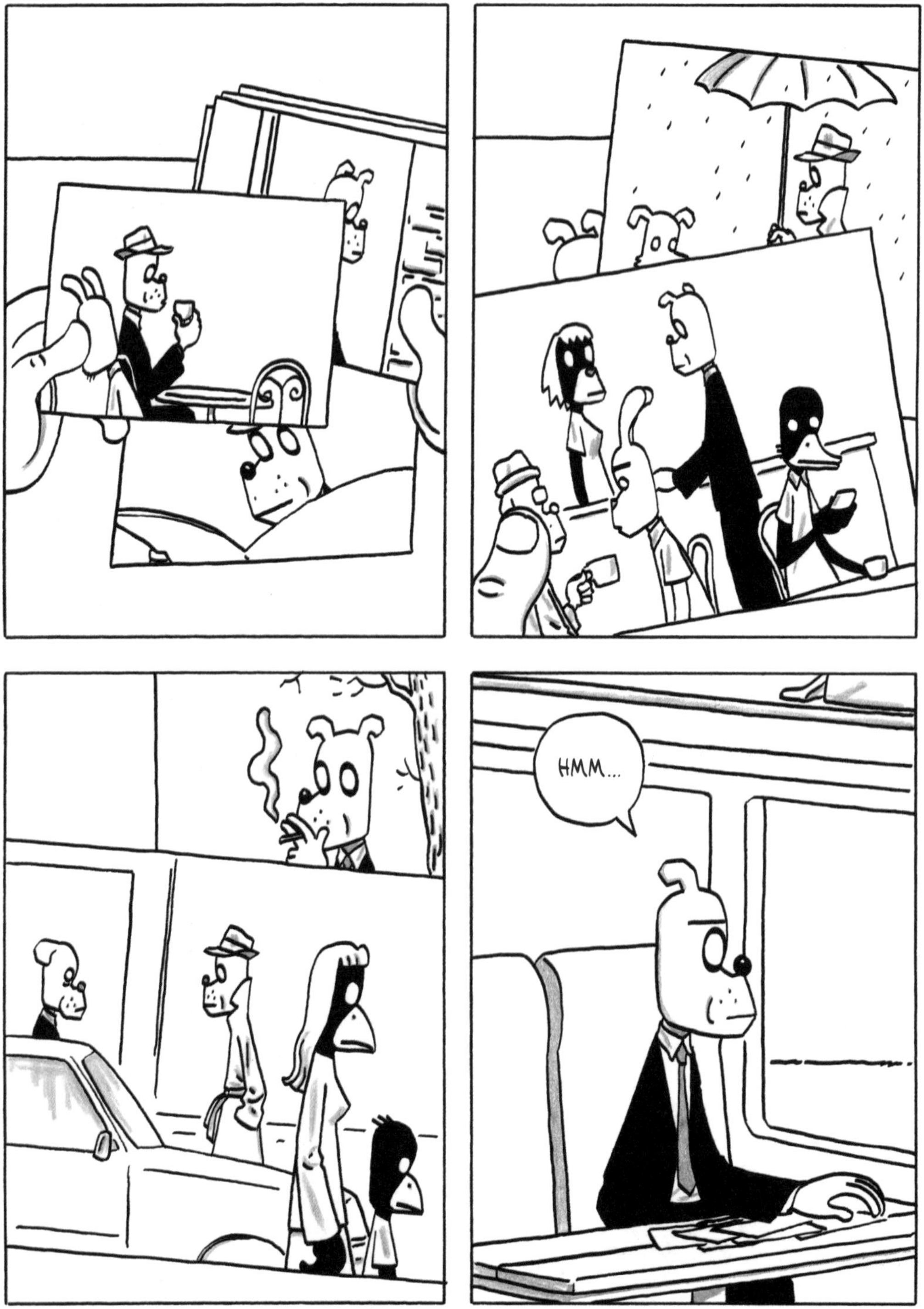
HMM...

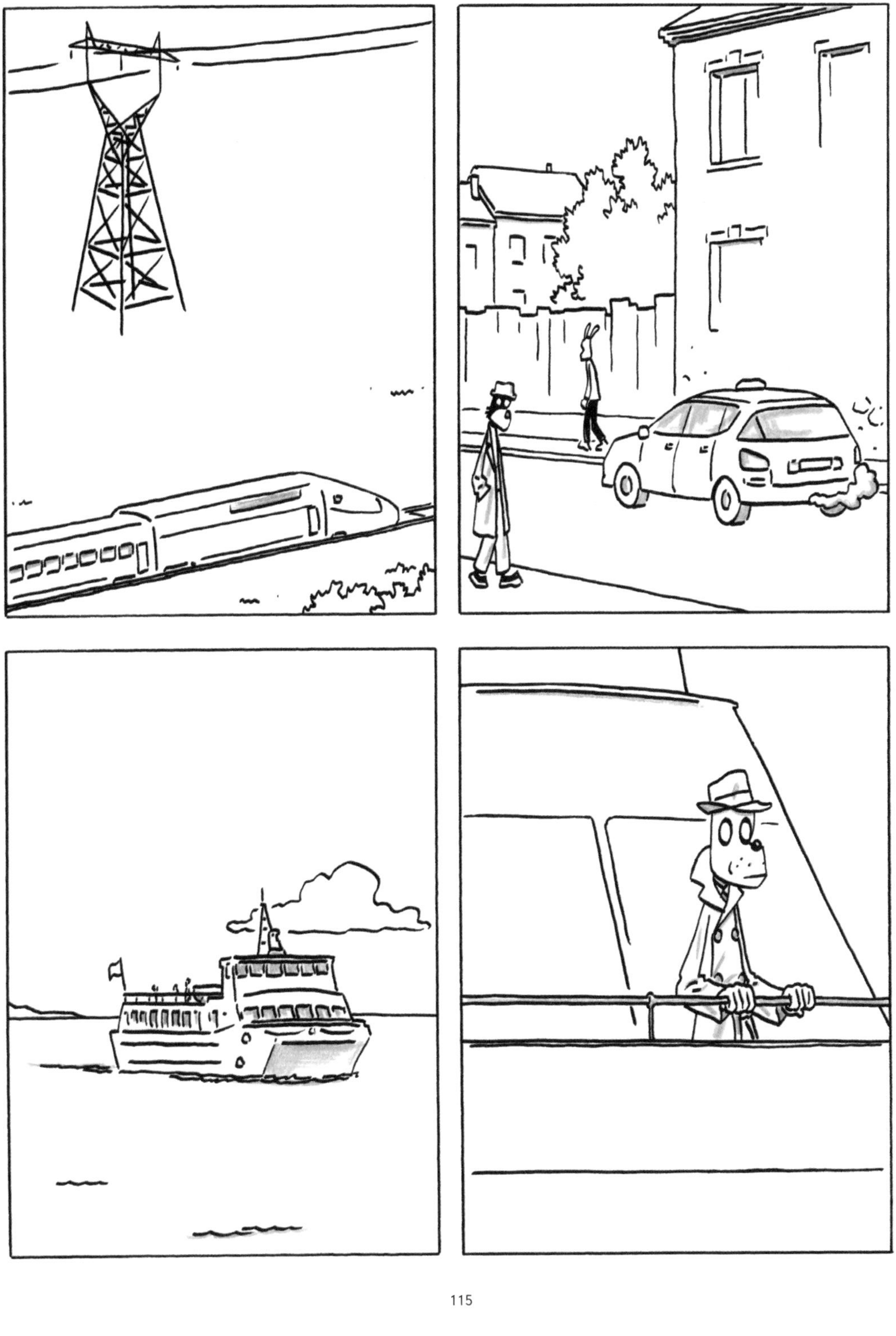

PERIE

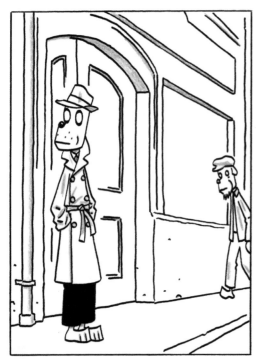

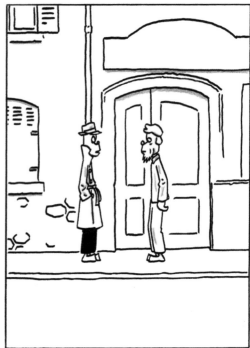

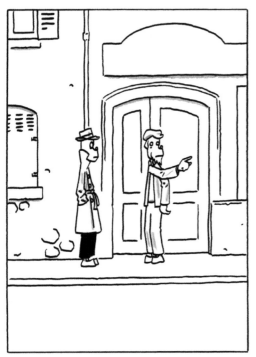

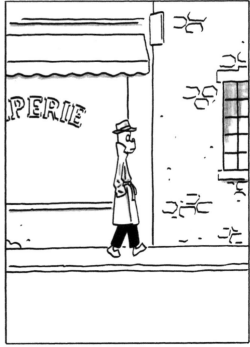

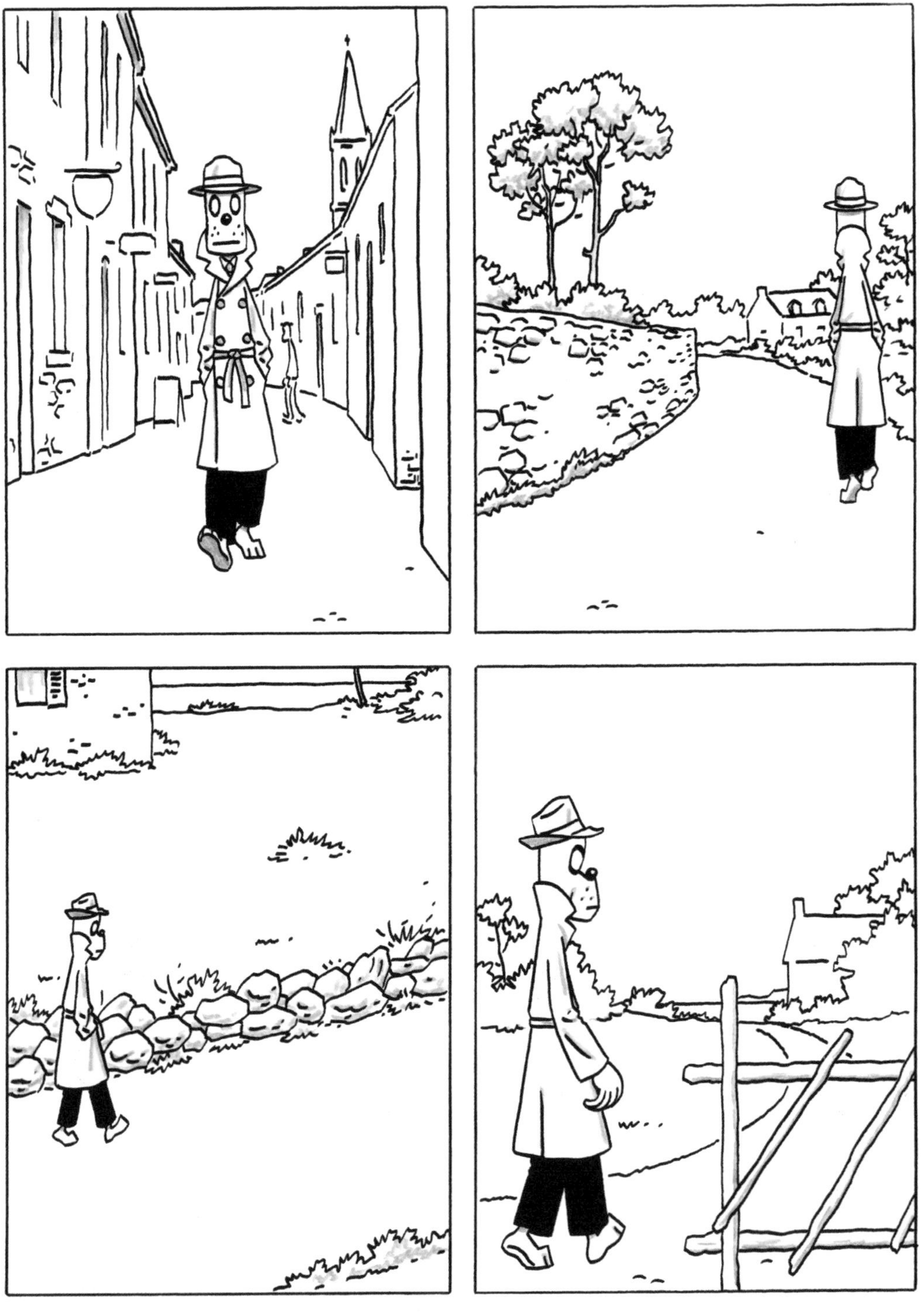

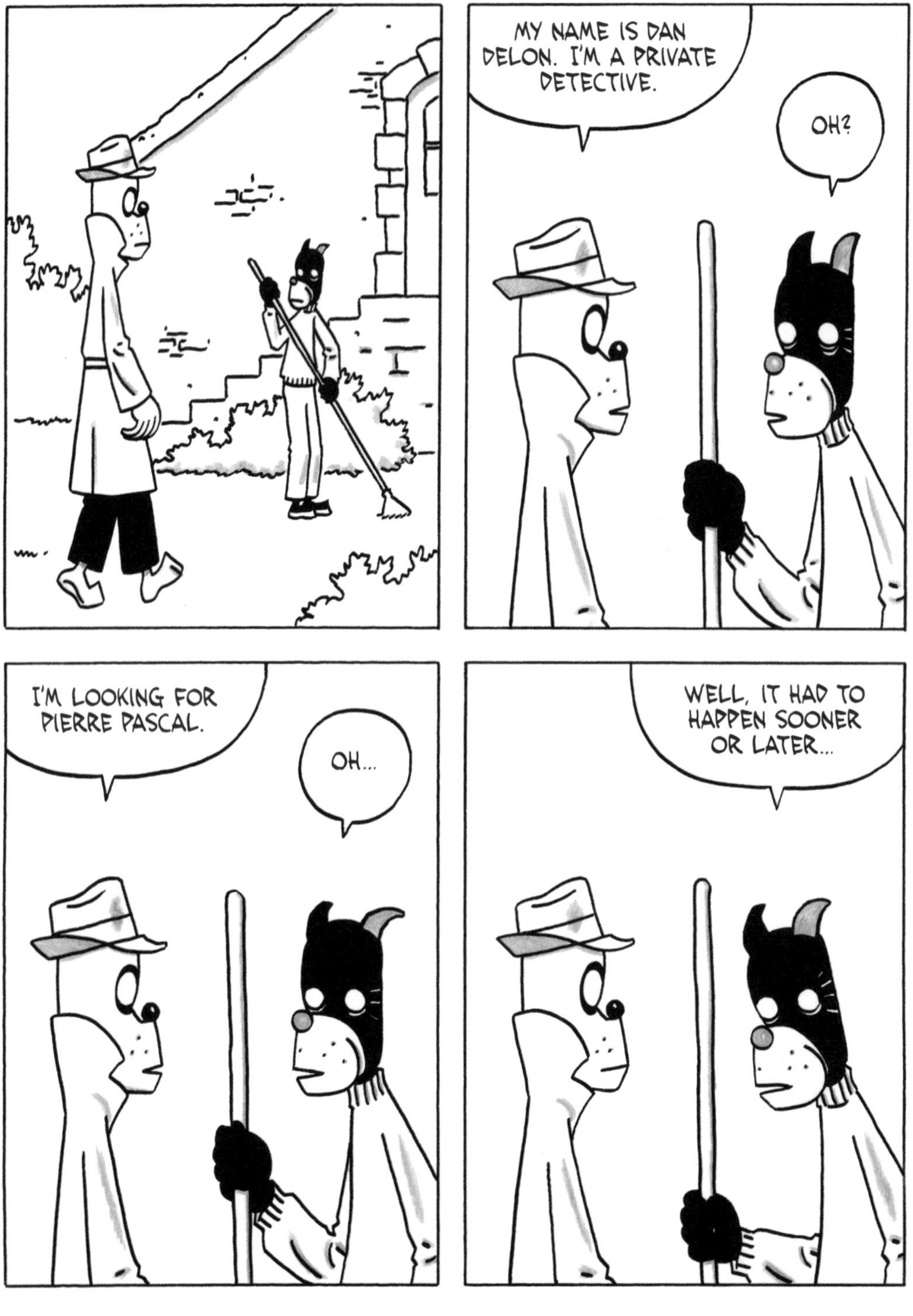
MY NAME IS DAN DELON. I'M A PRIVATE DETECTIVE.
OH?
I'M LOOKING FOR PIERRE PASCAL.
OH...
WELL, IT HAD TO HAPPEN SOONER OR LATER...

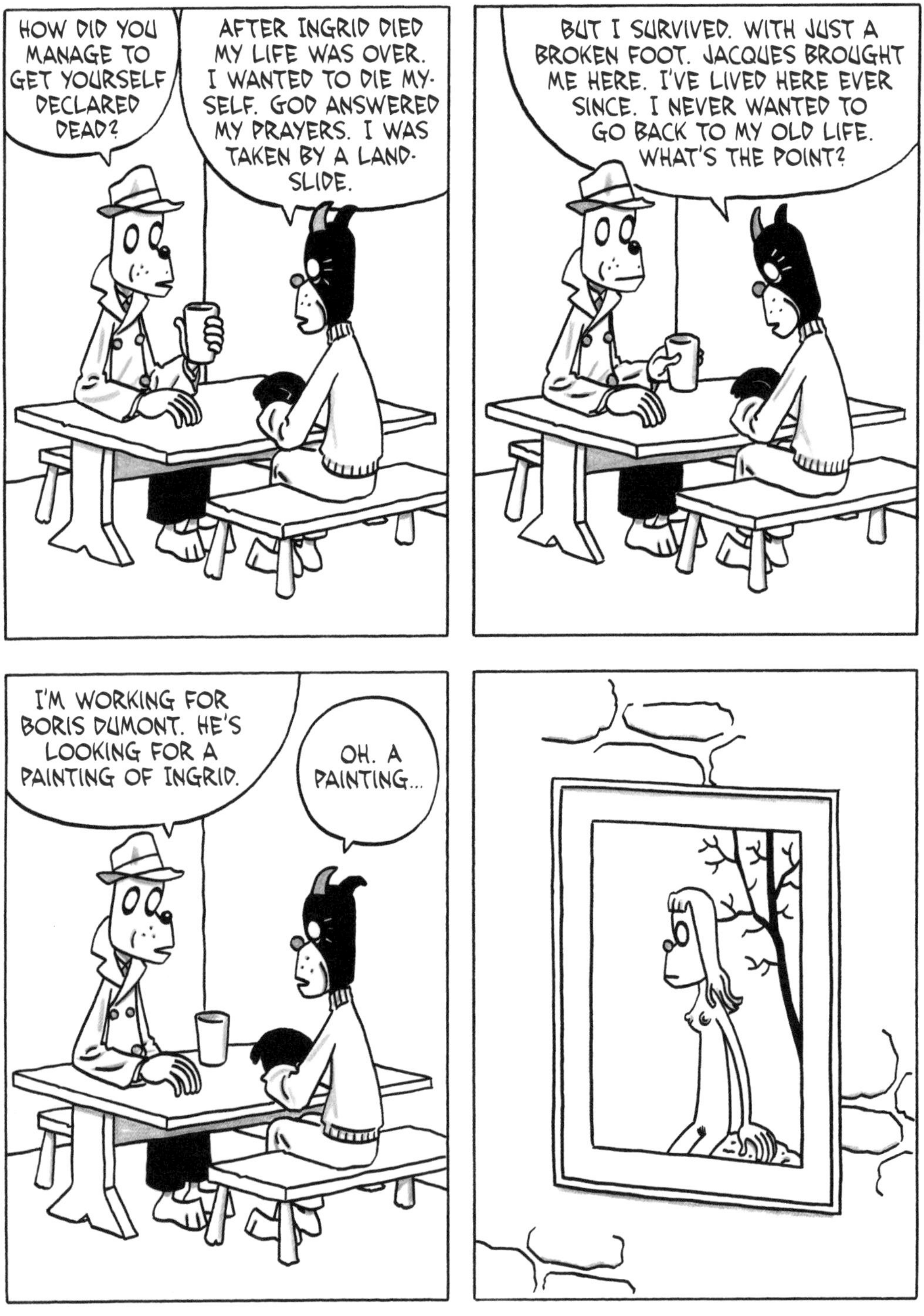
HOW DID YOU MANAGE TO GET YOURSELF DECLARED DEAD?
AFTER INGRID DIED MY LIFE WAS OVER. I WANTED TO DIE MY-SELF. GOD ANSWERED MY PRAYERS. I WAS TAKEN BY A LAND-SLIDE.
BUT I SURVIVED. WITH JUST A BROKEN FOOT. JACQUES BROUGHT ME HERE. I'VE LIVED HERE EVER SINCE. I NEVER WANTED TO GO BACK TO MY OLD LIFE. WHAT'S THE POINT?
I'M WORKING FOR BORIS DUMONT. HE'S LOOKING FOR A PAINTING OF INGRID.
OH. A PAINTING...

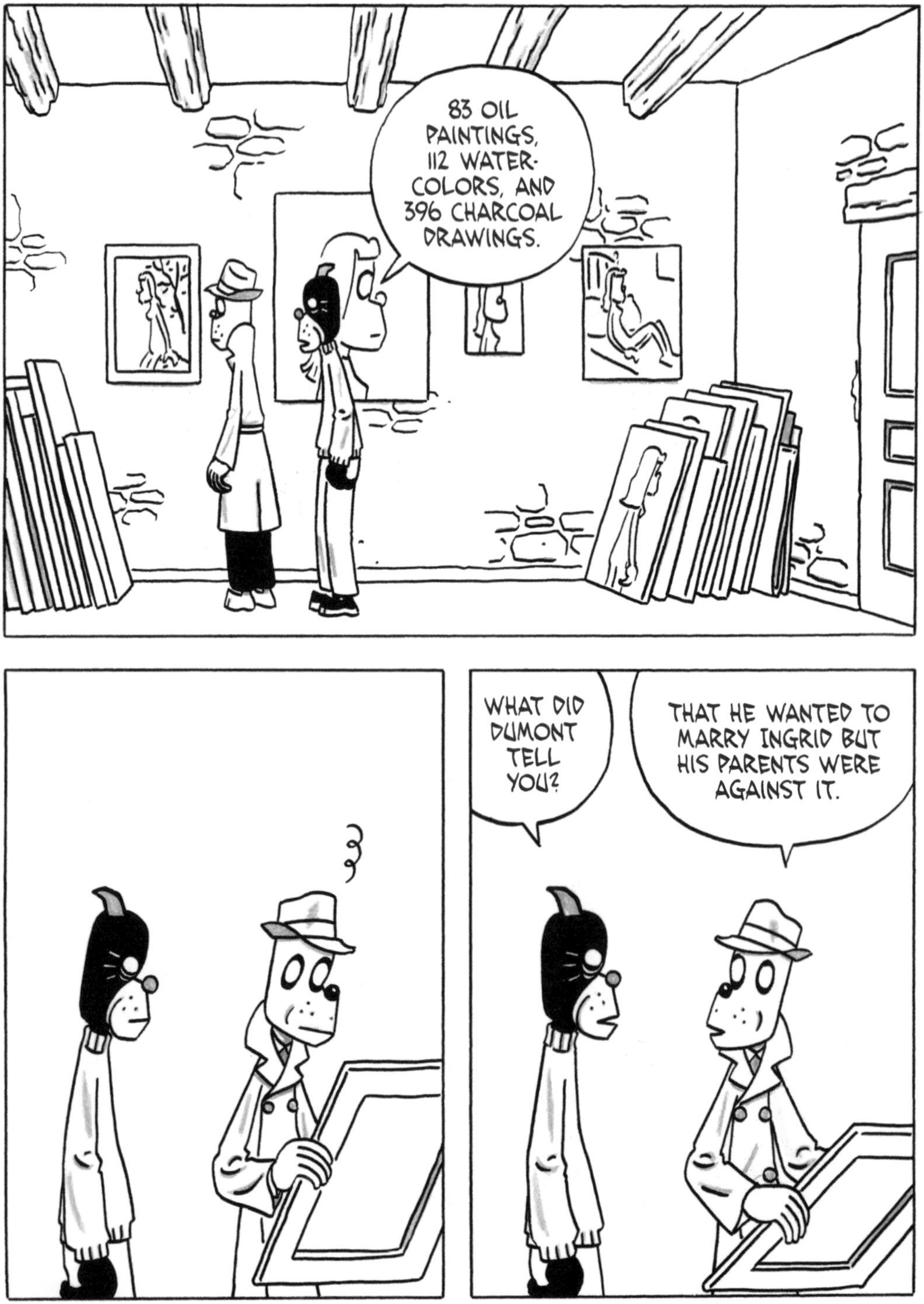
83 OIL PAINTINGS, 112 WATER-COLORS, AND 396 CHARCOAL DRAWINGS.
WHAT DID DUMONT TELL YOU?
THAT HE WANTED TO MARRY INGRID BUT HIS PARENTS WERE AGAINST IT.

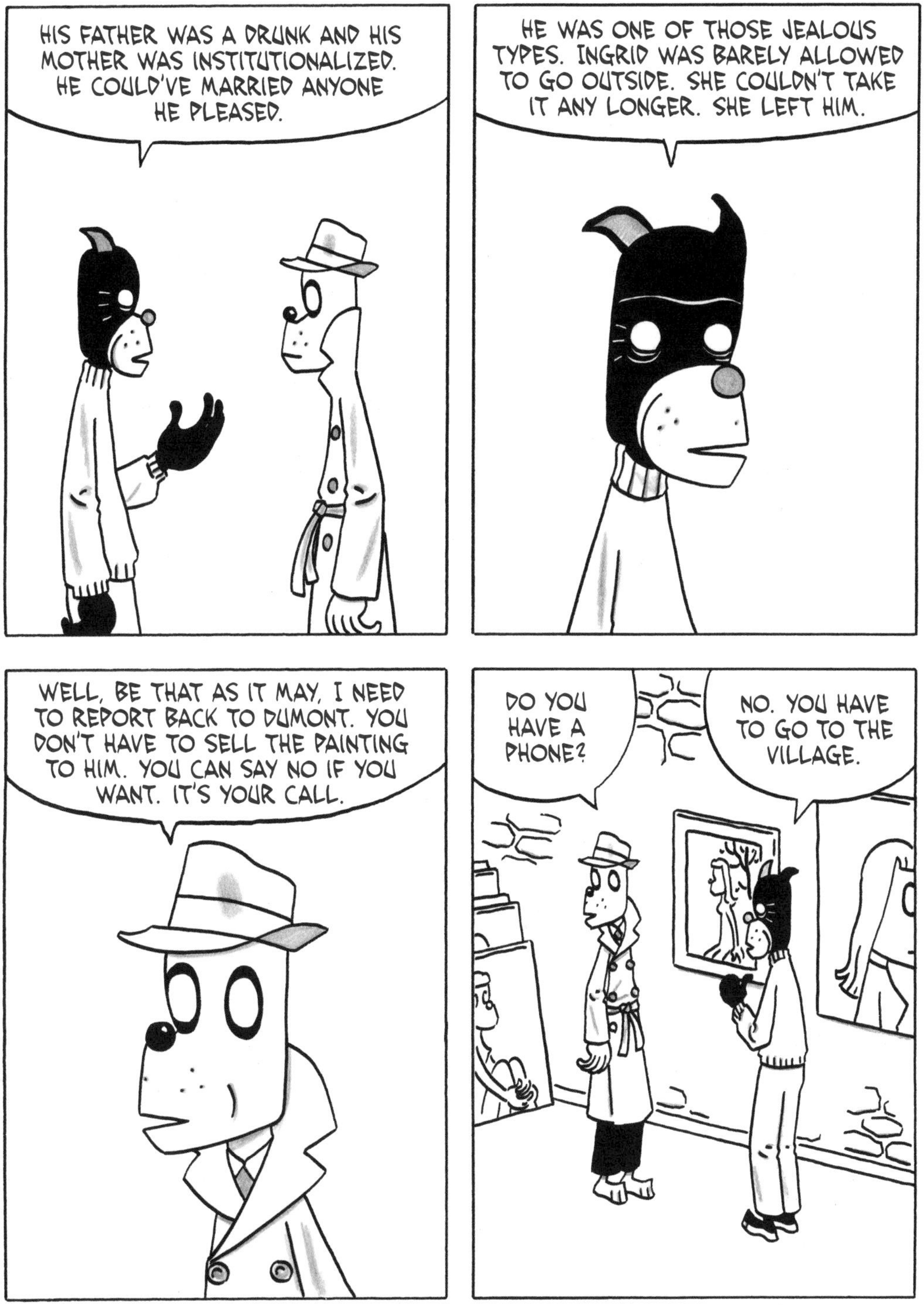
HIS FATHER WAS A DRUNK AND HIS MOTHER WAS INSTITUTIONALIZED. HE COULD'VE MARRIED ANYONE HE PLEASED.
HE WAS ONE OF THOSE JEALOUS TYPES. INGRID WAS BARELY ALLOWED TO GO OUTSIDE. SHE COULDN'T TAKE IT ANY LONGER. SHE LEFT HIM.
WELL, BE THAT AS IT MAY, I NEED TO REPORT BACK TO DUMONT. YOU DON'T HAVE TO SELL THE PAINTING TO HIM. YOU CAN SAY NO IF YOU WANT. IT'S YOUR CALL.
DO YOU HAVE A PHONE?
NO. YOU HAVE TO GO TO THE VILLAGE.

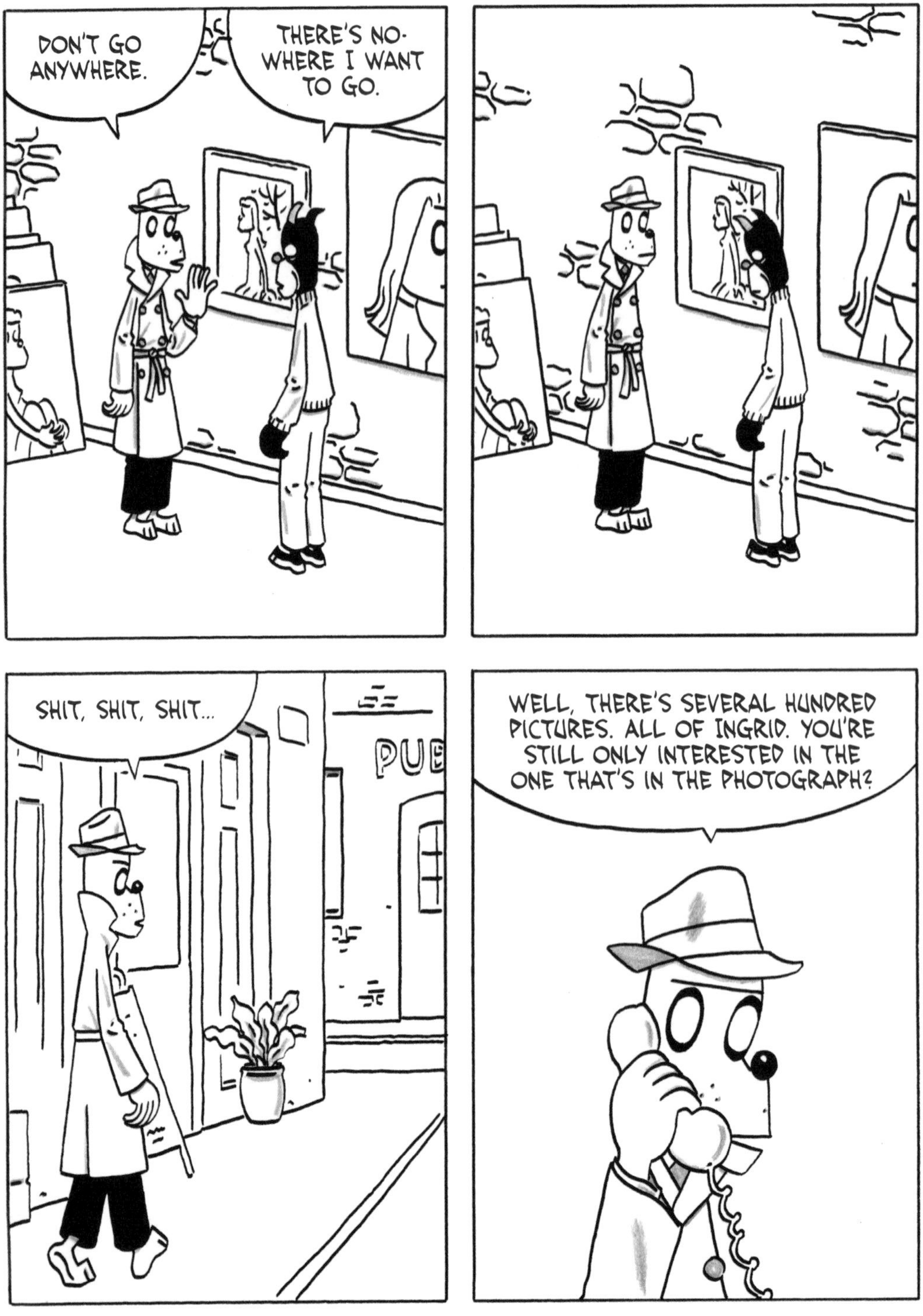
DON'T GO ANYWHERE.
THERE'S NO-WHERE I WANT TO GO.
SHIT, SHIT, SHIT...
PUB
WELL, THERE'S SEVERAL HUNDRED PICTURES. ALL OF INGRID. YOU'RE STILL ONLY INTERESTED IN THE ONE THAT'S IN THE PHOTOGRAPH?

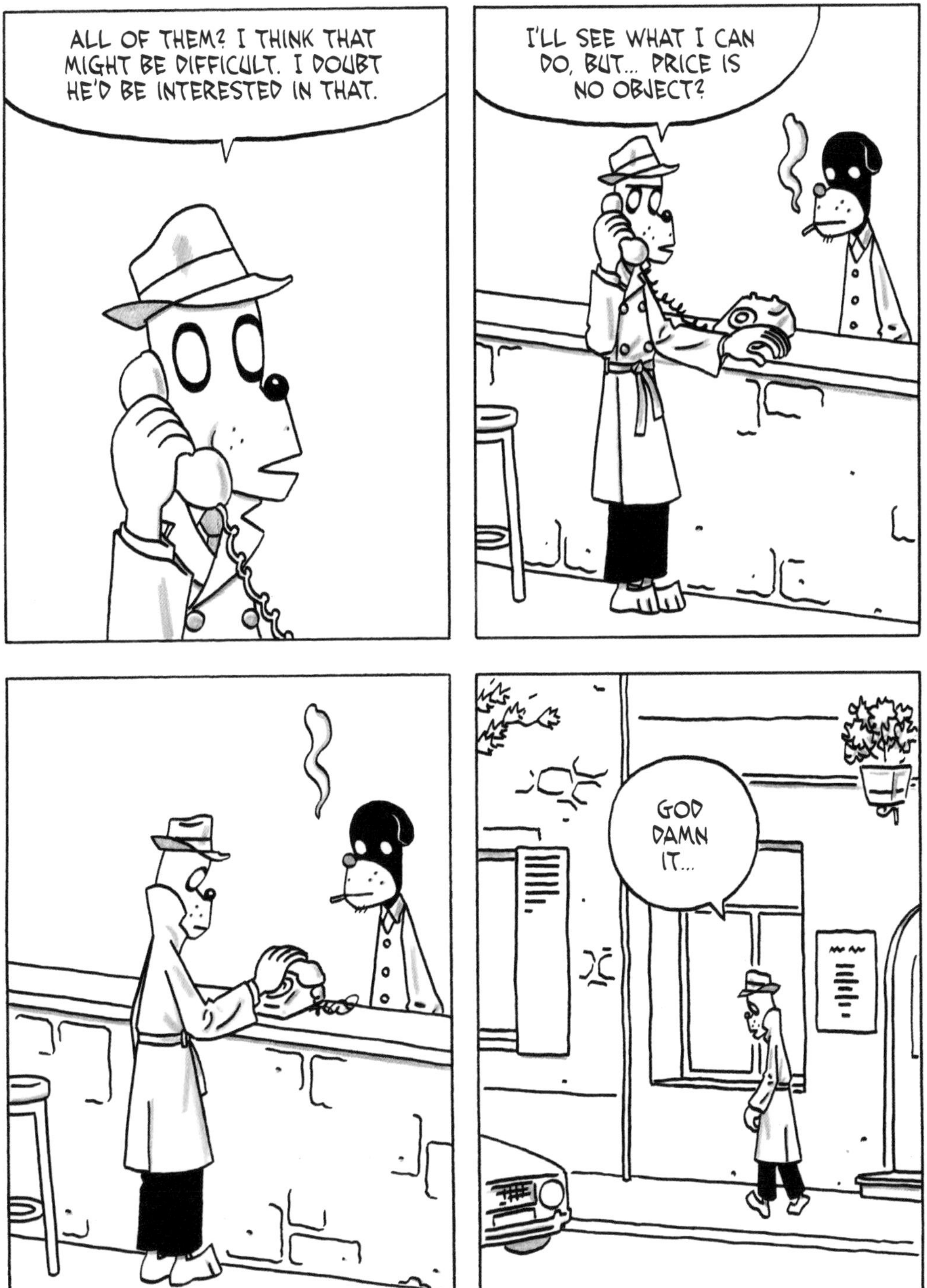
ALL OF THEM? I THINK THAT MIGHT BE DIFFICULT. I DOUBT HE'D BE INTERESTED IN THAT.
I'LL SEE WHAT I CAN DO, BUT... PRICE IS NO OBJECT?
GOD DAMN IT...

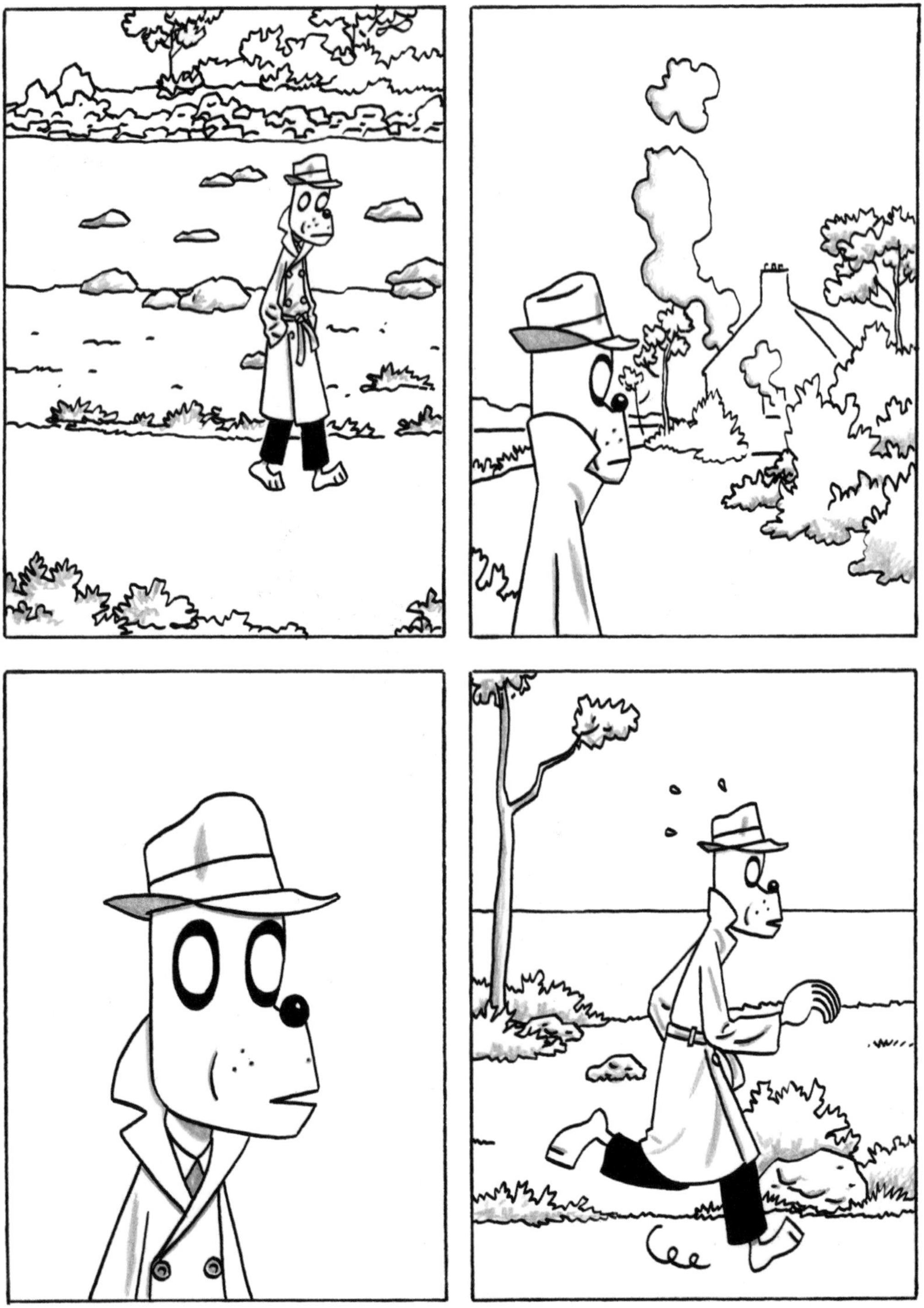

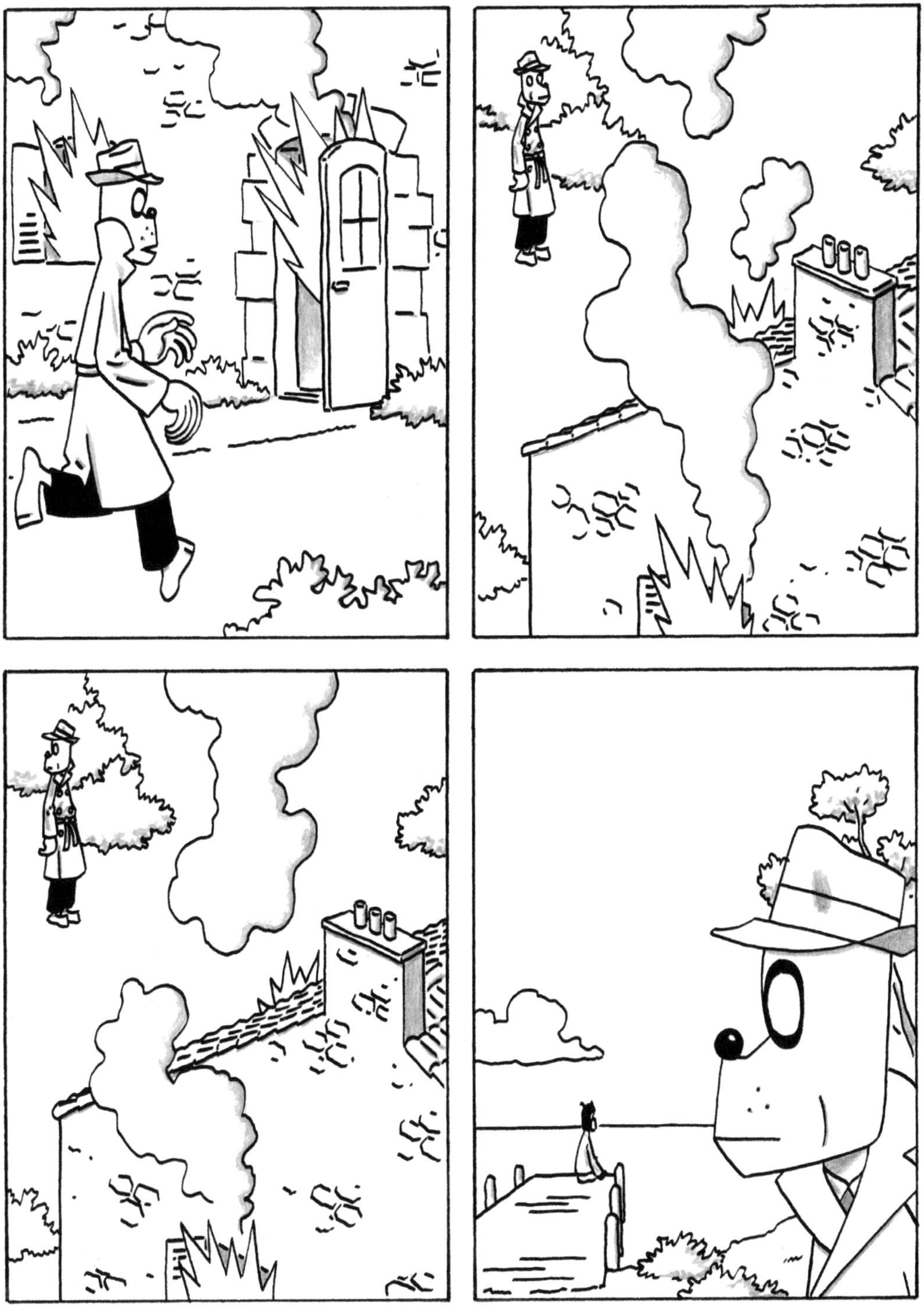

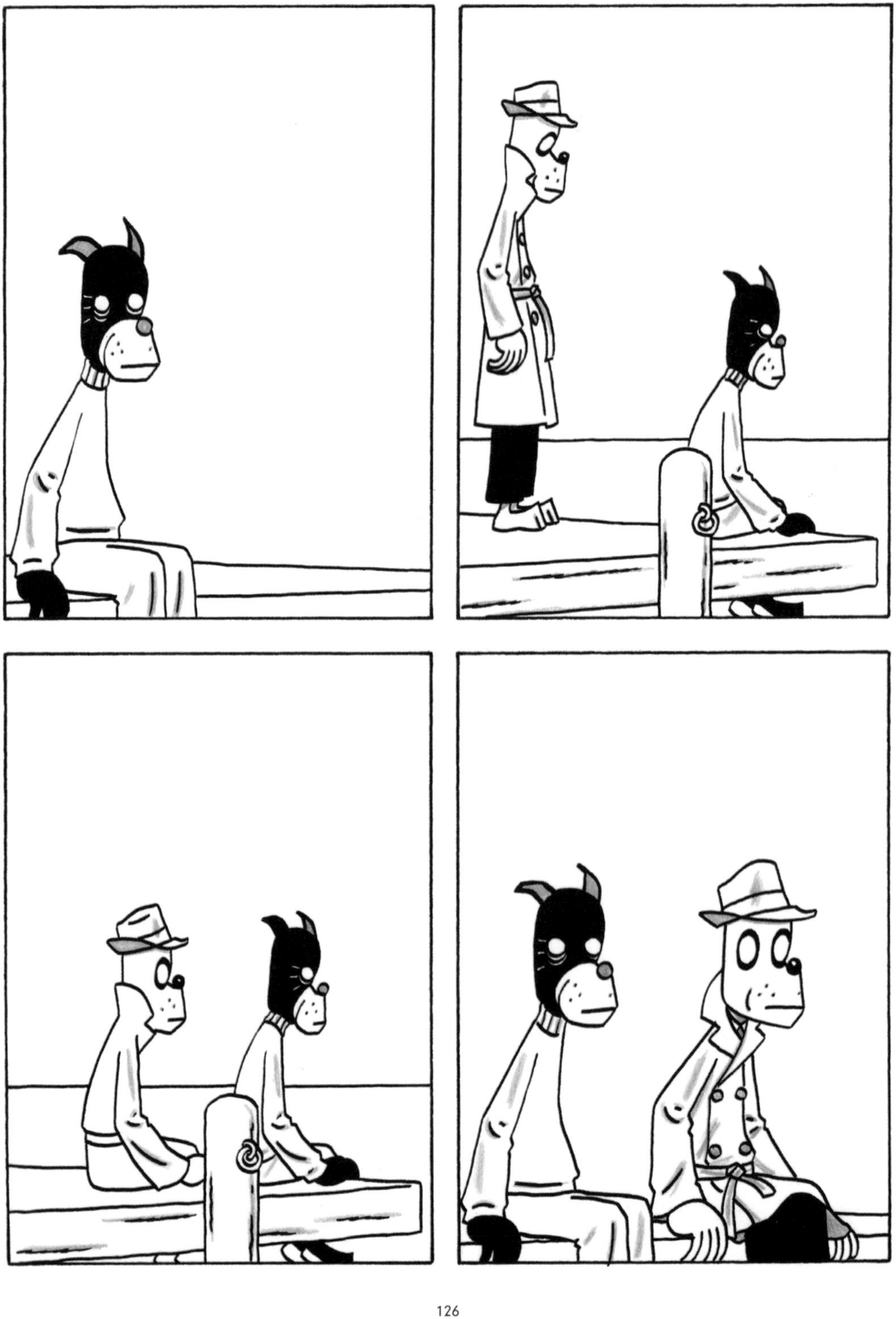

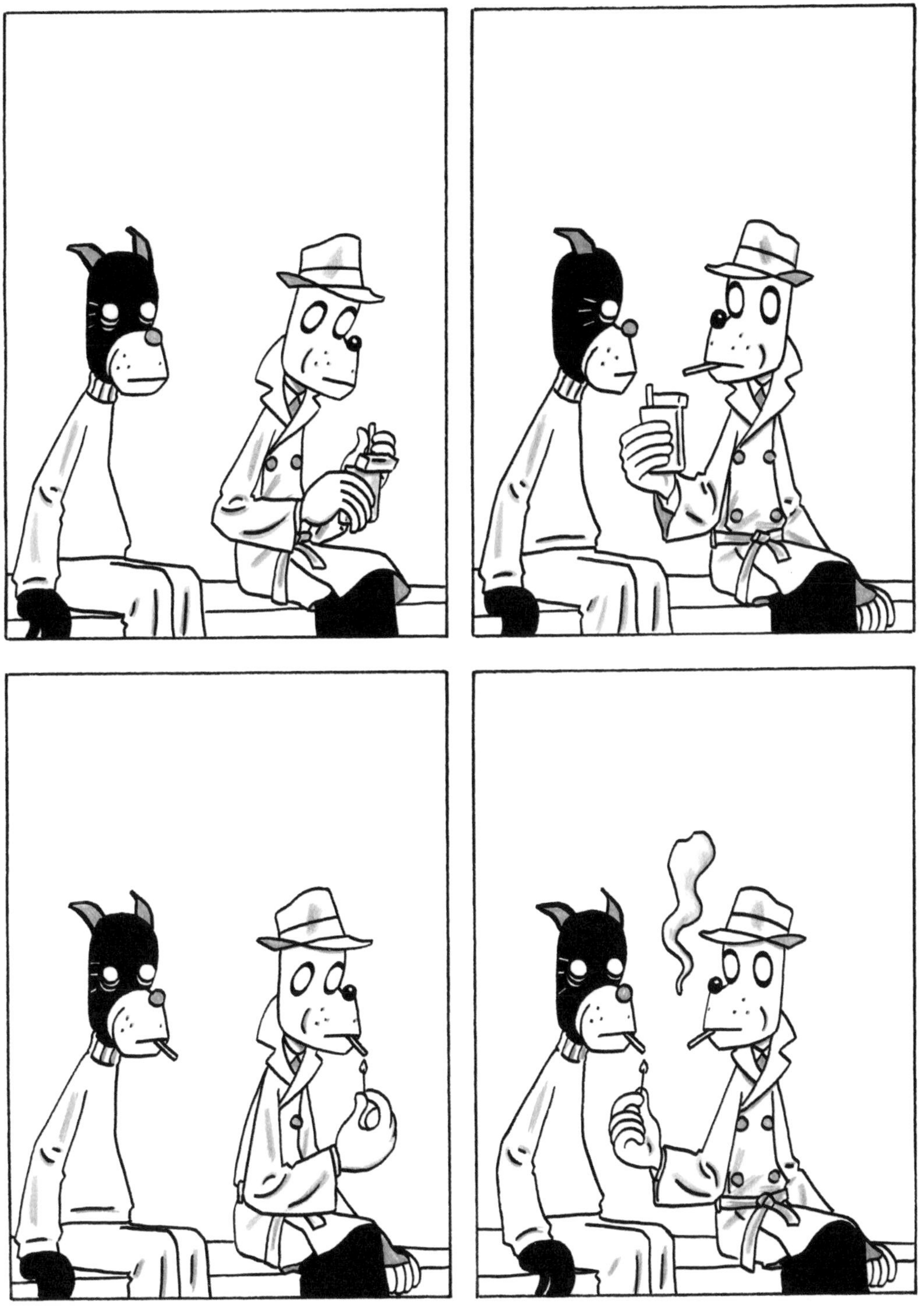

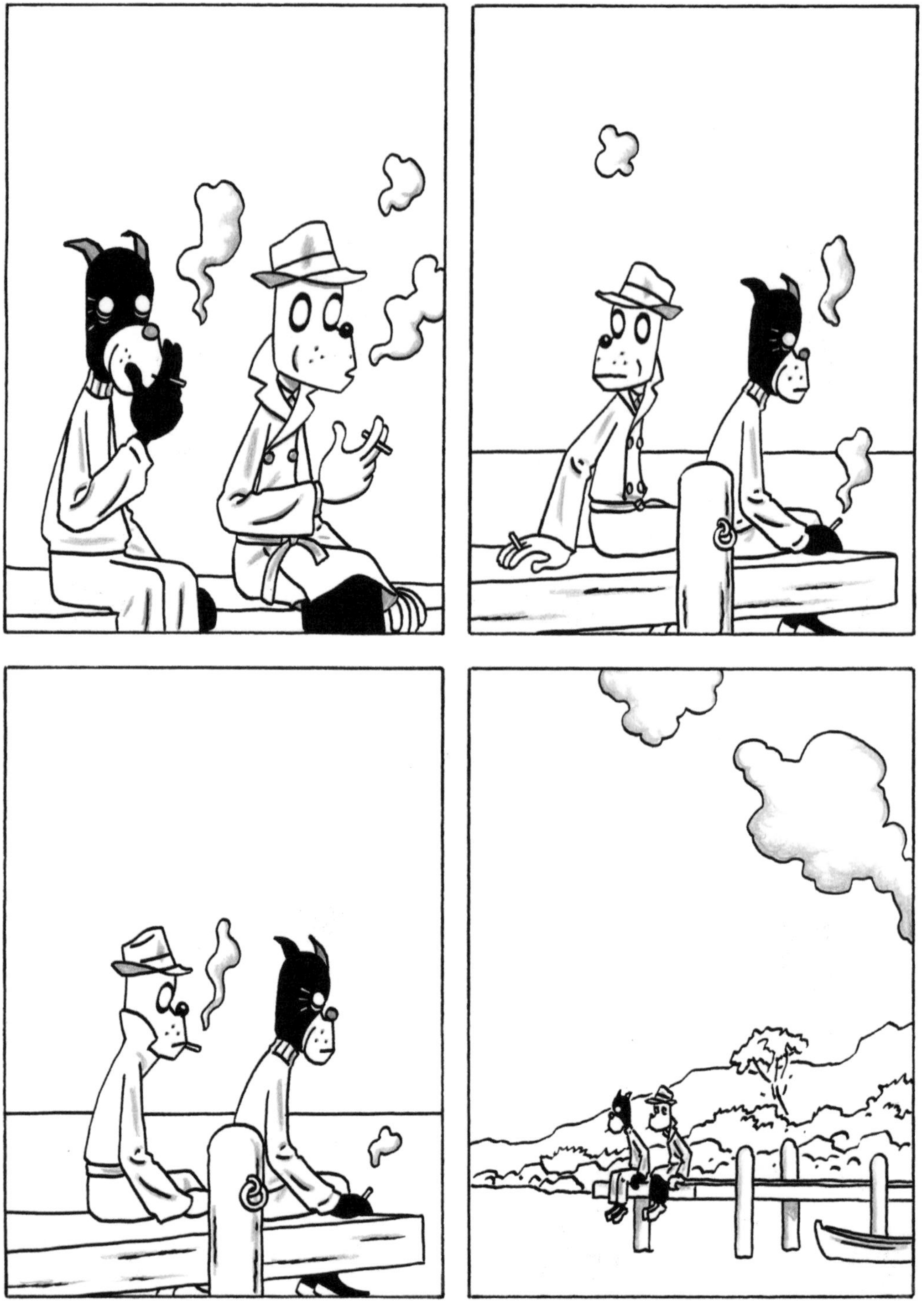

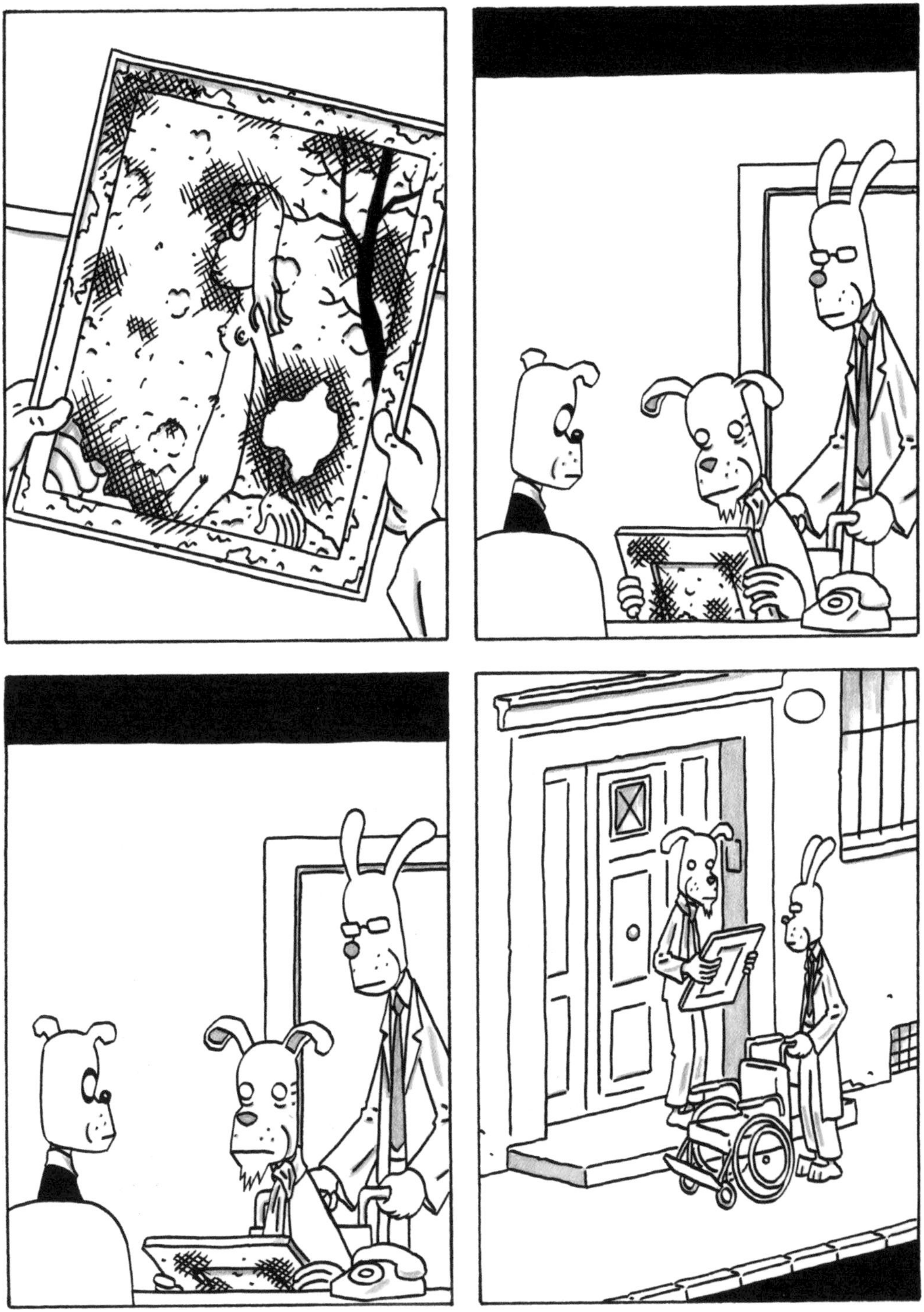

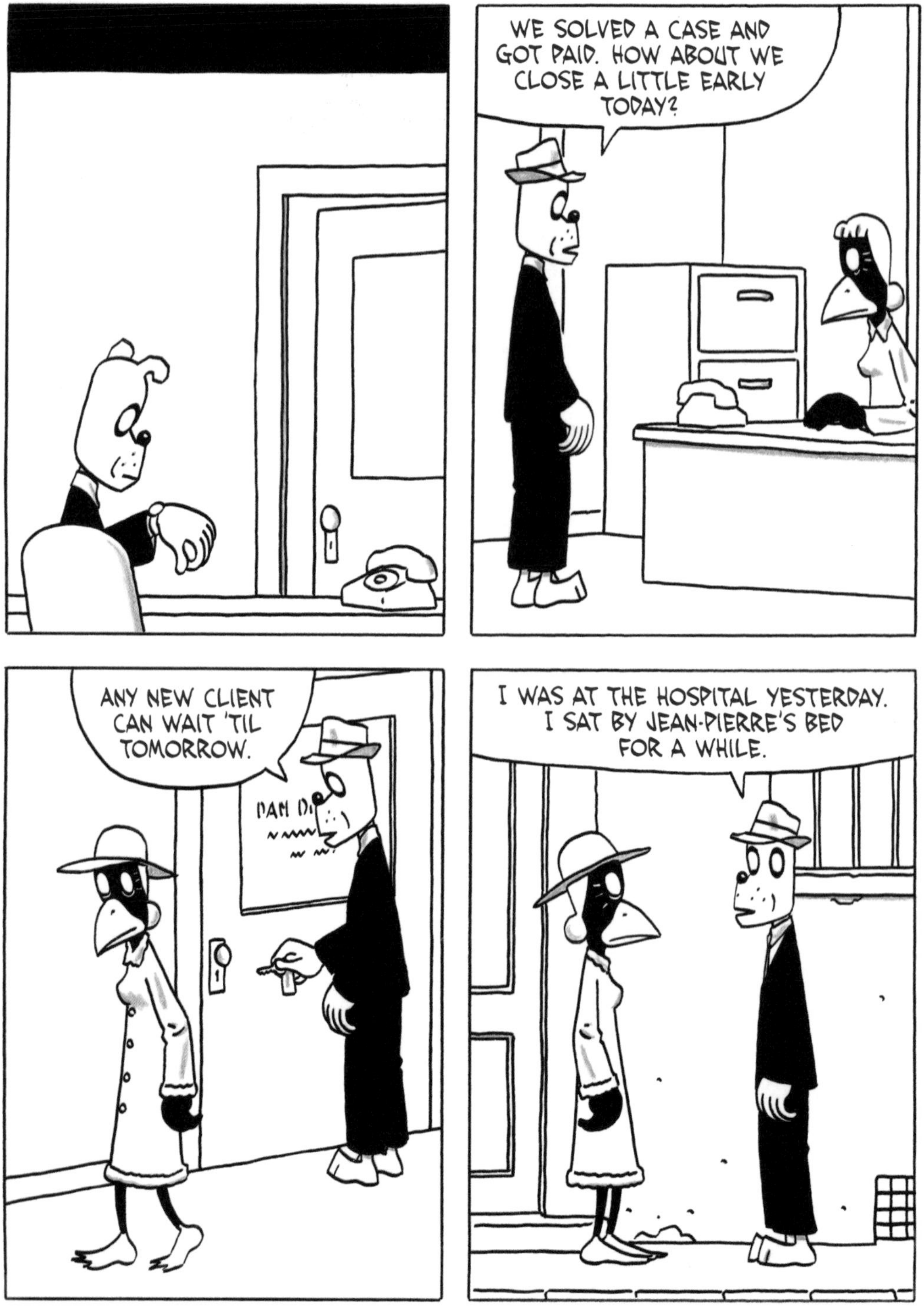
WE SOLVED A CASE AND GOT PAID. HOW ABOUT WE CLOSE A LITTLE EARLY TODAY?
ANY NEW CLIENT CAN WAIT 'TIL TOMORROW.
I WAS AT THE HOSPITAL YESTERDAY. I SAT BY JEAN-PIERRE'S BED FOR A WHILE.

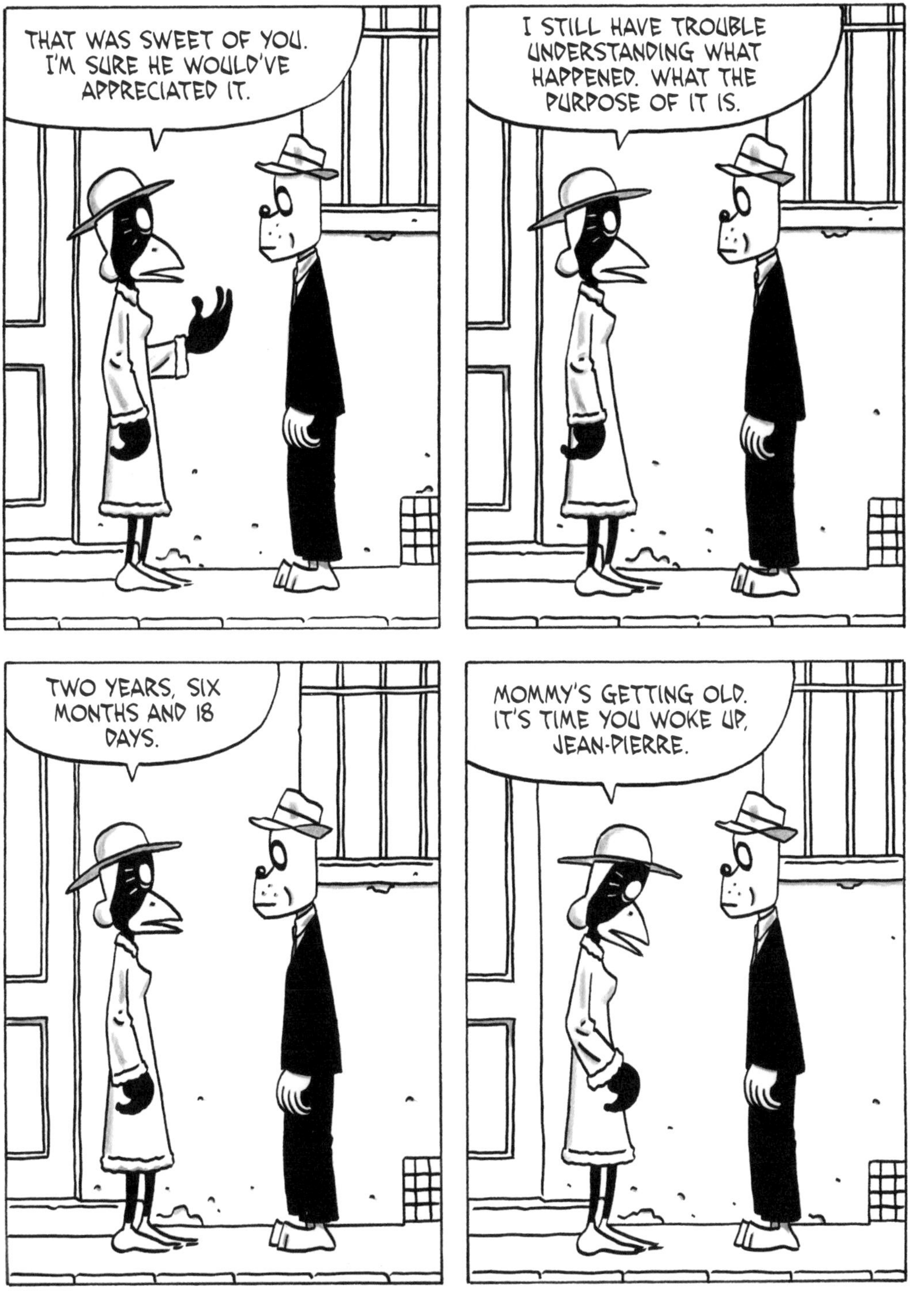
THAT WAS SWEET OF YOU. I'M SURE HE WOULD'VE APPRECIATED IT.
I STILL HAVE TROUBLE UNDERSTANDING WHAT HAPPENED. WHAT THE PURPOSE OF IT IS.
TWO YEARS, SIX MONTHS AND 18 DAYS.
MOMMY'S GETTING OLD. IT'S TIME YOU WOKE UP, JEAN-PIERRE.

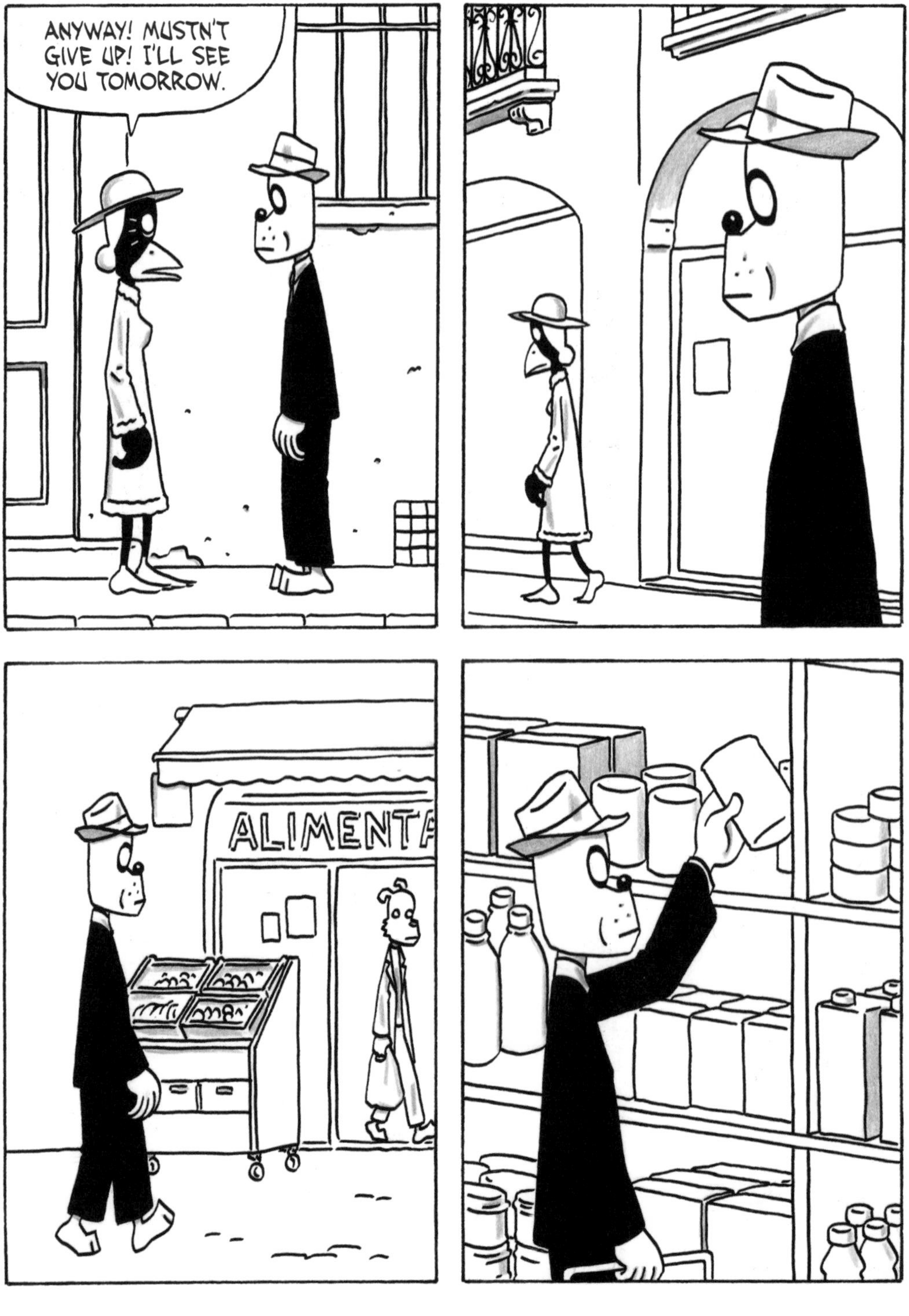
ANYWAY! MUSTN'T GIVE UP! I'LL SEE YOU TOMORROW.
ALIMENTA

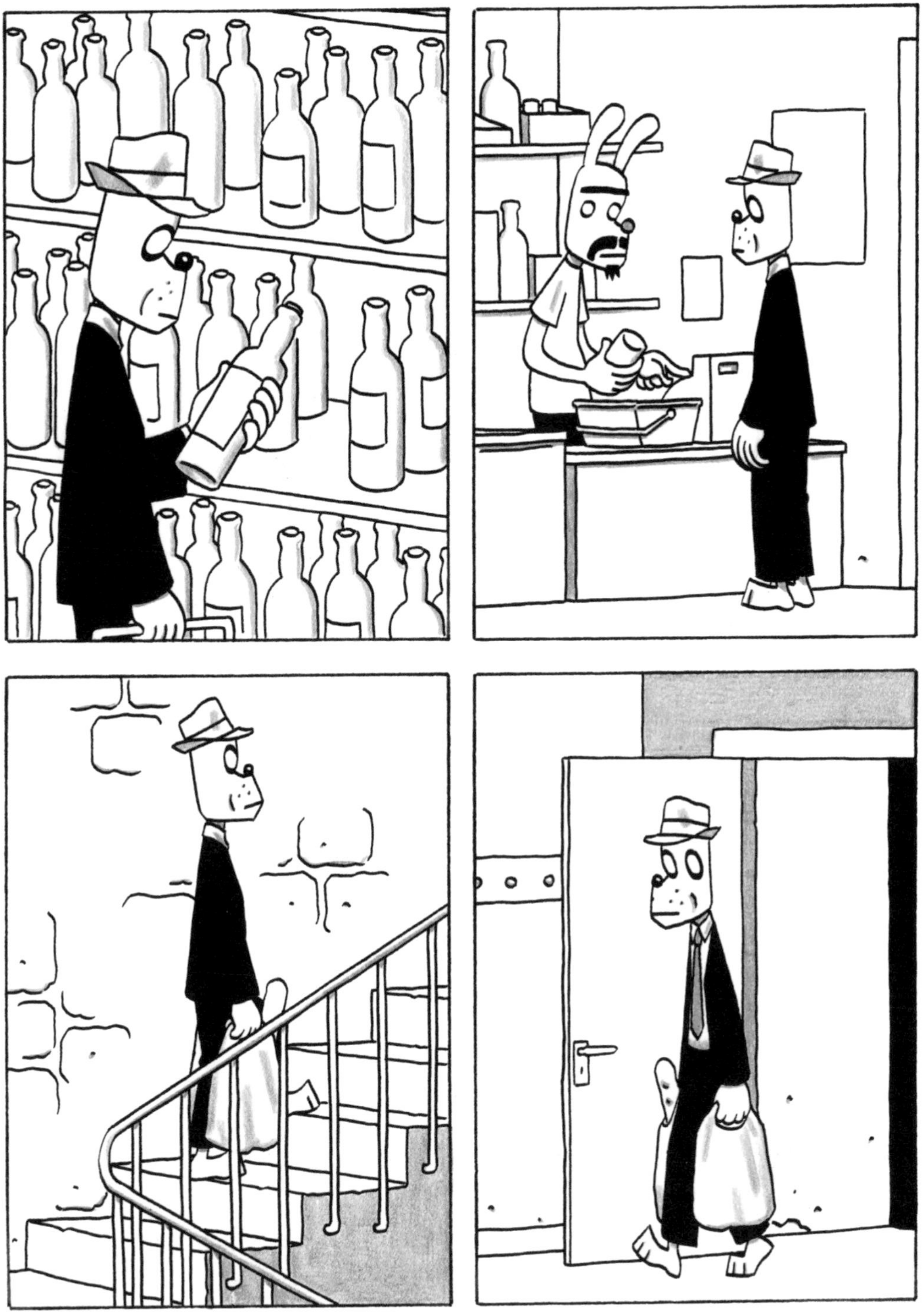

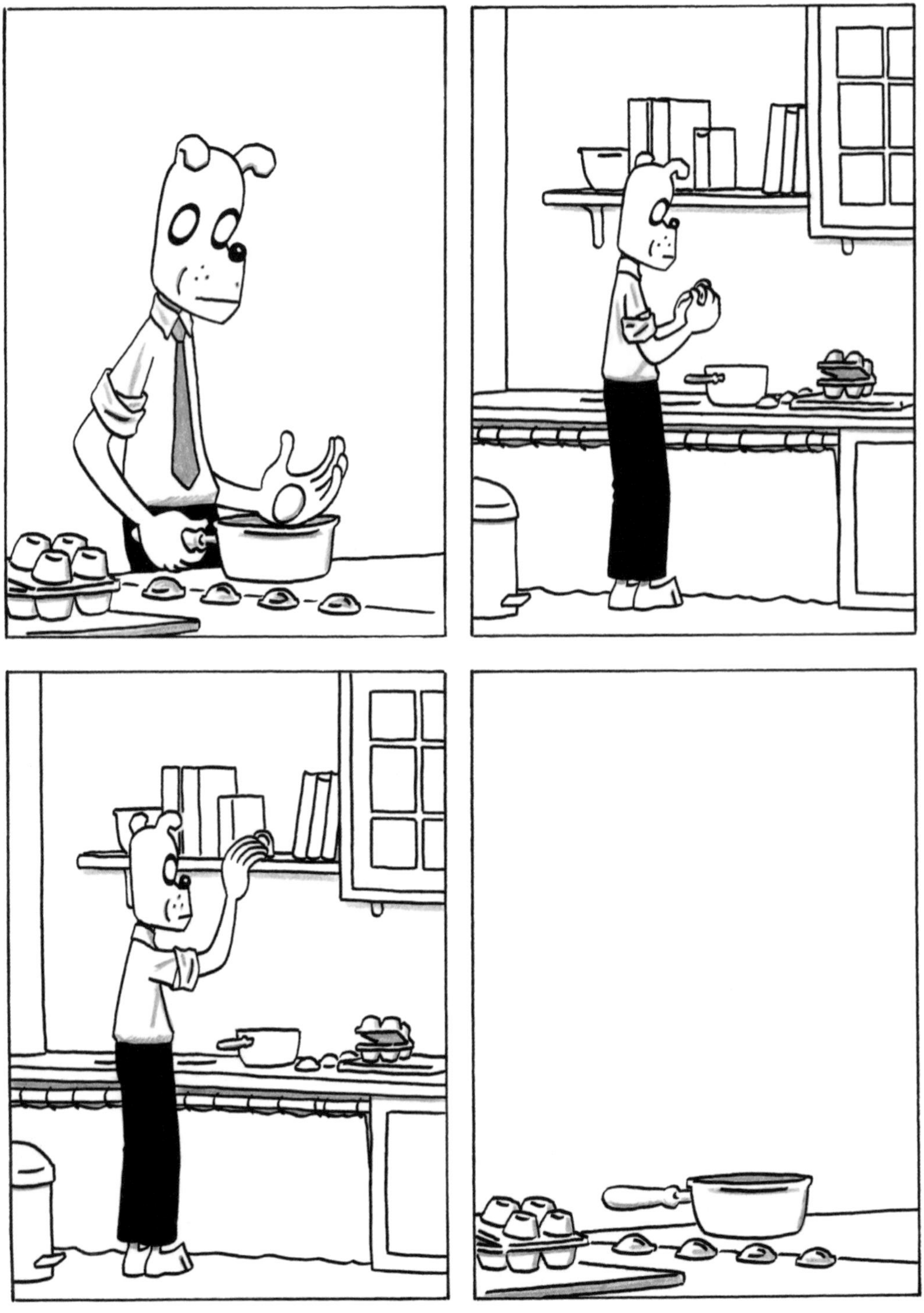

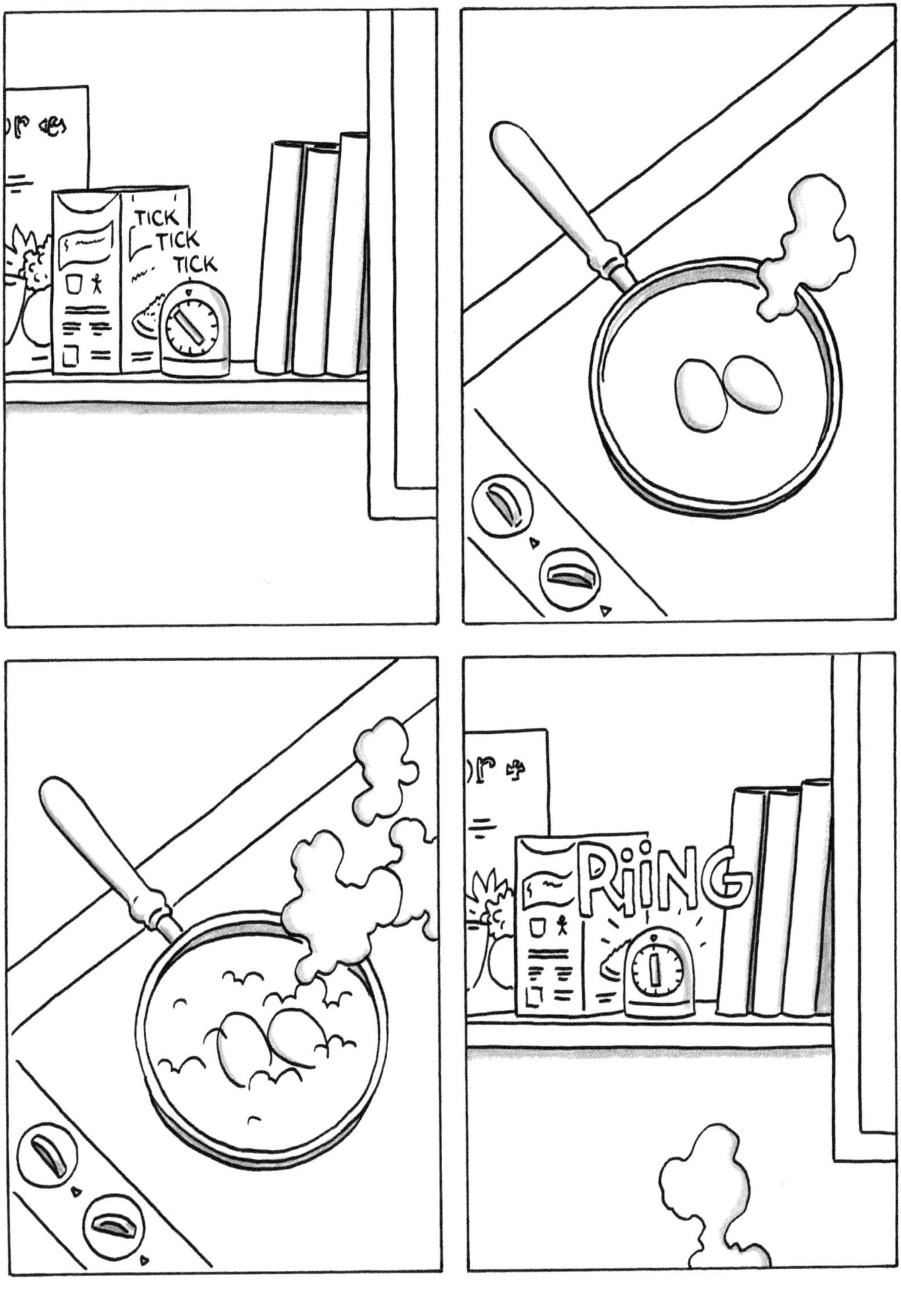
TICK
TICK
TICK
RING

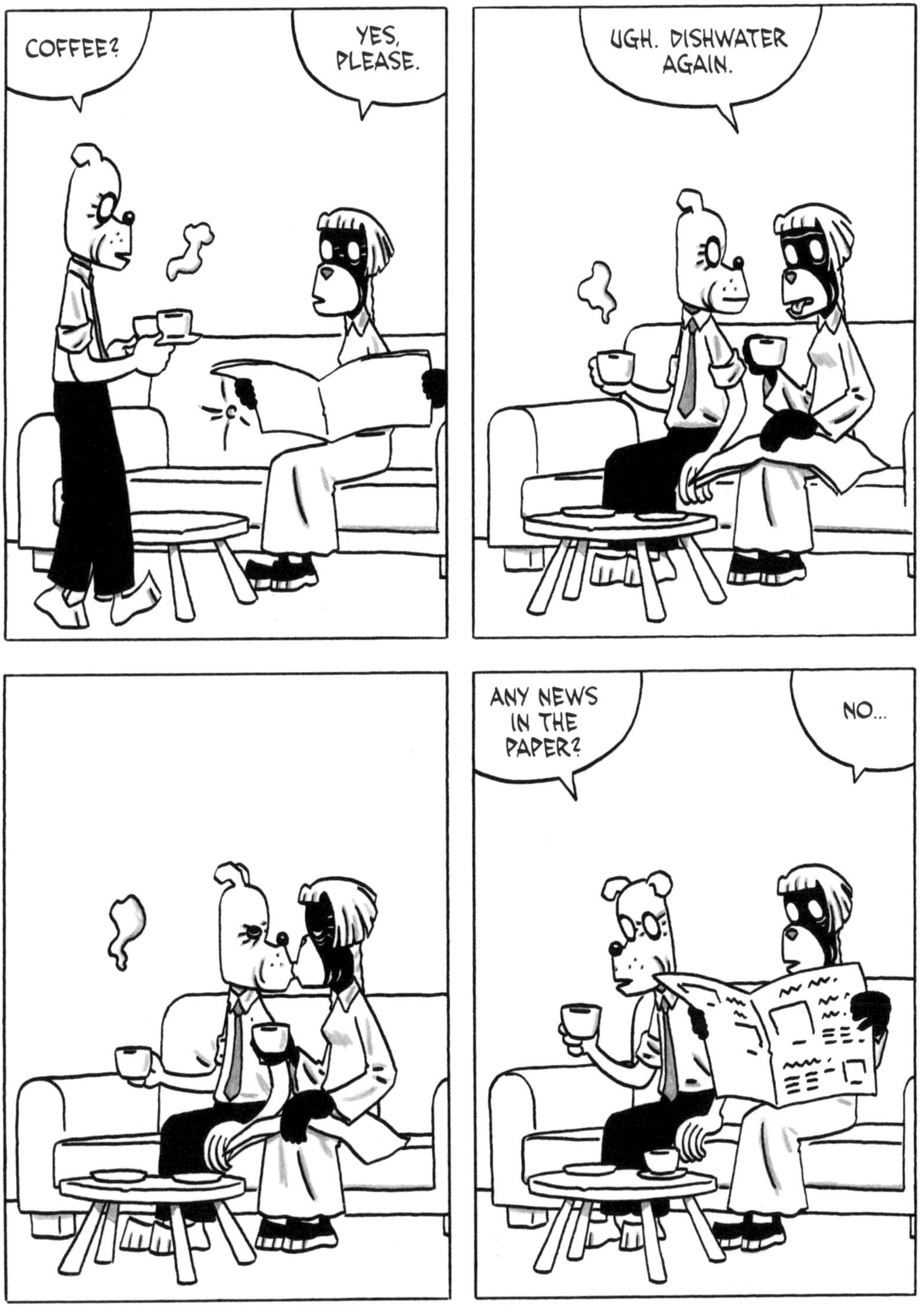
COFFEE?
YES, PLEASE.
UGH. DISHWATER AGAIN.
ANY NEWS IN THE PAPER?
NO...

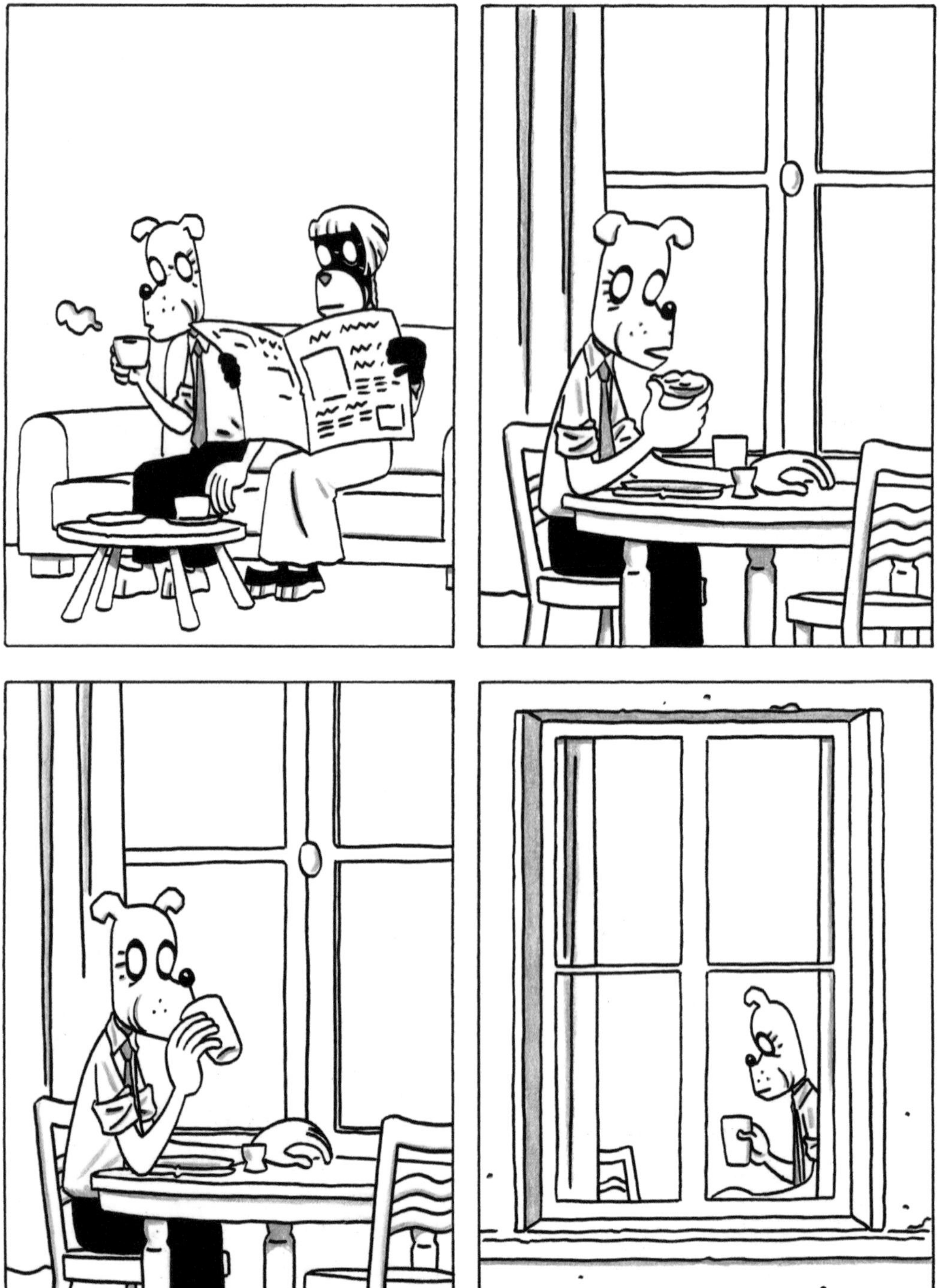

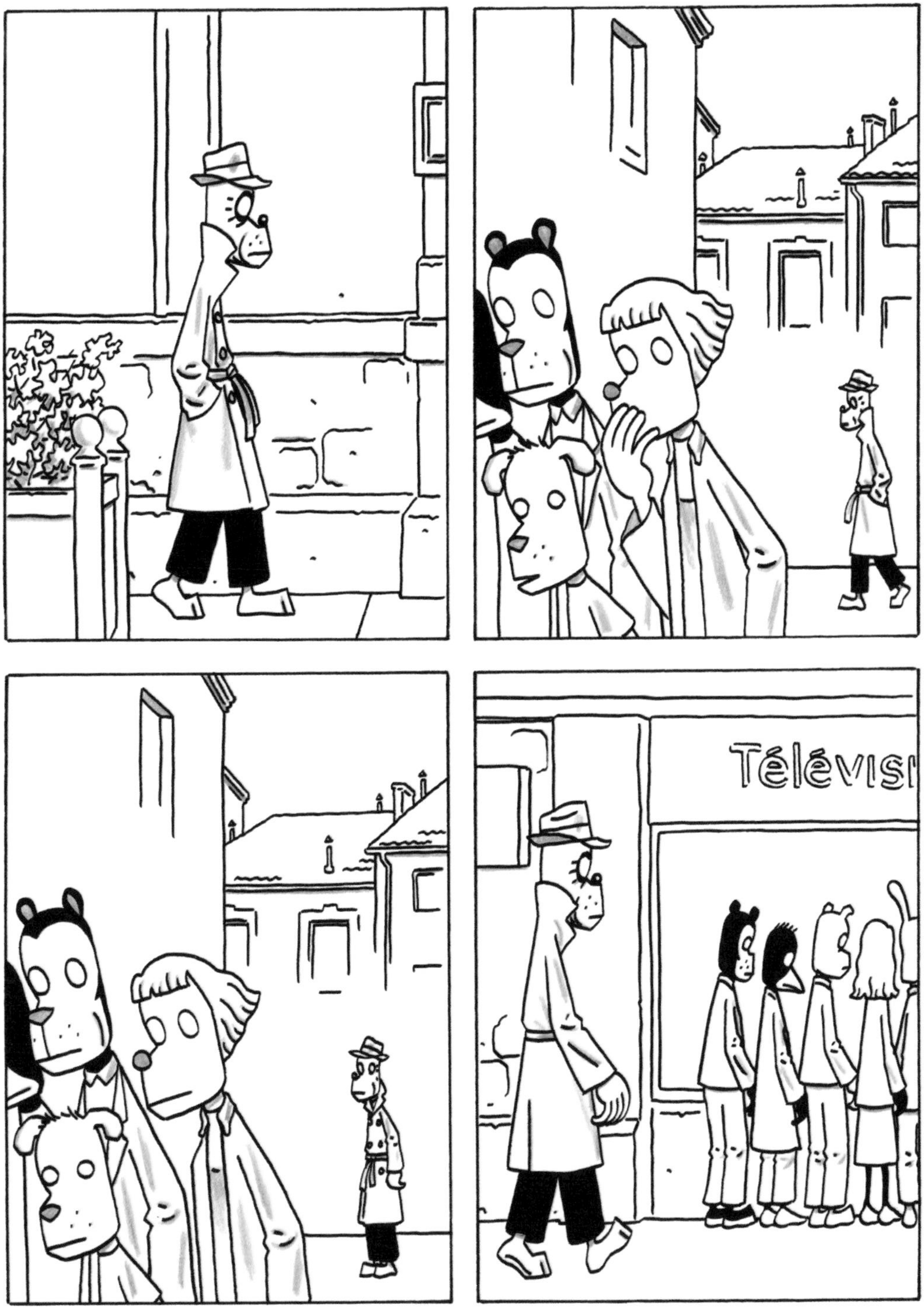
Télévisi

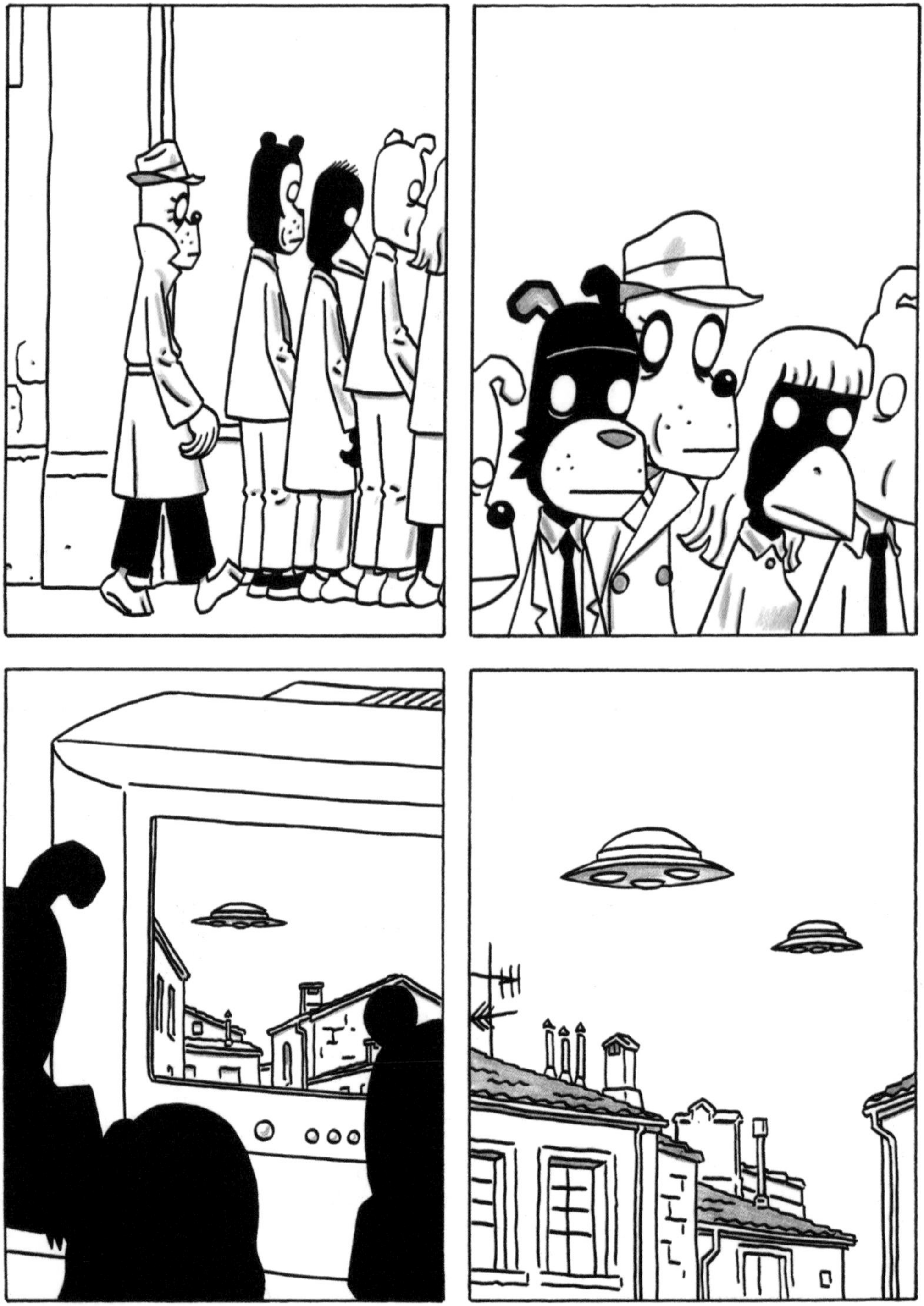

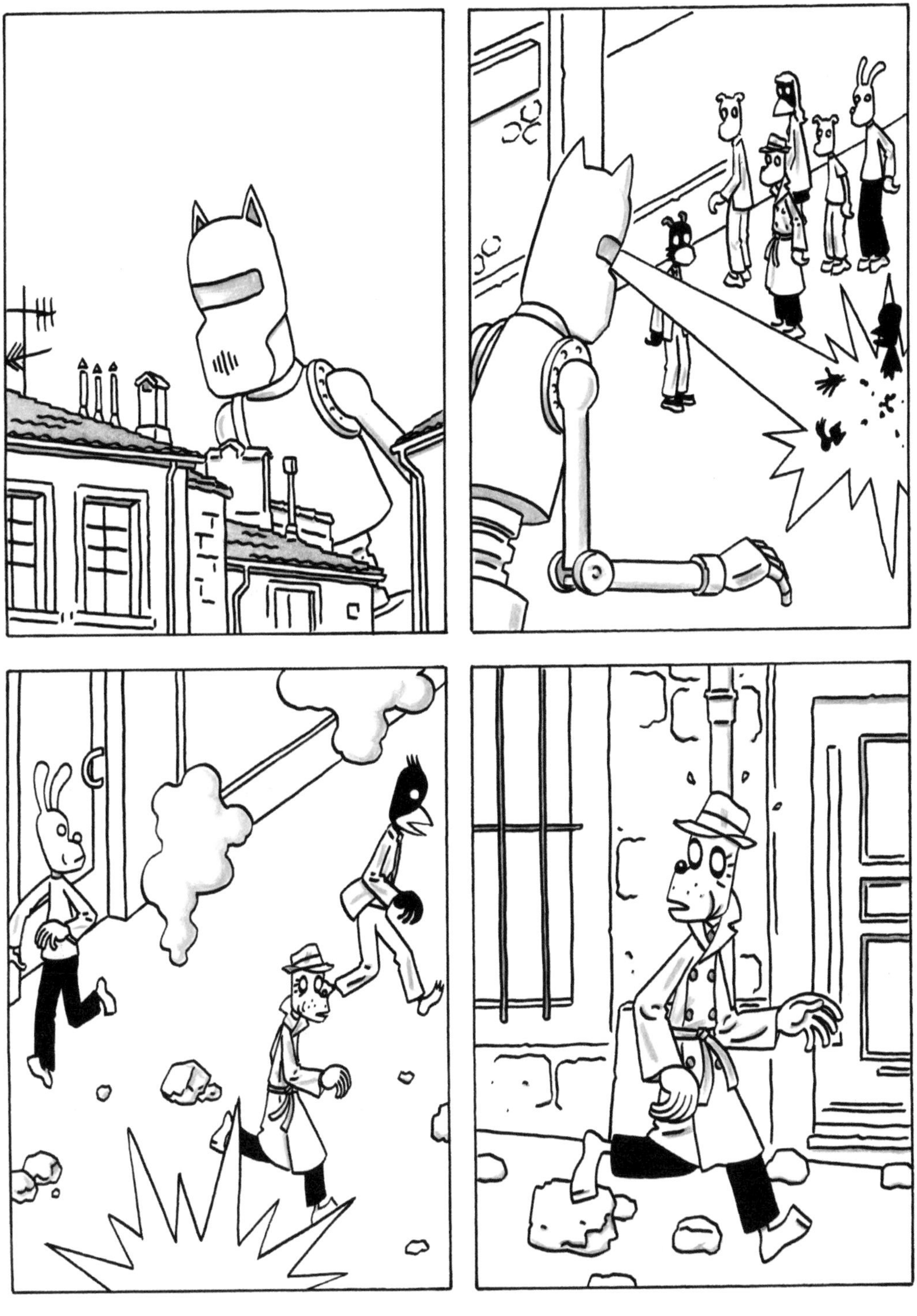

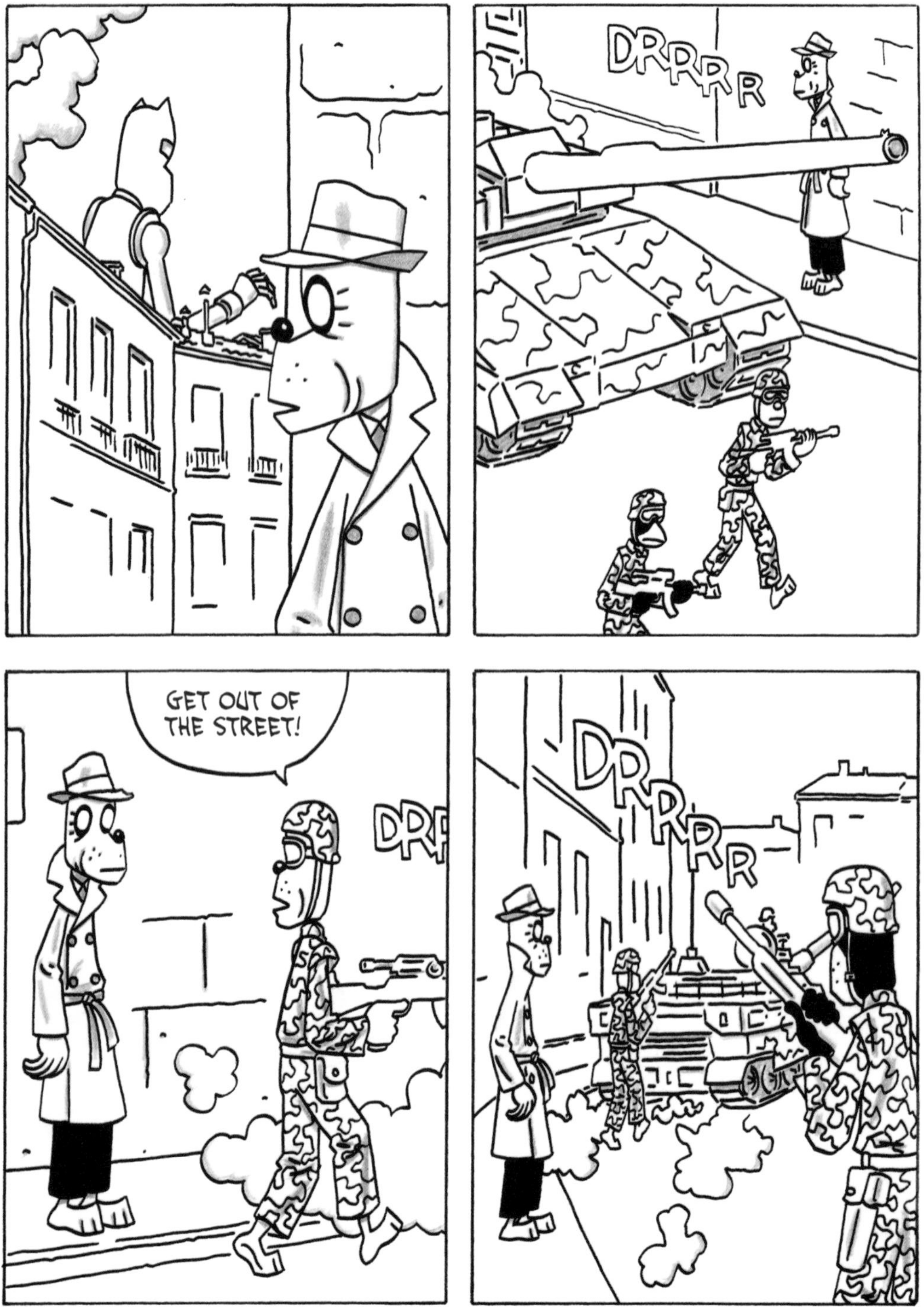
DRRRRR
GET OUT OF THE STREET!
DRR
DRRRRR

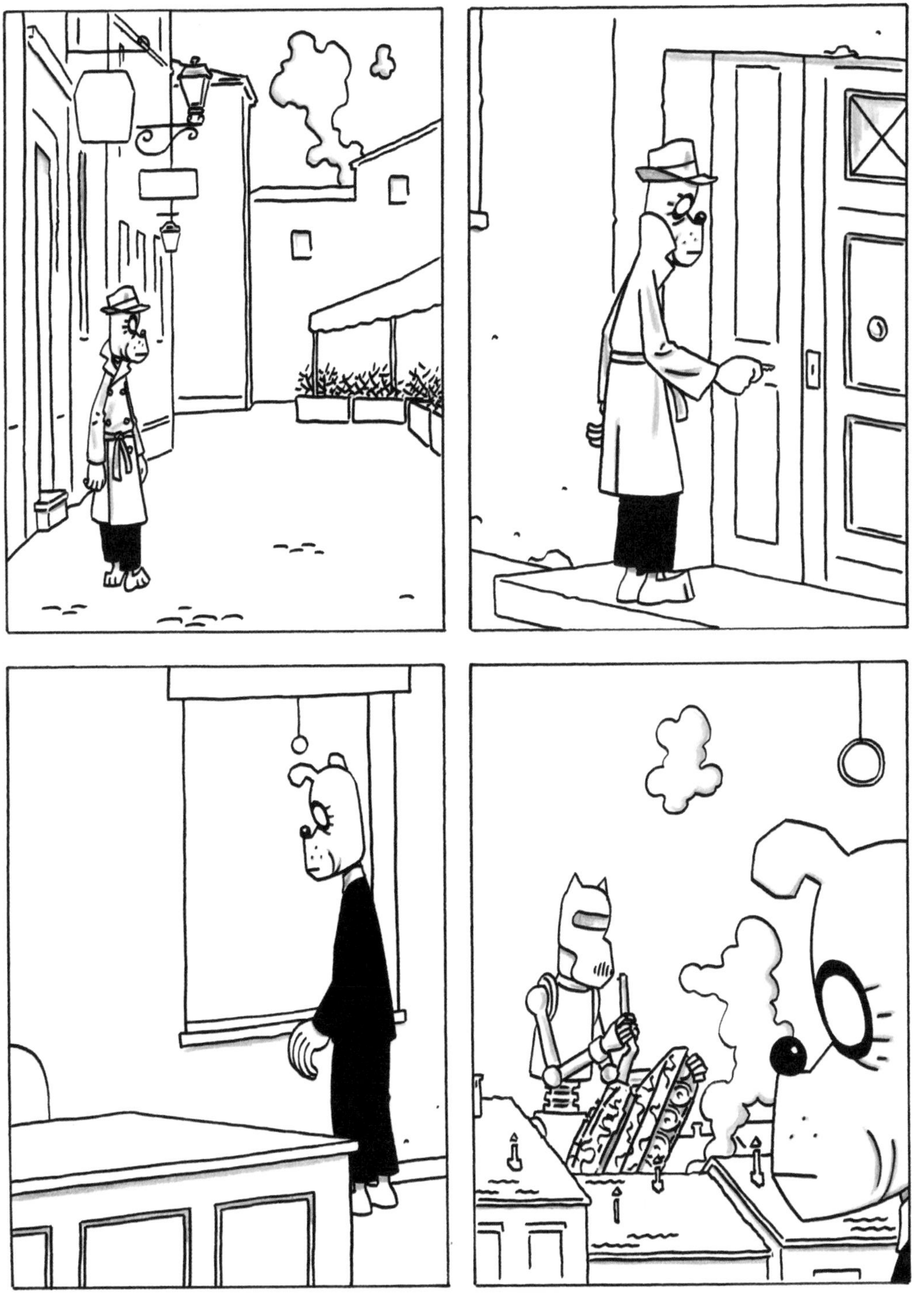

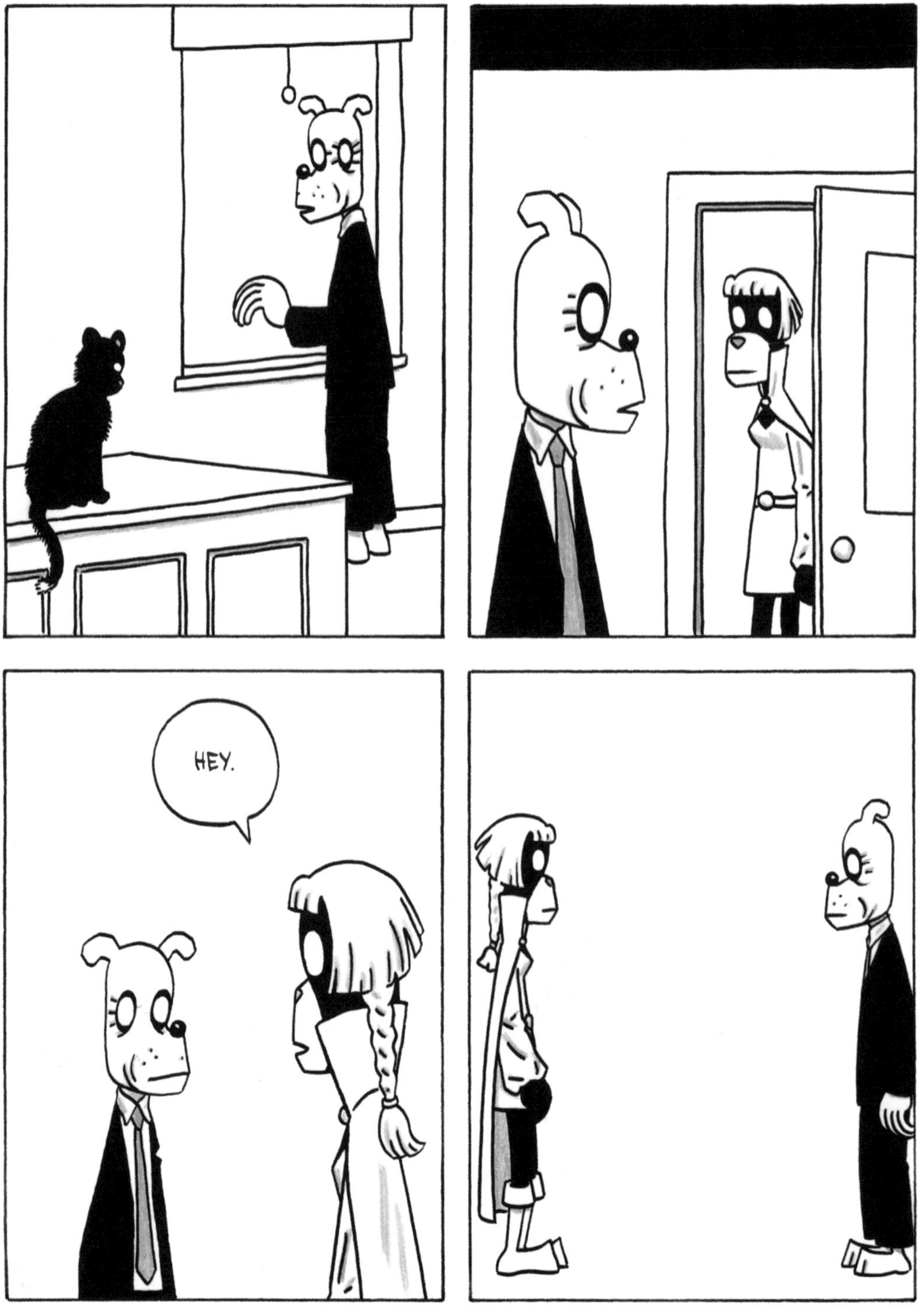
HEY.

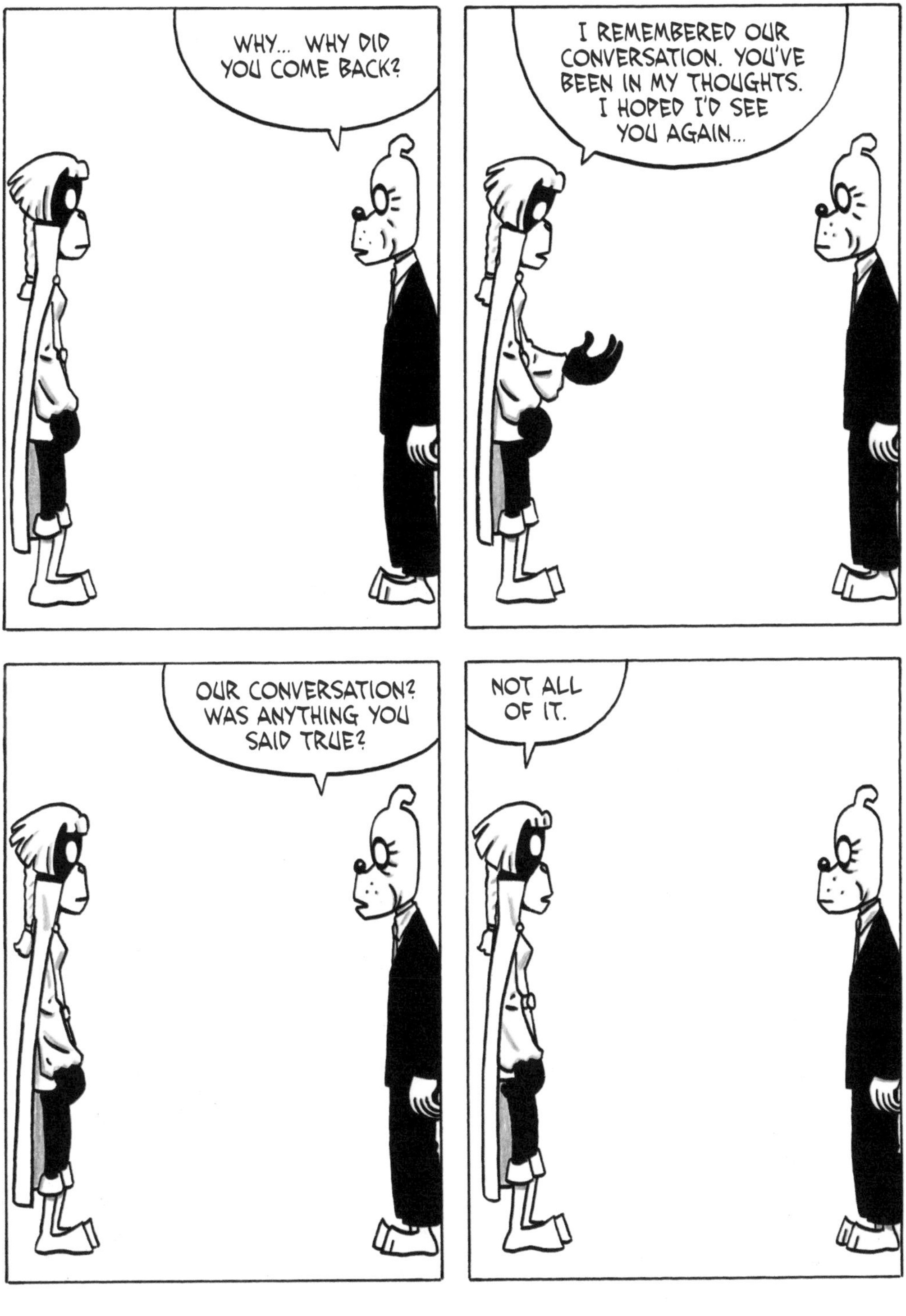
WHY... WHY DID YOU COME BACK?
I REMEMBERED OUR CONVERSATION. YOU'VE BEEN IN MY THOUGHTS. I HOPED I'D SEE YOU AGAIN...
OUR CONVERSATION? WAS ANYTHING YOU SAID TRUE?
NOT ALL OF IT.

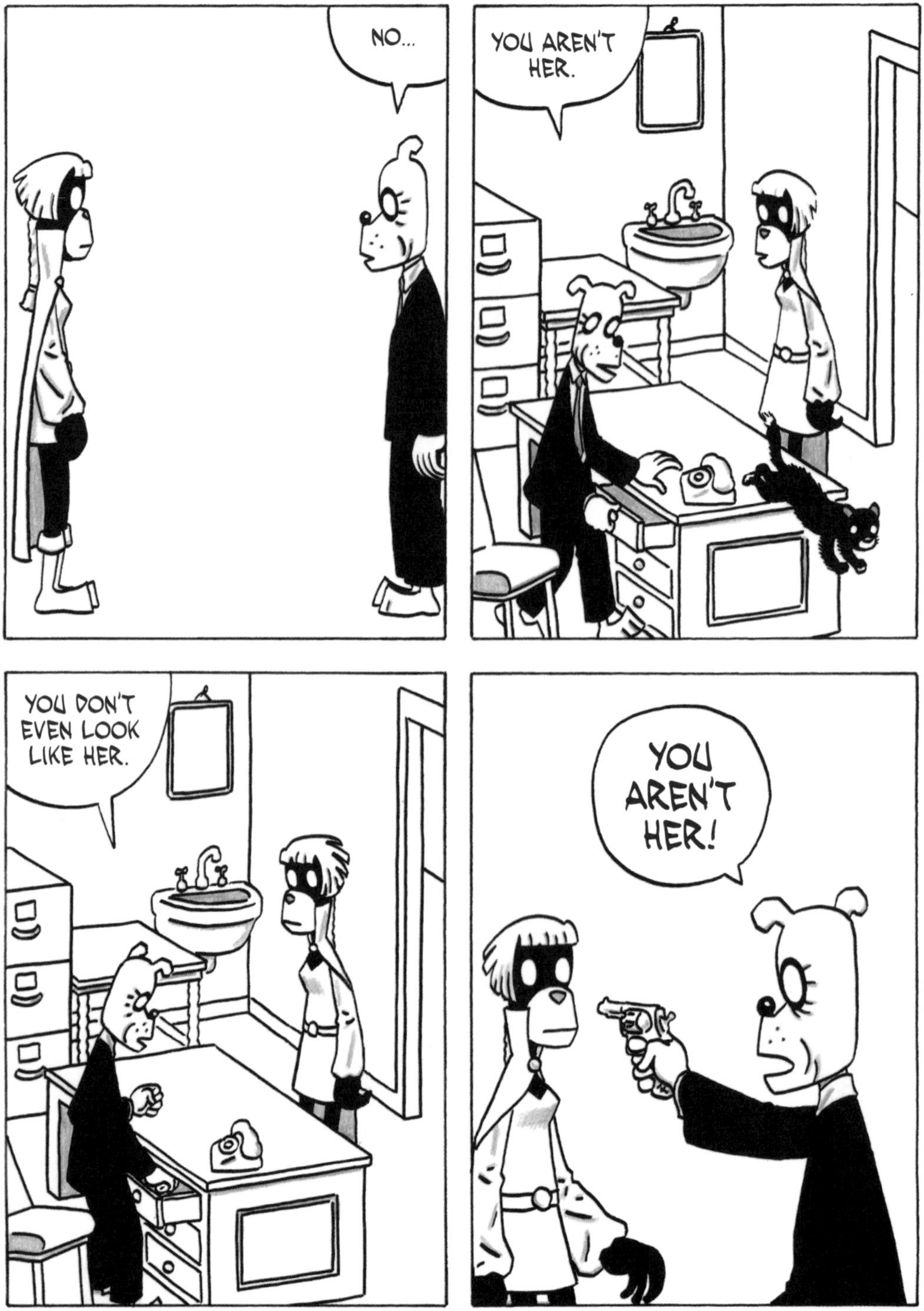
NO...
YOU AREN'T HER.
YOU DON'T EVEN LOOK LIKE HER.
YOU AREN'T HER!

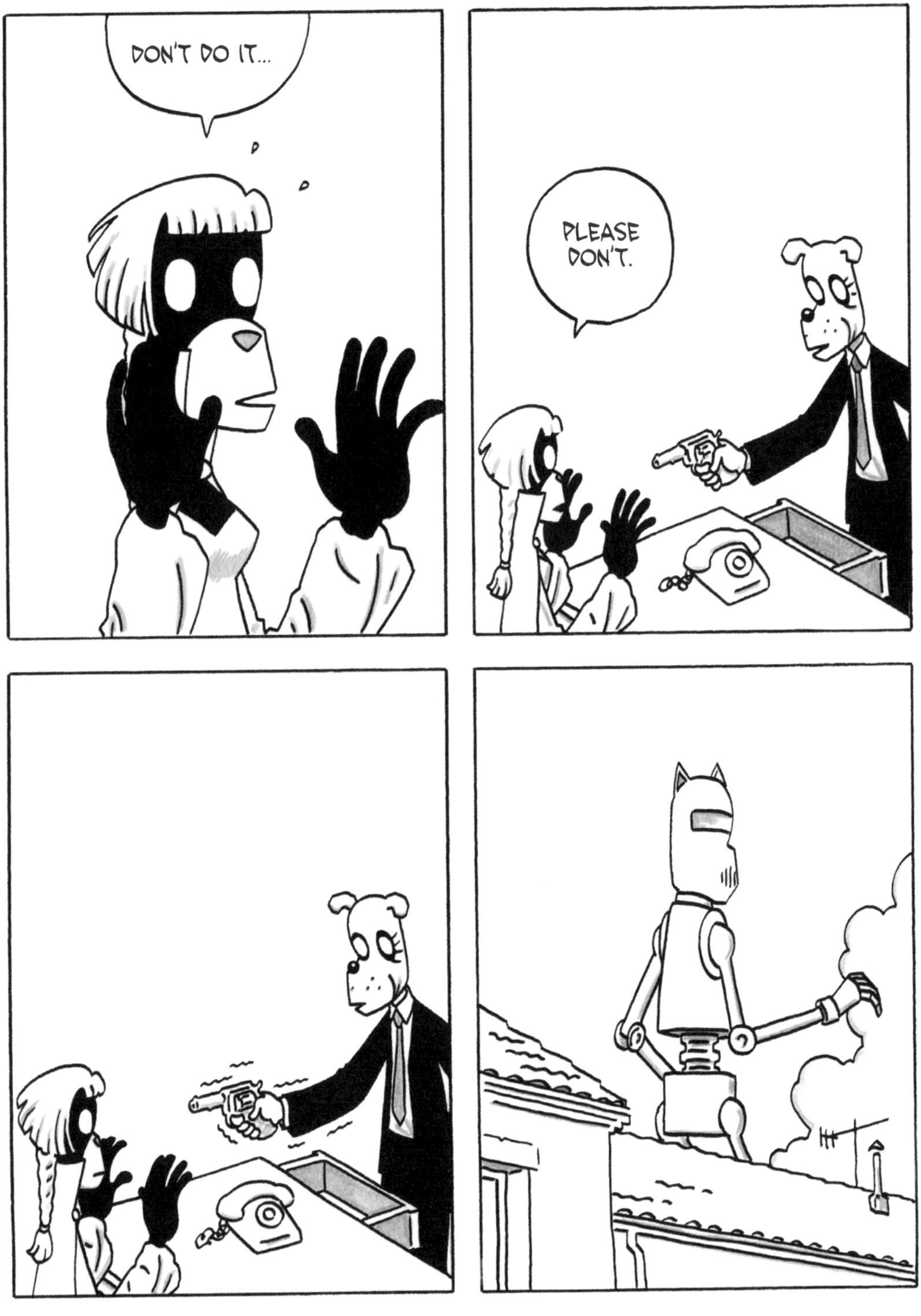
DON'T DO IT...
PLEASE DON'T.

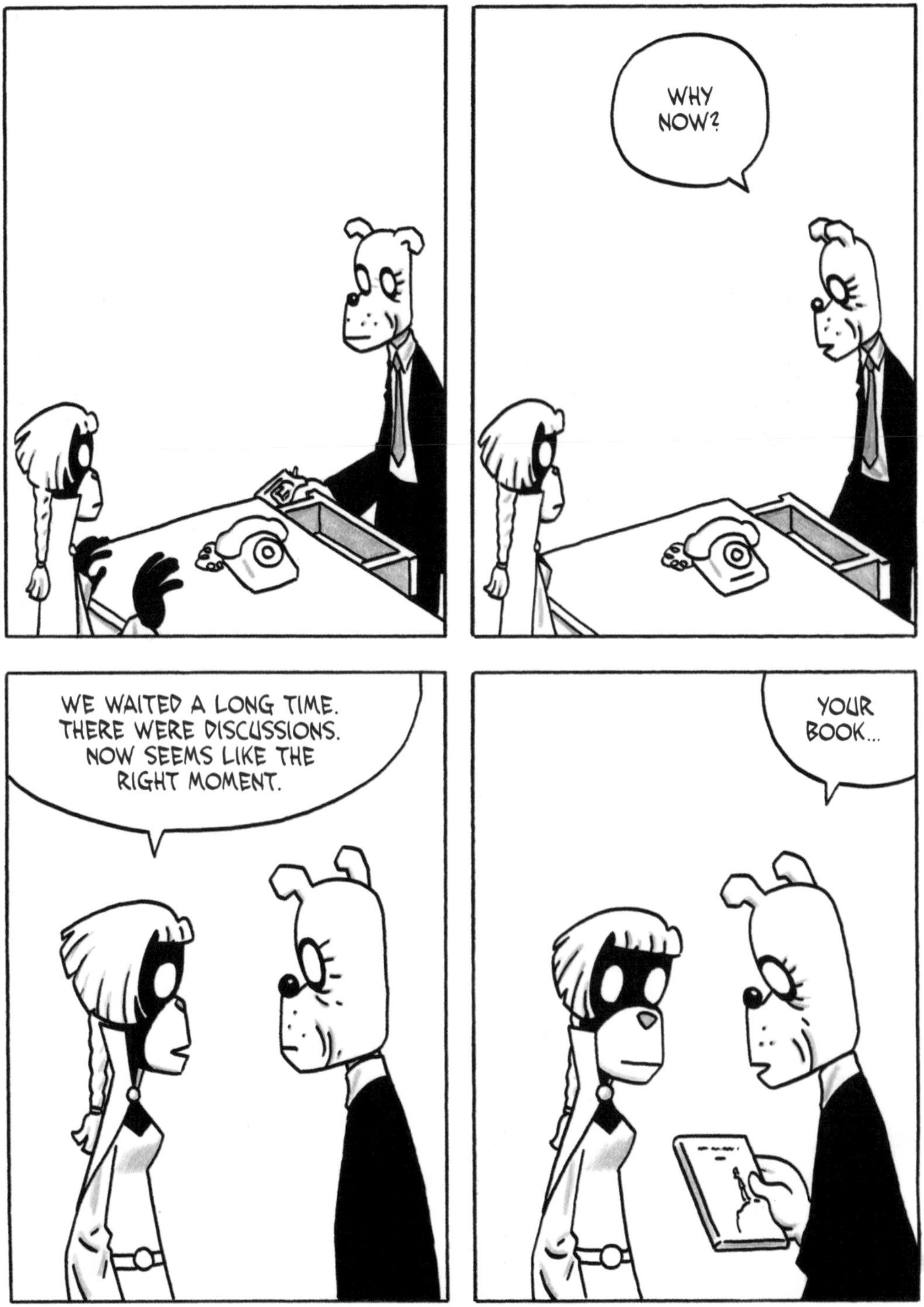
WHY NOW?
WE WAITED A LONG TIME. THERE WERE DISCUSSIONS. NOW SEEMS LIKE THE RIGHT MOMENT.
YOUR BOOK...

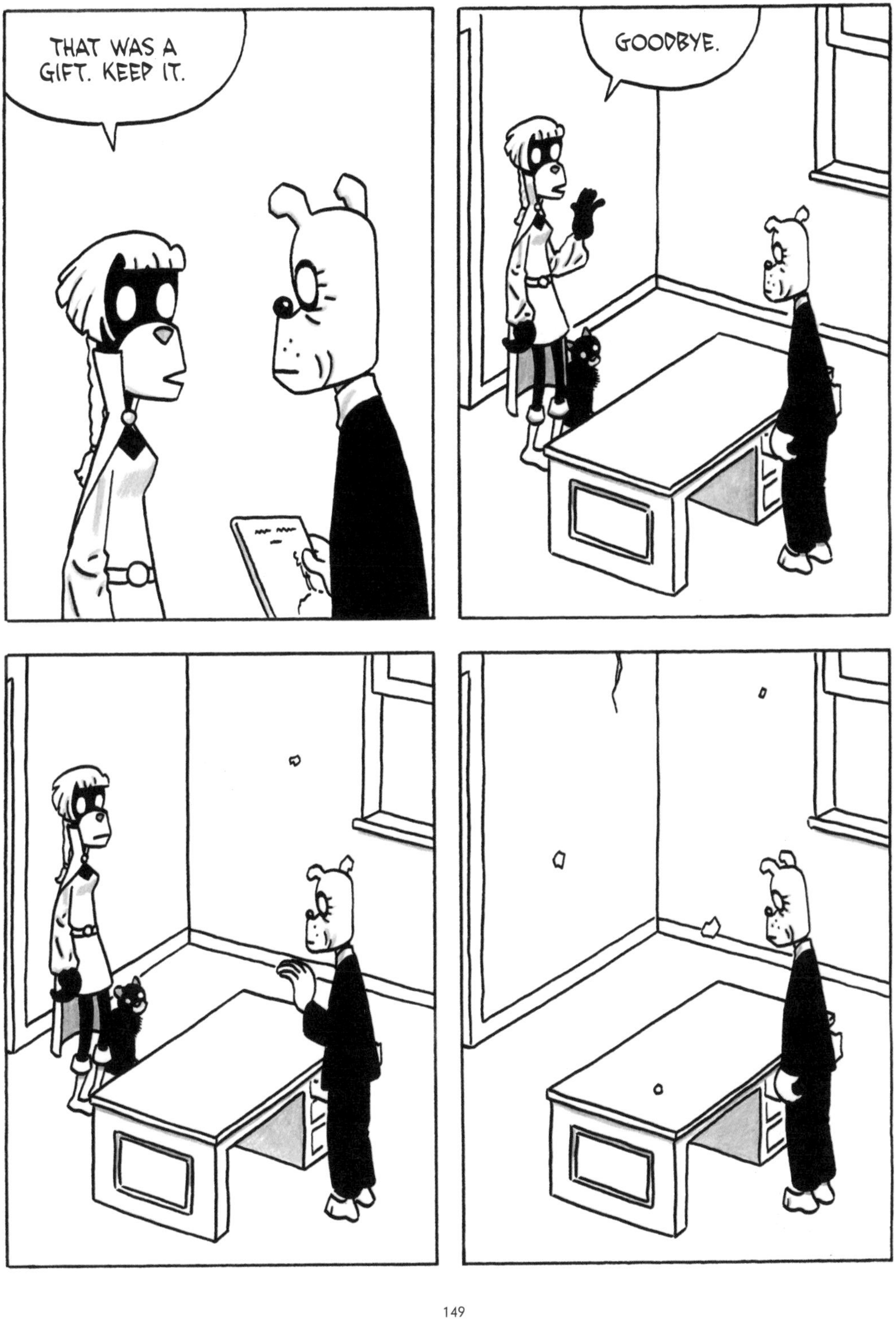
THAT WAS A GIFT. KEEP IT.
GOODBYE.

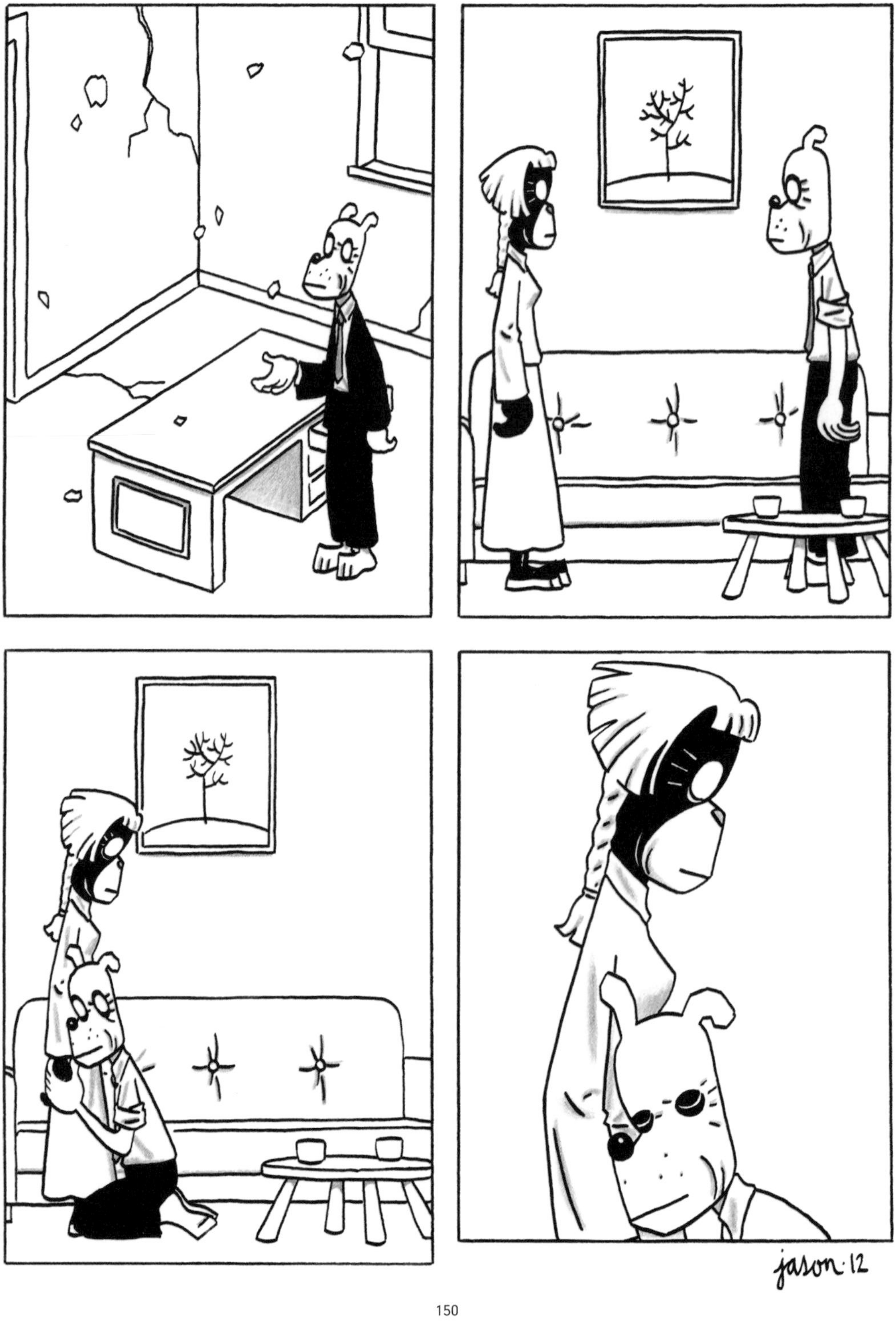
jason·12

FANTAGRAPHICS BOOKS • 7563 Lake City Way NE • Seattle, WA 98115 • Translated by Kim Thompson • Series Designed by Jason and Covey • Production and lettering by Paul Baresh and Emory Liu • Deskman: Jason T. Miles • Associate Publisher: Eric Reynolds • Published by Gary Groth and Kim Thompson • All characters, stories, and artwork © 2013 Jason. • All rights reserved. Permission to quote or reproduce material must be obtained from Jason or Fantagraphics Books Inc. • To receive a free catalog, call 1-800-657-1100, write us at the address above, or visit our website at fantagraphics.com. Visit beguiling.com, where Jason's original artwork can be purchased • First printing: July, 2013 • ISBN: 978-1-60699-642-3 • Printed in Singapore

Our beloved cartoonist Jason (born in Norway, 1965) disappeared one day when the outer door was left open. He is 6' 3" tall, wears glasses, and has ink stains on his fingers. If you find him please call Fantagraphics, 206-524-1967. No reward.

More Jason from Fantagraphics Books...

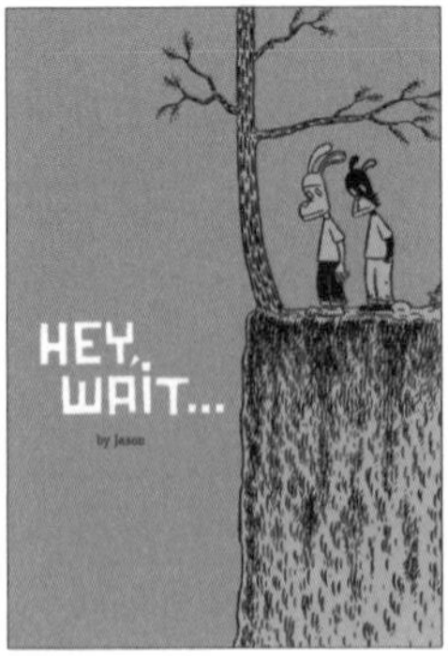
HEY, WAIT...
by Jason

Hey, Wait...
BLACK AND WHITE
68 PAGES / $12.95

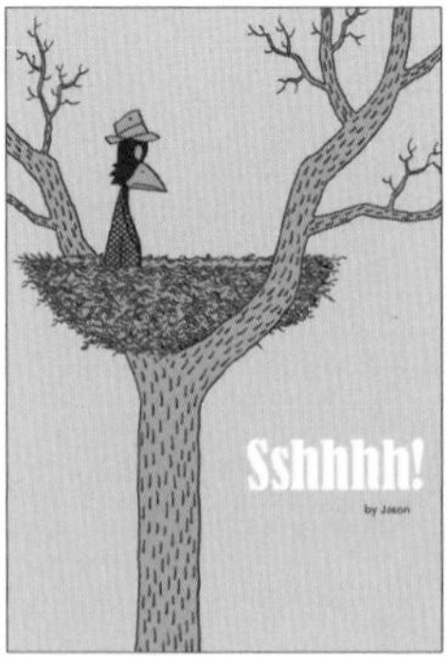
Sshhhh!
by Jason

Sshhhh!
BLACK AND WHITE
128 PAGES / $14.95

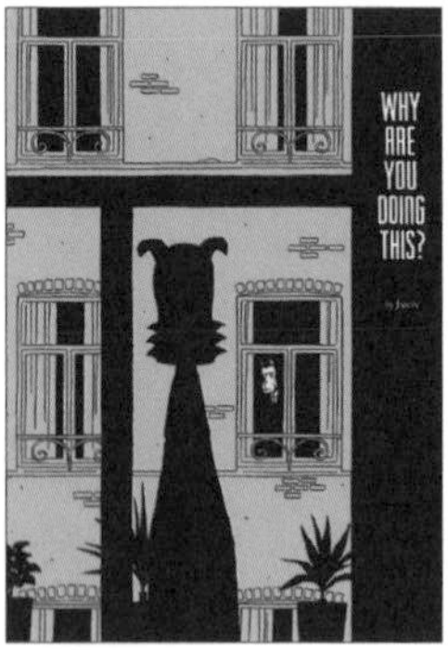
WHY ARE YOU DOING THIS?

Why Are You Doing This?
FULL-COLOR
48 PAGES / $12.95

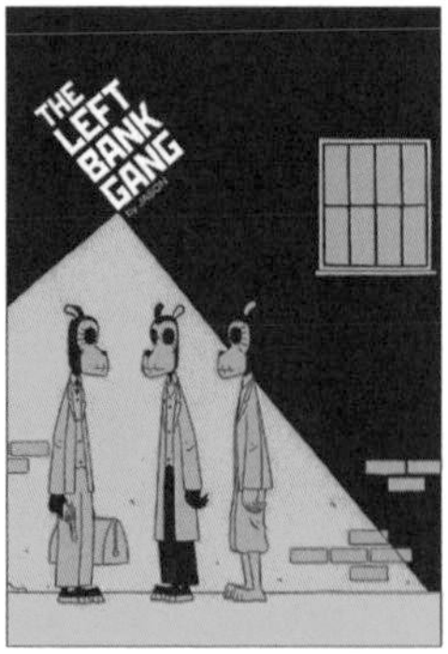
THE LEFT BANK GANG

The Left Bank Gang
FULL-COLOR
48 PAGES / $12.95

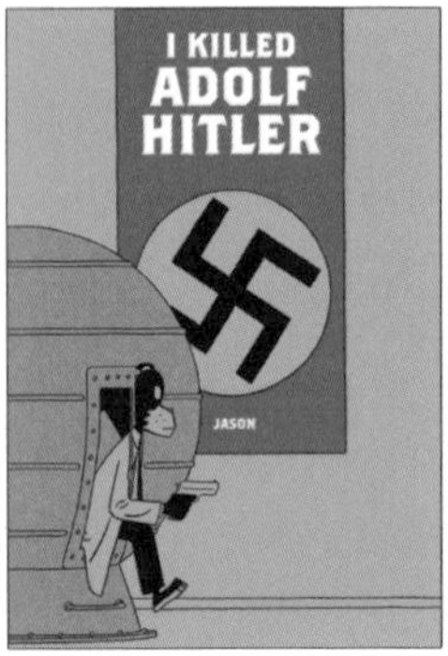
I KILLED ADOLF HITLER
JASON

I Killed Adolf Hitler
FULL-COLOR
48 PAGES / $12.95

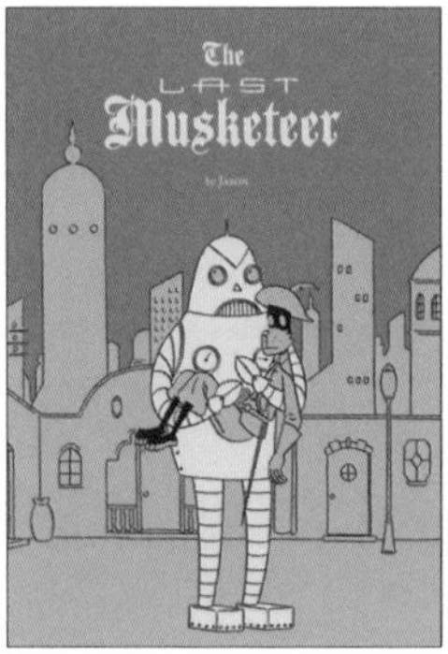
The LAST Musketeer

The Last Musketeer
FULL-COLOR
48 PAGES / $12.95

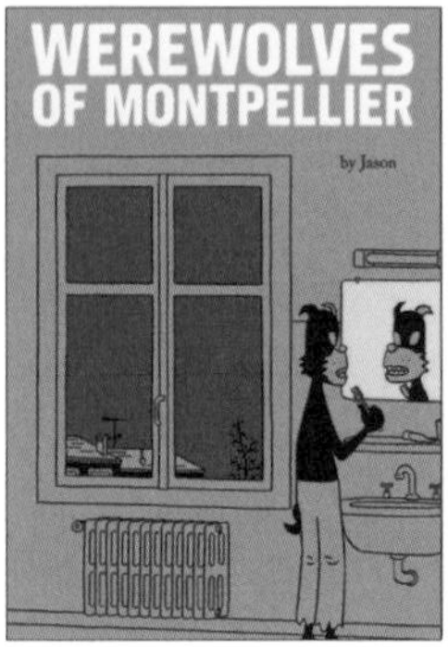
WEREWOLVES OF MONTPELLIER
by Jason

Werewolves of Montpellier
FULL-COLOR
48 PAGES / $12.99

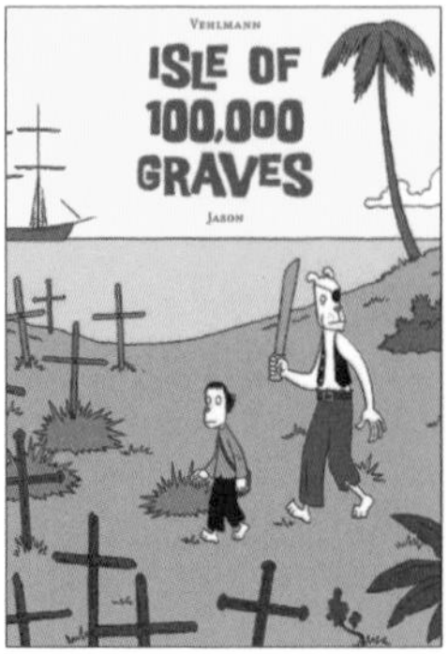
VEHLMANN
ISLE OF 100,000 GRAVES
JASON

Isle of 100,000 Graves
FULL-COLOR
56 PAGES / $14.99

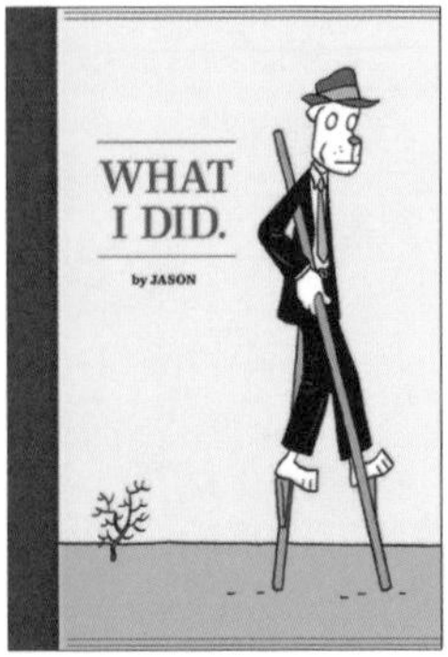
WHAT I DID.
by JASON

What I Did
BLACK AND WHITE/DUOTONE
272 PAGES / $24.99

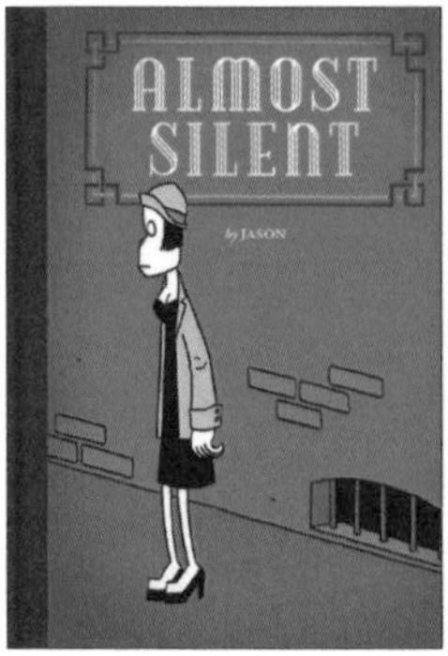
ALMOST SILENT
by JASON

Almost Silent
BLACK AND WHITE/DUOTONE
304 PAGES / $24.99

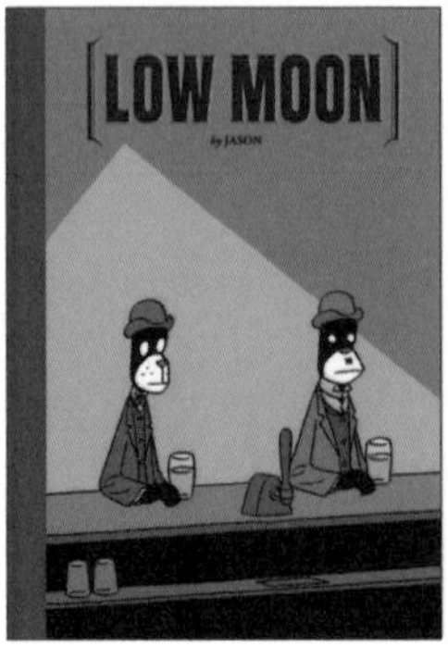
LOW MOON

Low Moon
FULL-COLOR
216 PAGES / $24.99

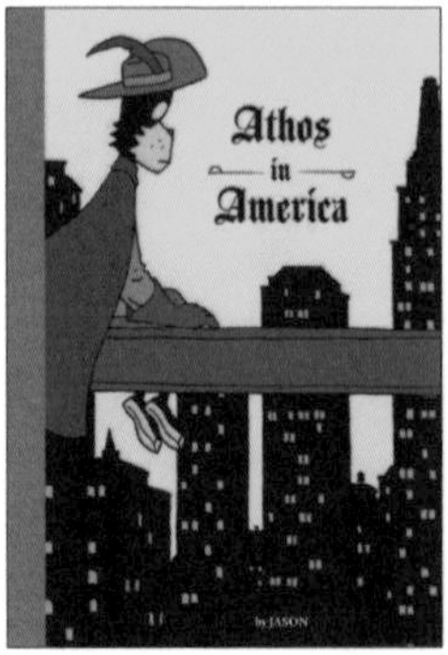
Athos in America
by JASON

Athos in America
FULL-COLOR
196 PAGES / $24.99